THE IRISH WAY

THE IRISH WAY

STUDIES IN IRISH SANCTITY
from SAINT PATRICK *to* MATT TALBOT

EDITED *by* F. J. SHEED

CLUNY
Providence, Rhode Island

Cluny Media edition, 2021

This Cluny edition is a republication of *The Irish Way*,
first published in 1932 by Sheed and Ward.

For more information regarding this title
or any other Cluny Media publication,
please write to info@clunymedia.com, or to
Cluny Media, P.O. Box 1664, Providence, RI 02901

VISIT US ONLINE AT WWW.CLUNYMEDIA.COM

ISBN: 978-1952826528

NIHIL OBSTAT:
GEORGIUS D. SMITH, S.TH.D., PH.D., *censor deputatus*

IMPRIMATUR: JOSEPHUS BUTT, *vic. generalis*
WESTMONASTERII, 30 APRILIS, 1932

Cover design by Clarke & Clarke
Cover image: Paul Henry, R.H.A., *The Potato Diggers*,
1912, oil on canvas

CONTENTS

FOREWORD i

SAINT PATRICK 1
by Alice Curtayne

SAINT BRENDAN 21
by Donal O'Cahill

SAINT COLUMBKILLE 35
by Raymond O'Flynn

SAINT COLUMBANUS 47
by Vincent McNabb, O.P.

SAINT MALACHY 73
by Vincent McNabb, O.P.

SAINT LAURENCE O'TOOLE 109
by C. P. Curran

DERMOT O'HURLEY 123
by Myles V. Ronan, C.C.

THOMAS FIHILLY, S.J. 135
by Aubrey Gwynn, S.J.

MICHAEL O'CLERY 147
by Victor Sheppard, O.F.M.

BLESSED OLIVER PLUNKET 177
by Philip Hughes

THADDEUS MORIARTY, O.P. 205
by Alice Curtayne

CATHERINE MCAULEY 217
by Fergal McGrath, S.J.

MARY AIKENHEAD 235
by C. P. Curran

THEOBALD MATHEW 245
by James O'Mahoney, O.M.Cap.

JOHN HAND 261
by Thomas O'Donnell, C.M.

MARGARET MARY HALLAHAN 267
by Eve Healy

WILLIAM DOYLE, S.J. 285
by James Brodrick, S.J.

MATT TALBOT 297
by F. J. Sheed

FOREWORD

by F.J SHEED

EVERY NATION HAS ITS OWN WAY OF BEING CATHOLIC, for the life of the Faith does not destroy the natural life and take its place, but elevates the natural life to a new level of activity. There is no good gift of Nature that is not thus retained and used at its highest by Grace: and as every nation pours its own characteristic qualities into the Church she welds them all and offers all humanity to God. The aim of this book is to show what Catholicism is in the Irish, and the method has been to take a number of great Catholics who were typically Irish and show what manner of people they were. These studies are not compressed biographies but portraits: their purpose is not so much to tell the reader what certain people did nor even what they were; but simply to show them to him.

In the choice of people to be studied, no fixed rule was followed save that they should be Irish and should be noted beyond the average for love of God. The idea came into being during a holiday in Kerry last summer, and the first concern was to find the writers rather than the subjects. The only condition here was that the writers should be of Irish blood. Once they were found and the idea explained to them, it was largely for them to decide whom they should write on, since obviously they were likely to write better on the saint of their own enthusiasm than on the saint of someone else's choosing. The result was the eighteen names treated of here. It is not meant to be a list of the eighteen best Irishmen. St. Brigid, for instance, is not here, nor St. Finian, nor a dozen others. It is simply a list of good Catholics, who were Irish, from whom, therefore, something might be learnt of Irish Catholicity.

What emerges from the whole book? Two truths principally. First, a man is a better Catholic for loving his own people; not to do so is to be deficient as a man, and deficiency in humanity remains as a deficiency in religion. Second, saints tend to be most characteristically national. National character shows most strongly where there is least weakness in personal character. If you would see any nation personified, it is always in a saint that you will see it best—there never was anyone more typically French than the Curé d'Ars (save, perhaps, St. Joan of Arc); the one unmistakable Englishman in all history is Blessed Thomas More. And so in Ireland. Of the people in this book, not one could possibly be anything but Irish.

What, you say, of St. Patrick? St. Patrick *is* Irish. The question where he was born has no bearing on the question where he belongs. St. Patrick's hold on the Irish heart is something without parallel in the world. It is not simply a matter of gratitude for a great favor received fifteen centuries ago. It is a matter of sheer personal affection—a thing of rich emotion, with warmth and excitement in it. Does any Irishman in the world think of St. Patrick as dead? As I have said, the thing is without parallel. Not so do other nations feel about the man who brought them the Faith. The reason for this special Irish feeling about the national saint is something special in the original relationship. St. Patrick belongs to the Irish in the sense that the Irish belong to him. The word Irishman meant something different after his coming. The Irish were born anew. Under God's providence they were born of St. Patrick and after fifteen centuries every generation of them still bears his imprint. Every nation has its own way of being Catholic. The Irish way is St. Patrick's way. And this book proves it.

I

SAINT PATRICK (389–461)[†]

by ALICE CURTAYNE

SAINT PATRICK'S OWN ACCOUNT OF HIS PARENTAGE IS the simplest imaginable and would apply to nearly half the population of Ireland today: he tells us in his *Confession* that his father, one of several sons, owned a small farm and lived in a village. A detail or two, less familiar, should be added. Patrick's father was a decurion, that is, member of the municipal council of a Roman town, and both he and his father before him appear to have been clerics. Concerning this, Bury hazards the suggestion that the decayed dignity of decurion had become so burdensome, attempts were frequently made to escape it by taking minor Orders.

Patrick further tells us that he was born in Banavem Taberniae. The identification of this place-name has perplexed the centuries. Modern scholarship appears to have settled down firmly to the opinion that it was in Monmouthshire, somewhere near the mouth of the Severn, rather than near Dumbarton in Scotland, although this conclusion is most repugnant to Scottish opinion. For a personal

† This personal study is based chiefly on the *Confession*. The quotations given are from Dr. J. D. Newport White's translation. Acknowledgment is also due to the works of Drs. Todd, Healy, Gwynn, Bury and Helena Concannon

appreciation of the Saint, it is all one whether he was born in Monmouth or Dumbarton. His Roman citizenship is what counts. He was thoroughly Romanized. All through life he displayed the typically Roman qualities of simplicity and endurance. And this it is that lends his life such marvelous unity: the pattern emerges exact.

Moreover, Banavem Taberniae, wherever it was, ceased early in life to have much significance for Patrick. When he was sixteen years old, that village was the scene of a great pirate raid. Patrick was captured near his father's villa and carried overseas, one of thousands of prisoners, who formed the best part of the pirates' booty. Landing on the coast of Antrim, his captors sold him to the petty king of the district, in exchange for a few kine. The boy's head was shaved as a sign of his status; he was given a slave's garb—a sheepskin tunic descending to the knees and leather sandals laced with thongs. He had to do the menial work of four Pagan households. One of his chief occupations was the herding of swine on the slopes of Mount Slemish.

It was a searing experience. The change of life was radical, drastic, and apparently final. Flung utterly helpless into the hands of heathen masters who held him in rigorous slavery, this son of a Roman decurion was shocked into a precocious gravity. His new life was so hard as to be a sort of daily castigation, as testified by the reminiscent shudder with which, in his old age, he described it: "I was chastened exceedingly and humbled every day in hunger and nakedness." Referring to the fate of those captives from Banavem Taberniae, he says briefly: "The Lord poured upon us the fury of His anger."

Before this occurred, Patrick tells us that "he knew not the true God"; that "he was ignorant of the living God"—perplexing phrases, since he was obviously the child of Christian parents and mentions priests as tutors of his childhood. The phrases can imply only that he was an average, careless youth (in his own estimation), to whom religion had no vital meaning, at least until he had completed his fifteenth year. Then, in his destitution, he turned to God and began for the first time to know Him with personal experimental knowledge.

> And there the Lord opened the understanding of my unbelief that, even though late...I might turn with all my heart to the Lord my God, who regarded my low estate, and pitied the youth of my ignorance, and kept me before I knew Him, and before I had discernment.... Now, after I came to Ireland, tending flocks was my daily occupation; and constantly I used to pray in the daytime. Love of God and the fear of Him increased more and more, and faith grew, and the spirit was moved....

I do not think that Patrick, in his terrified "conversion" on Slemish, formed the purpose of returning to Ireland as a Christian missionary, for in his old age he referred to that enterprise as "a great grace...that formerly, in my youth, I never hoped for nor thought of." But he received a divine, very personal and very precious, initiation in his loneliness, and his response was a resolution to serve God perfectly. This became "the fixed purpose of his soul," from which he never afterwards swerved. The divine plan in his regard, the method of that service, was but gradually unfolded to him. Every time a part of the road was disclosed, he saw an obstacle confronting him, each appearing more formidable than the last. These barriers were six in number: servitude, ignorance, the hostility of superiors, the forbidding magnitude of the task suggested to his mind, the treachery of a friend, temptation to despair. He displayed utter singlemindedness in his efforts to coerce exterior circumstances into conforming with inner divine direction. That is the whole story of his long life. It could be shown symbolically as a drama of six scenes.

Patrick as a slave-boy was utterly powerless to accomplish any good. His master being a Druid, the youth was hemmed in by the inhibitions of a strong Pagan creed, of unquestioned ascendancy throughout the land. Probably, to his awakening religiousness, the core of his destitution was his complete severance from the sacramental life of the Church, from all communion with his kind. It is unnecessary to enter into the material rigors of his life. Slaves, in the

Ireland of his day, were hardly accorded human rights. Fiacc tells us that Patrick, in captivity, never ate human food. In a land where no money appears to have been coined, a slave was the unit of barter. One slave-girl was reckoned the equivalent of three cows. As an indication of the absolute ownership exercised, a master could send his slave even to kill a man and the slave was bound to obey. A glimpse of the treatment meted out to this class of the community is found in that episode of Patrick's later life: he met some slaves cutting down yew trees with such blunt instruments that the palms of their hands were bleeding freely. Intimately interested, he questioned them, and they told him they were not allowed to sharpen their irons on the flagstone, as that would make their work too easy.

In short, Patrick felt himself morally bound to find a way out. But six years passed before he attempted his escape. Then it was in response to divine guidance and from no exterior suggestion that he made his dash for liberty. He was told the direction to take in order to find a ship. By this time a man of twenty-two, he disappeared unobserved from his master's household and walked two hundred miles through unknown country, terrors encompassing him, the fear of pursuit and re-capture behind him. During all that way he says he met with nothing to alarm him.

When he reached the port, the ship that his inner voices had told him of was casting its moorings, but the captain indignantly refused to allow the exhausted slave to board her. After a discussion with his crew, however, he changed his mind and recalling Patrick, who had already taken refuge in prayer, he allowed him to clamber on. The runaway had not the least notion of their destination, but he cast himself into the hands of God Almighty, having learned, as he said, "that He can be utterly trusted."

There began an odyssey in which hardship was the chief note. Patrick, in this passage, is like an athlete engaged in physical combat with an adversary, with such awful persistence did slavery fetter him. He soon found that he had changed one form of servitude for another of a more disagreeable sort. To the human eye, that state threatened to engulf him; his name seemed about to be obliterated from the world of doers. Writing of it in his old age, he becomes confused in his recital of those strange vicissitudes. After three days at sea, they disembarked on some unknown coast and then journeyed for twenty-eight days through a desert, where food failed them and they were on the verge of death by starvation. The heathen crew taunted the Christian youth that his almighty God had forsaken him, because they were not likely to see a human being again. Patrick affirmed his unshaken confidence and then a herd of swine appeared and the wanderers had food in abundance. What occurred subsequently is uncertain, but it seems that after another fourteen days, during which they always found food and fire and dry quarters in which to sleep, the company reached the habitations of men and shortly afterwards Patrick escaped, having spent two months with his new masters. He found out his kindred in Britain, who received him as a son and gave sympathetic ear to the tale of his tribulations. He had overcome the first obstacle to his perfect service of God, the helplessness of servitude. But immediately the second barrier arose before him: his ignorance.

With that fixed purpose of his soul no other way of life was possible save a dedicated one. Patrick resolved to be a priest. Now the swineherd of twenty-two had had a valuable moral training on Slemish, but from the academic point of view, his incompetence was disastrous. His studies having ceased when he was fifteen, he was wholly uneducated. Nevertheless, with ardor and patience, he immediately began making up for his deficiency.

Despite the most painstaking research, the twenty-year interval between Patrick's escape from Ireland and his voluntary return is still darkly mysterious. In his *Confession* he says no word about that interval. Four names are mentioned as the centers of his training: Marmoutier, near Tours, Lérins, Arles, Auxerre. The monastic foundations of Marmoutier, Lérins and Arles were of European fame and their pupils considered privileged. Four saints are mentioned among

Patrick's exemplars or preceptors: St. Martin of Tours, St. Honoratus, St. Amator, St. Germanus. These men were not notable for piety only; they were among the foremost scholars and ecclesiastical organizers of the day. If they contributed to the formation of Patrick, then he lacked no external stimulus to cast off the impediment of ignorance.

Even a fleeting acquaintance with St. Germanus of Auxerre would have a deep effect on Patrick. Educated in Rome for law, he joined the army instead and later became a priest. He was an officer in the army up to the very day of his ordination. A character of outstanding originality, he was sent to Britain by the Pope in 429 to combat the heresy of Pelagius. That campaign was not fought by preaching only, but on at least one occasion by actual physical combat, during which the military prowess of Germanus reasserted itself and ended in his winning what is known as the "Alleluia" victory. It is often asserted that Patrick accompanied Germanus on that mission to Britain, though the primal authority for the statement is slight.

Regarding Patrick's training, there is certainty in two respects. He was happy during that period, because he longed unutterably in after life to revisit the places known to him in Gaul. In that congenial monastic atmosphere, the soul of the crushed and despised swineherd expanded in gracious tranquility. He emerged profoundly versed in at least one branch of study—Scripture—which appeared afterwards as though woven into the texture of his thought, so that he habitually expressed himself in the language of Holy Writ. He developed other gifts too that are rarer, because inborn: one of these was construction and another, administration.

In that period when he was thus laboriously overcoming the barrier of ignorance, he began to have dreams of a sharp-cut distinctness in one of which a courier appeared with countless letters; one of these he gave to Patrick. The missive was superscribed with the words, "The Voice of the Irish." As the student was wonderingly unfolding it to read, he heard the voices of many, crying to him as with one mouth, "We beseech thee to come and walk once more amongst us." He heard that plea so often that it became very familiar in his ears. He even knew the very people who thus called to him, theirs was "the voice of those who live beside the Wood of Foclut which is nigh unto the western sea." And in his dreams that cry to Patrick possessed a quality of such urgency that it seemed to break his heart. His awakenings were confounded with the mystery of it. He began to understand that his work as a priest was to be missionary and the field, Ireland.

The moment Patrick understood it, the third barrier arose in the opposition of his superiors. They thought such an enterprise at once too hazardous and too responsible for him, beyond his capacity. His statement of the position is clear.

> The Lord showed mercy upon me thousands of times, because He saw in me that I was ready, but that I did not know through these (revelations) what I should do about my position, because many were forbidding this embassage. Moreover, they used to talk amongst themselves behind my back and say "Why does this fellow thrust himself into danger amongst hostile people who know not God?" They did not say this out of malice, but it did not seem meet in their eyes, on account of my illiteracy, as I myself witness that I have understood.

Yet he must have urged the evangelization of Ireland with unabated persistence. The question of raising him to a bishopric was finally mooted, in order to permit him to embark on the mission of his choice, and then the opposition that broke out was even fierce in its nature. Patrick tells us that a friend of his "fought" for him in his absence. Opponents must have even imputed to him unworthy motives to account for his persistent determination to go to Ireland. This is evident from his protestation:

> I testify in truth and in exultation of heart before God and His holy angels, that I never had any cause except the Gospel and His

> promises for ever returning to that nation from whence previously I scarcely escaped.

But at length Patrick overcame the opposition of his superiors sufficiently to enable him to proceed. As a consecrated bishop, he returned to Ireland in the year 432.

Immediately the fourth barrier presented itself in the sheer magnitude of the work he had undertaken. When Patrick leaped ashore at that inlet of Strangford Lough, he must have seen himself infinitesimally dwarfed in comparison with the enormous complexity of his task. We do not know who his companions were, but they were few in number. He had not come to savage tribes, but to a country with a highly organized religion which had become fused with a strongly developed native culture. There were in Ireland only a tiny number of scattered knots of Christians, whom Palladius had either baptized or brought with him. They were completely disorganized. Patrick had practically to begin at the beginning. He had no native power whatsoever on his side, nor even any access to its goodwill. In fact, the moment he disembarked the authority with which he was invested fell from him in the eyes of a people who did not comprehend it, and he reassumed the status of a fugitive slave. Patrick's first attempt at a solution was *activity.* In the way he set to work, he was like a Titan released.

His methods were characterized by boldness. He did not try to work by quiet diffusion, by peaceful propaganda. He lighted an enormous bonfire on the top of Slane in defiance of the royal edict and then had to appear before the High King to give an account of himself. Thus he joined issue at once. Everyone knows the story of that paschal fire lighted by Patrick on the first Easter of his mission. But Tirechan in the telling of it has a wonderfully expressive phrase. He says Patrick kindled the fire "in the nostrils of King Laoghaire." So strong was the tribal sentiment in Ireland and so accurate the missionary's memory, he knew it was useless to try to work upwards from the people. He attacked the chieftains and when he won, the tribes followed. But Patrick's was no timidly proffered apologetic. He flung Christianity in the face of Druidism.

His preaching and his baptizing were on a superhuman scale. It is related that he once preached for three days and three nights without pause. The old accounts add piously that to his audience the time seemed but as one hour, to all save one of his hearers at least, a girl—Saint Brigid—who fell asleep. The delightful detail is added that when Patrick noticed her slumbers, he would not allow her to be awakened. He baptized hundreds of thousands with his own hands and signed the chrism of confirmation on their brow. In his old age, he liked to ruminate on those companies of the newly-baptized who had passed through his hands. With unabated energy year after year, he labored on from tribe to tribe and left them in every case as a people reborn:

> I am a debtor exceedingly to God, Who granted me such great grace that many peoples through me should be regenerated to God and afterwards confirmed, and that clergy should everywhere be ordained from them for a people newly come to belief....

In truth the rapid ordination of a strong corps of native clergy proved, as was to be expected, a most powerful factor in promoting the confidence of the people. Even he himself was amazed at it. He never underestimated the magnitude of his work, but he humbly ascribed it directly to God:

> Wherefore then in Ireland they who never had the knowledge of God, but until now only worshipped idols and abominations—how has there been lately prepared a people of the Lord, and they are called children of God? Sons and daughters of Scottic chieftains are seen to become monks and virgins of Christ.... Their number increases more and more—and as for those of our race who are born there, we know not the number of them....

This latter fruit of his work, the blossoming of monasticism, was as striking as the emergence of a native clergy, and was like a divine guarantee of stability.

The conversion of Ireland to Christianity is a golden page in history. But the tendency in Patrician literature has been to exaggerate somewhat the ease of that conversion. True there was not the slightest attempt at organized persecution of the Church, but there was plenty of sporadic, isolated hostility. One instance is the plot to assassinate Patrick, which resulted in the death of his devoted charioteer. We know of at least one attempt made to poison him. Once he and his companions were stoned. His own account of the hardships of his mission shows that physical courage played a large part in his work:

> On occasion, I used to give presents to the kings, besides the hire that I gave to their sons who accompanied me; and nevertheless they seized me with my companions. And on that day they most eagerly desired to kill me; but my time had not yet come. And everything they found with us they plundered, and me myself they bound with irons. And on the fourteenth day the Lord delivered me from their power.... Daily I expect either slaughter, or to be defrauded, or reduced to slavery, or an unfair attack of some kind....

There is even more kinship between this Apostle of an agricultural country and the laborer in the fields than is derived from rural birth and farmer parentage. Notice how readily intelligible to such a one is Patrick's simile describing the grace of his mission:

> I was like a stone lying in the deep mire; and He that is mighty came, and in His mercy lifted me up, and verily raised me aloft and placed me on the top of the wall....

Moreover, Patrick was a toiler. Every ploughman is a symbol of him, and the more stubborn the glebe to be broken, the more profuse the sweat, the more perfect the symbol. *Toil* is the keynote of his mission. He himself described it as "my laborious episcopate," "labor which I had learned from Christ my Lord." He worked like a man possessed. Afterwards, when he tried to describe it, he shrank from the hugeness of the recital; "It would be a tedious task to explain it all in detail, or even in part. . . ."

The old "lives" are full of numerical evidence of the sheer laboriousness of Patrick's work. The founding of a new church is a favorite episcopal dream, but what of a bishop who founds *seven hundred* places of worship, ordains five thousand priests, gives minor orders to an unnumbered host of clerks, and consecrates three hundred and seventy bishops? Those are the figures given in the Tripartite Life. Dr. Todd has discussed exhaustively the ecclesiastical machinery that allowed room for so many bishops over so small an area. I need not dwell upon that here. Suffice it to say that at least every tribe had to have its bishop.

To appreciate his labor, it must be borne in mind, too, that when Patrick founded a church, the act was something very much more strenuous than blessing a foundation stone. He did not go about his missionary work with a companion or two, in the later Franciscan manner. You must see him with his travelling "household" ranged around him. This household comprised an assistant bishop; a chaplain; a brehon or judge, to advise him in legal matters; a "champion," or "strong man," for bodyguard; a psalmist; a chamberlain; a bell-ringer; a cook; a brewer; a sacristan; two table attendants; a driver; a firewood-man; a cow-herd; three smiths; three artisans; three embroideresses; three masons. This household was modelled on those of the petty kings, an instance of how Patrick adapted himself to native customs, and maintained his dignity. In his ceaseless missionary travels, he and his company were like a small township on the move. They thundered up to a chieftain's dun, with their train of chariots, wagons, tents, baggage, equipment. The churches were mostly built of timber, or wattle and clay, and when Patrick founded one, he nearly always assisted with his own hands in the building of it. His household then provided the furnishings. His coppersmiths made altars, chalices, patens and quadrangular book-covers. His smiths made the nails used in the building, the door-hinges and handles, the bells. His embroideresses made the vestments and altar-cloths.

Patrick was the first hedge-schoolmaster in Ireland. In addition to the retinue detailed above, there travelled always with him in his journeys his "school"; a group of likely Irish boys, suitable candidates for the priesthood, whom he trained in practical missionary work, while he taught them the psalter, missal and ritual in preparation for the conferring of Holy Orders. When he founded a church center, he nearly always had one member of this "family" ready to take charge of it.

Results best proclaim him. He came to Ireland in the year 432, and before ten years had passed he had the Irish Hierarchy established under the primacy of Armagh! In the firmament of the Church, he had made Ireland a bright star. Already, in that brief span of years, he saw the whole country linked up, even to its remotest parts, with churches and monastic foundations, to which a great tide of conversions was flowing steadily, with a strong native clergy in possession. The thing was accounted miraculous and the eyes of Christendom were turned on his work. Impressed by the mission organization in that northern island, Rome had raised it to the status of an ecclesiastical province, making Patrick its Metropolitan, with his seat at Armagh. And when Patrick wrote in his old age from his retirement at Saul, he had the gratification of seeing a native bishop his Metropolitan successor—Benignus, whom he had trained from boyhood.

But before these things came to pass, Patrick had passed through the last trial of his vocation—the treachery of a friend—and the most grievous crisis of his life—a temptation to despair. It seems that, in his superiors' view, Patrick had never wholly made up the defect of ignorance. Since that ignorance was of a special kind, namely, an inability to converse and write with ease in classical Latin, it had better be designated by the less offensive term, *rusticitas.* A deep awareness of this, for the deficiency had almost disqualified him for the mission, made Patrick sorrowfully self-conscious about it to the end of his life. In his *Confession,* written when he was an old man, he emphasizes his *rusticitas* with almost wearisome iteration:

> I am the most illiterate and the least of all the faithful, and contemptible in the eyes of very many...a fool...the abhorred of this world...I had long since thought of writing; but I hesitated until now, for I feared lest I should fall under the censure of men's tongues, and because I have not studied as have others, who in the most approved fashion have drunk in both law and the Holy Scriptures alike, and have never changed their speech from their infancy, but rather have been always rendering it more perfect. For my speech and language is translated into a tongue not my own, as can be easily proved from the savor of my writing, in what fashion I have been taught and am learned in speech.... Now in mine old age, I earnestly desire that which in youth I did not acquire... When a youth, nay, almost a boy, I went into captivity in language (as well as in person) before I knew what I should earnestly desire, or what I ought to shun. And so today I blush and am exceedingly afraid to lay bare my lack of education; because I am unable to make my meaning plain in a few words to the learned. Perchance it seems to not a few that I am thrusting myself forward in this matter with my want of knowledge and my slow tongue....

It must be remembered about Patrick that he was bilingual, and his "slowness of tongue" can have applied only to his converse in Latin. During his captivity in Ireland, he had to learn the Gaelic speech of his masters, and this acquirement was of enormous benefit to him when he returned as missionary. He preached to the people in the language of their homes. His feats as a preacher must be offset against his protestations of *rusticitas.* One recalls that sermon of three days and nights during which the time seemed to his audience to be but one hour. That does not argue a lack of fluency or intelligibility. The only conclusion is that Patrick was perfectly at home with his Irish converts, so much so that he became gradually less at home when communicating in Latin, whether by tongue or pen, with his ecclesiastical colleagues.

His *rusticitas* must also be considered in conjunction with his extraordinary zeal for the promotion of learning. An illustration of his method is seen in the story of the conversion of Ernaisc and his son Loarn. These having signified their readiness to hear of the new faith, Patrick immediately sat down with them under a tree and proceeded to teach them what is called in the "Lives" the alphabet, but what was in reality a written compendium of Christian doctrine. That picture of master and pupils under a tree illustrates every stage of his missionary progress. He not only taught orally, but he taught the written word too, and with extreme diligence he taught his pupils how to write the Gospel. There is another extraordinary picture one likes to hold in mind. On one occasion the pagan inhabitants of a district through which Patrick and his band were passing showed the greatest alarm, believing that the Christians had descended upon them with arms for aggressive purposes. But what the Christians were carrying in their hands were, not weapons, but wooden boards, rather like the Irish short sword in shape and size. On these harmless staves the "alphabet" was inscribed and the pupils were learning as they marched along the road Patrick had literally armed his converts with the doctrine of Christ.

Yet when the success of his mission was admittedly phenomenal, Patrick was still far from winning the unanimous approval of his colleagues and superiors. Before he became Metropolitan, an enquiry was actually instituted into his fitness to be head of the Church in Ireland. Now among those appointed to "try" Patrick was his best friend, unnamed in the *Confession,* but concerning whose loyalty he never previously had any doubts. The Unnamed had been his friend in student days, even before Patrick had been made a deacon. To him, Patrick, before his ordination, had confided a secret. It concerned some error into which he had lapsed, or imagined he had lapsed, before he was fifteen. The Unnamed had strongly supported Patrick for the bishopric, had urged his merits against all opponents. Then came the astounding reversal. At that "trial" of Patrick, this friend suddenly turned against him, and even betrayed the secret—that ancient confidence of some thirty years' standing—and urged it as a reason for Patrick's removal from office.

Here is the saint's own account of the unhappy episode:

> After the lapse of thirty years they found, as an occasion against me, a matter which I had confessed before I was a deacon. Because of anxiety, with sorrowful mind, I disclosed to my dearest friend things that I had done in my youth one day, nay, in one hour, because I had not yet overcome. I cannot tell, God knoweth, if I was then fifteen years old...

He writes of it in his old age, perhaps some twenty years after the occurrence, and it is clear that the wound he then sustained was not yet healed. That blasting disillusionment in friendship had filled him with a bewilderment which the passage of years had not cleared from his mind:

> I am grieved for my dearest friend...a man to whom I had even entrusted my soul! ... How did it occur to him (or, how could he bring himself) to put me to shame publicly before everyone....

The arraignment resulted in Patrick's deposition from office. As he phrased it, he was "rejected." He was even superseded for a brief period. This was the supreme crisis of his life. It occurred in the full tide of his success; he had just brought the organization of the Church in Ireland to the point where he could press for the establishment of a hierarchy. When the unjust sentence smote him, he was fearfully tempted to acquiesce, to abandon his lifework; this to him was a counsel of despair. He believed afterwards that if he had yielded to the formidable pressure then exercised upon him, he would have jeopardized his soul's salvation. He referred with a kind of dread to that anguish of indecision; with dread and gratitude, as in speaking of a horrible abyss from which a friendly hand had at the last moment restrained him:

> Certainly on that day I was sore thrust at that I might fall both here and in eternity. But the Lord graciously spared the stranger and sojourner for His name's sake; and He helped me exceedingly when I was thus trampled on, so that I did not come badly into disgrace and reproach.... Hence, therefore, I render unwearied thanks to my God Who kept me faithful in the day of my temptation....

Instead of submitting therefore, it would seem that he forced himself to go to Rome, where he was reinstated in office. He immediately returned and resumed his labors for the conversion of Ireland.

Saint Patrick was advanced in years by the time he had overcome those six obstacles to his free service. Henceforth he walked in liberty, but he had not far to go. The long level rays of sunset were already shining on his road. He died at peace in the midst of his adopted people. It is characteristic of him that his grave is unknown. Disputes about its location arose not very long after his burial and the uncertainty persists to the present day. In the annals of Christian history, he is an example of the prophet who was not stoned. In the history of the country he evangelized, his name shines out as the one patriot who was undefeated.

The legends woven around Patrick are the most sheerly poetic and the most beautiful in Christian hagiography. The mind that elaborated those stories was beautiful: a glad, utterly guileless mind, always grateful for the vision. It is the mind Patrick bequeathed to

Ireland. Both legend and authentic record show that, despite his great constructive gifts and volcanic energy, he was a man of the easiest approach, who inspired intense love and loyalty. The shining simplicity of his life must have been reflected in an abiding tranquility of expression, which won the world to him. When the chieftain Dichu heard of his landing, he sallied forth in battle array to bar his passage, but "when he saw the face of Patrick, he loved him." After the seasoned old warlord, it is a child who joins him. As he was mounting his chariot, taking leave of the parents of Benignus, the child clung to his foot in such a passion of grief that Patrick was forced to take him too. A delightful legend tells of another boy going to him in tears and the great missionary, gravely arresting those tears with his finger on the boy's cheek, turned them into gems. The two princesses, Ethne and Fedelm, trust him at sight and converse with him without a shadow of restraint.

His humble and cheerful comradeship with all classes once saved his life. The charioteer, Odran, overhearing a druidical plot to assassinate him, did not reveal it to his master but suggested instead that they should change places: in other words, Patrick would drive and Odran would recline at ease behind. Patrick at once assented, though the request must have seemed extraordinary. The result was that Odran was killed by a spear thrust and the saint escaped. The stories of Bishop MacCartan and Trea illustrate the same characteristic. When MacCartan had been serving Patrick for fourteen years, he thought it was time he had a rest. Being the saint's champion, his work was to assist him over the fords of rivers, over difficult roads, and in general to act as bodyguard and defense. Patrick was attached to him, and therefore it did not occur to him to give MacCartan promotion to easier work. But MacCartan conveyed the position by uttering the most dismal groans every time his services were required. "What's the matter with you?" said Patrick. "Age and infirmity," replied the other. "And all my comrades are now in churches whereas I am still on the road." "True," replied Patrick after a pause, and he immediately gave him a church.

When Trea came to be baptized, her veil was down over her face. It would seem that the angels had arranged it like that. The usual fashion was back over the head, and when Patrick reached her, he instinctively raised his hand to adjust the veil. "Is it not good that it should remain as it is?" said the maiden a trifle pertly. "It is good," said the Bishop submissively.

Patrick identified himself so closely with his converts that the world has almost come to regard him as an Irishman. But he was an exile among a people whom his compatriots in Empire regarded as barbarian. And frequently his state of exile pressed bleakly in upon him. He had recurrent attacks of homesickness in which the thought of revisiting his own people in Britain and Gaul rose with irresistible allurement before his mind:

> Wherefore then, even if I should wish to part from them, proceeding thus to Britain—and glad and ready was I to do so—as to my fatherland and kindred, and not only that, but to go as far as Gaul in order to visit the brethren and to behold the face of the saints of my Lord—God knoweth that I used to desire it exceedingly.

His peaceful conquest of Ireland was never touched with the least suggestion of exploitation. He must have drawn heavily upon some missionary funds upon the continent, for he seems to have personally financed the whole enterprise in order to win the people's confidence. He accepted nothing from them, not even the "laborer's hire." He had a horror of receiving any material reward for his work. He tells us himself that when pious women gave him gifts to express their recognition, he returned them. He returned them even when those gifts were cast upon the altar, preferring to cause a little transient hurt than to permit the initiation of a doubtful practice. He served his newly-ordained clergy without accepting from them, as he phrases it himself, "even the price of my shoe." "I did this so as to keep myself warily in all things.... and that I should not, even in the smallest matter, give occasion to the unbelievers to defame or disparage." His entire independence in all matters of material benefit made a profound impression on the pagans, as is illustrated in that amusing story of Daire and his cauldron. This unswerving attitude was one of the sources of Patrick's power.

Probably the greatest tribute ever paid to Saint Patrick occurs in Fiacc's Hymn, where such emphasis is laid on his power of overcoming by example where he had failed to convert by the spoken word. The greatest sermon he ever preached was his own life. That Hymn has preserved a remarkable picture of a man, who was "not deterred by cold, not possessed by hunger or thirst, sleeping on a bare stone, with a wet cloak around him, a rock for his pillow...enduring great toil."

SAINT BRENDAN (483–577)

by DONAL O'CAHILL

THE BIRTH OF BRENDAN WAS NOT WITHOUT PRESAGE. Patrick, standing on a Limerick hill and stirred by the grandeur of Kerry, had foretold it. Cara, Brendan's mother, had had a vision in which her bosom was bright with heavenly radiance and her breasts shone like snow. Erc, her bishop, had explained it saying she should bear a son great in power and rich with grace of the Holy Ghost. Airde, a wealthy neighbor, had invited St. Becc Mac De to prophesy some important event and he had answered: "There shall be born this night, between you and the sea, your true and worthy king whom kings and princes will honor, and whom he shall guide to heaven."

That night, in the year 483, the district north of Tralee was full of strange portent. A wondrous light blazed over Barra, near Fenit, illuminating the minds of men even as it struck the sea or lit the hills. For Brendan, son of Finnlugha and predestined patron of Kerry and Clonfert, was born… Early next morning Erc and Airde came, like the eastern kings five centuries before, to do homage to the promised child. Taking him in his arms, the bishop blessed him and claimed him as fosterling. Airde, rejoicing, made an alms of thirty cows with their thirty calves and offered his protection forever. Then the infant was taken to Ardfert and baptised at Wethers' Well, a place still honored by seasonal pilgrimage. Mobhi was the name first given him, but a mantle of white mist (broen finn) was seen to descend until it veiled all Fenit, and henceforth he who was white in soul and body was called Broenfinn or Brendan.

The Ireland into which Brendan had been thus ushered was fraught with great change. War's terrible intoxication was losing its attraction for the Irish, who were everywhere accepting the doctrines of Christ. The descendants of warriors who had harried the Romans to the Alps had yielded to the pleadings of Patrick and were even then raising throughout their land the foundations of a Spiritual Empire that was to last to the end of time.

When Brendan was a year old Erc, complying with custom and desirous of keeping him within his own jurisdiction, had him sent to fosterage in Killeedy, County Limerick. There but a very few years before, Saint Ita—the youthful Brigid of Munster—had founded her convent and gathered a number of women whose austerities and ministrations won the esteem of many saints. The nun whose mortifications inspired St. Cummian's writings naturally exercised a profound influence over Brendan. Her special interest in him is perhaps proof of the promise given even by his earliest years. He returned her affection by a devotedness that deepened with time and drew him back to her in later life for sympathy and counsel in all his undertakings.

After five years Brendan returned home and was placed under the care of Erc. In the early ages of the Church the duty of educating youthful aspirants to Holy Orders usually devolved on the bishops themselves. Thus it was with Saint Augustine in Hippo, with Saint Ambrose in Milan, and the same system obtained in the early instruction of the Irish Saints. To this preceptorship amid native surroundings we must turn if we would trace the growth of that fervor and love of perilous emprise which were to fructify so marvelously in the manhood of the saint. Erc—the boy's patron and earliest bishop of whom there is record in Kerry—has been identified with the "sweet-voiced" brehon who fearlessly acclaimed Patrick at the court of King

Laoghaire. Years before, on the withdrawal of Benignus to Connaught, he had come from Slane to continue the mission amongst the tribes of West Munster. None more fitted, Erc fired the boy's imagination with stories of Patrick's achievement and stirred the childish soul with a longing for emulation. Here, too, Brendan's wanderings by the sea bred a familiarity with its moods that mitigated its terrors, and its eternal thunderings sowed in his consciousness the seeds of a wanderlust not merely daring but divine. Of those years of pupilage in Kerry—and they continued for fourteen years—only the most meagre accounts have come down. These, however, convey an impression of Brendan's great application to study and of a character unusually strong.

The old legends linger upon those early days. Contrasting with the paucity of authentic record, they tell with much detail of his providential protection in times of danger and of his sustenance in need. In the drought of summer fresh springs burst forth for him, birds flew to his succor, and a doe came each morning from the upland of Luchra to yield him her milk. Once when ten years old, he accompanied Erc on a visit of ceremony. While the bishop was preaching, the boy—who had been left waiting in a chariot—proceeded to recite the psalms. A little girl, attracted by the sweetness of his voice, jumped in beside him and asked him to play. But Brendan, considering his dignity slighted, gave her a sound thrashing and regretted it immediately. He confessed his guilt to the bishop and received the stiff penance of spending that night in a cave. There the young penitent passed the time in prayer or in chanting the psalms, and his voice was so powerful even then, it was heard at a distance of a thousand paces. Erc was both pleased at the prompt obedience and amazed at the boy's courage. In Brendan's ready, almost gay compliance with the bishop's command there is evident not only the early development of his humility but the first proof of that fearlessness so striking in later years. Of this period of his life, and indeed of the subsequent ten years, but one fact is known: that he had the occasional companionship of his sister Briga. Perhaps this may be the reason for assuming that she too received her early training under Erc.

Having completed his preliminary studies at home, Brendan, at the age of twenty, went northward to the theological school of Clonfoish. While on the way he encountered the heathen warrior Colmán Mac Lenin. If the hardened soldier was not impressed by the student's bearing he was certainly fascinated by the imperiousness of his mission. For Brendan bade him forsake the ignoble calling of war and invited his service under the captaincy of the Universal King. He kindled the warrior's imagination with his story of a banner tattered, maybe, but unsullied and above surrender, and promised him a place in the Christian Army whose legions were to rise on the edges of the earth and whose glory should endure forever. The warrior yielded to the student. Together they travelled into Connaught, and Mac Lenin, kneeling before the aged Jarlath, became Brendan's first convert. He it was who founded Cloyne, became its first bishop, and is now venerated under the name of Saint Colmán.

Under the presidency of Jarlath the seminary of Clonfoish, near Tuam, had won a great reputation for the teaching of Scripture and it was to pursue such study that Brendan had enrolled. That his demeanor and application soon attracted notice is shown by the friendship that sprang up between master and pupil despite the disparity in their ages. Indeed Jarlath's removal of the See to Tuam—the seat of the present Archdiocese—was due to Brendan's suggestion when leaving.

Before Brendan's ecclesiastical studies were completed a large number of his kinsmen had settled at Magh Enna in Mayo. So large was that migration, the district chosen became known as "Upper Kerry." Thither Brendan next turned, probably at his kinsfolk's request and with a disciplinary eye to the more intractable members of the tribe. But subsequent events give the journey an even deeper significance. It is said that an angel appeared to him and dictated the Rule by which he was to govern his life and the lives of the multitudes later subject to him. Although the original is no longer extant, similar rules have come down from the immediate successors of Saint Patrick who were the pioneers of Irish monastic discipline. Of these early codes the most important is that of Saint Ailbe of Emly which is said to resemble in a general way the Rule of Saint Brendan. It enjoined absolute obedience and the observance of silence each day until the hour of one o'clock, for "two-thirds of piety consist in silence." The monks had to subsist on the most meagre fare and sleep on the floors of their cells, dressed in their habits, and with little covering. Hospitality was stressed but no lay person was allowed to enter the monastery enclosure. This rule of Ailbe's runs into sixty-nine strophes enumerating the minutest details of community life and shows a severity without parallel save in the records of Egyptian asceticism.

During Brendan's stay in Magh Enna there occurred an event which shattered the quietude of his visit. A young man had died and Brendan met the funeral cortege on the way. Filled with sorrow, he bade the relatives have faith and prayed over the corpse. The incredible happened—the dead man was restored, to the joy of an amazed throng. This stupendous news spread like wildfire and Brendan had to flee from the importunities of the people and from the inducements of the king who wished him to remain in their midst. But a wider conquest than that of the plains of Magh Enna was luring Brendan.

He returned home in the year 513 and being thirty years old—the age required by the canons of the early Church—he was ordained by his old preceptor, Erc. His gravity of purpose from the beginning is proved by his self-imposed abstinence. For he never afterwards partook of food that had had the breath of life although he imposed no such law upon his disciples. Immediately after ordination he set about stimulating in his native county that monastic spirit he had seen practised so imposingly elsewhere in Ireland. There can be little doubt that his labours were greatly facilitated by the influence of his family who were of noble lineage and several of whom became saints. It is probable that he was helped in no small degree too by those tribal whisperings of the miraculous powers he had exercised in the west. In a short time many followers gathered to his Rule and the growth of cells, oratories, and churches was a natural sequence. Though no date is ascribed to the foundation of Ardfert it is generally considered to have been his first. Barrow, Rathoo, Kilfenora, and a cell on Brandon Hill followed in quick succession. Thus there grew up, always under his guidance and not seldom built by his own hands, those various villages of huts with their common refectories and churches, and self-sustaining communities who devoted themselves to the monastic life.

The spontaneity of the response astonished Brendan. In the steady stream of disciples he saw proof of the enduring strength of Irish monasticism, and doubtless this initial success brought home to his mind the ultimate limitations of insular endeavor. He saw growing up throughout the land many institutions like those of Clonfoish and Clonard. Men and women, inspired by the same ideal, were thronging to them until Ireland, loud with psalms, became a gigantic hive of religion whose members' chief need was fresh fields to which they might bear their honeyed faith. It was a reversal of the Gospel state of things: harvesters were not lacking; the need was a new terrain where souls might be garnered for God. The situation did not leave Brendan unaffected for long. His practical mind probed the problem; it was appropriate that he should find a solution in the sun. Ever since childhood he had seen it blaze a path of glory over the wastes to the unknown west. Since the world began that sight had stirred even the least imaginative among men and, inevitably, it filled with dreams of discovery the missionary soul of Brendan. There, to the west, might be the haven he was hoping for—a possible outlet for that surging tide of the missionary Gael. "Everyone who hath left father, or mother, or sister, or lands, shall receive an hundredfold..." The words of the Gospel rose to his mind and thus, after something like twenty years' labors at home, Brendan thought of other lands.

Popular imagination has for long represented Brendan as an aimless wanderer, a sort of vagabond of the sea. Conventional accounts needed but a few judicious touches to portray him as a soft but successful pirate who had, somehow or other in a blanket of mist, captured a place in the Christian Calendar. No conception could be more remote from reality. In an age that was practical enough to produce multitudes of saints, Brendan was supremely practical. Even as a child he had shown signs of it in those odd moments of leisure snatched for study, and on the morning of his ordination too by those self-imposed rigors. He is Saint precisely because he was a navigator with the highest possible purpose, because he was in fact a conquistador for Christ.

A voyage of exploration had many attractions for one of Brendan's mold. It appealed to that spirit of daring he had shown even as a child in the cave, and it held too the alluring prospect of that perfect contemplation possible in a ship at sea. But even stronger reasons impelled him. The early Celtic peoples had an immemorial belief in the existence of an Elysium set beyond the rim of the western ocean. Bearing a variety of names this island shone in the amber light of romance, reflecting the desires of the different races. Even in Christian times there was a tradition current along the western seaboard of Ireland that the "Land of Promise" could be seen every seventh year. Brendan could not remain wholly indifferent to such tales. It seems however that his greatest incentive came from a brother monk, Barinthus, who was a navigator credited with western voyages. Having heard this monk's account of his travels, Brendan withdrew to his cell on Brandon Hill. There, for three days, he fasted and prayed for guidance—alone, with the ocean beneath him rolling outward to the alluring west.

At the end of the vigil Brendan announced his decision to sail and ordered three boats to be built. The crew of sixty were selected, provisions were gathered, and the day named. Then, with a courage that equaled his faith, he sailed from the Kerry bay that still bears his name and disappeared into romance and mist.

For periods varying between two and seven years Brendan is said to have explored the western ocean. Although the traditional accounts of his adventure are made grotesque by fable there is evidence that he reached a delightful land. Some accounts place his landing in Newfoundland and others mention the Virginian Capes. While these are not authoritative, there is said to be proof in indigenous remains that Irishmen had settled in America centuries before the Spanish sighted its shore. It is said too the Darien Indians spoke a language akin to that of the primitive Irish, and that an eighth century people in Florida were speaking the Irish tongue. Furthermore, the early Mexicans were undoubtedly acquainted with Christianity's central truths. When Cortez and his six hundred landed there in 1519 they were amazed to find their arrival hailed as the fulfilment of a native tradition, strong as it was certainly old. They were told that, many centuries before, one whom the natives called *Quetzalcoatl—the Precious*—had come from some "holy island" of the northeast, in a boat with "wings" or sails. According to their centuried tradition he was a tall white man, advanced in years, with broad forehead, black hair and beard, and he wore a long garment, over which hung a mantle marked with crosses. For several years he remained in their country teaching the divine faith. So greatly was he venerated by the people, they attributed his subsequent departure to the workings of some malign influence and were comforted only by his promise to return or to send some of his disciples instead.

This man was certainly a Christian missionary from Europe and it seems probable he labored among these Toltecs sometime between the sixth and eighth centuries. At that period there was great missionary activity among the nations of Europe, and those familiar with ecclesiastical history know that Ireland—*Insula Sanctorum*—was foremost, aflame with apostolic zeal, her sons shrinking from no peril, by land or sea, in their labor for the salvation of souls. If *Quetzalcoatl* was not Brendan—and the assumption that he was involves no serious inconsistency—then it seems fruitless to seek his identity. Nor is there lacking external evidence of Ireland's early maritime enterprise in the west. Icelandic sagas of great antiquity chronicled the western voyaging of Irish monks, and the Scandinavians knew the elusive island as *Irland it Mikla* or Ireland the Great. In many ancient maps Saint Brendan's Island, under various denominations, was marked in the western sea and to some extent influenced Columbus. So recently as 1634 the French geographer, Tassiu, drew a map in which he placed the island of Hy-Brazil to the west of Ireland.

Of the actual land discovered by Saint Brendan nothing authentic is known. An old legend, after picturesquely enumerating the perils of the voyage, tells of a lovely land with extensive meads decked with flowers and laved by many rivers, of thickly set trees, fruit-laden, swaying before scented winds in a light that always shone. Brendan explored the country in every direction and at last came to a great river which he was unable to cross. Here a heavenly messenger appeared to him and, telling him that the land would be made manifest to his successors, bade him depart.

Brendan's return home was the signal for great rejoicings. Crowds flocked to welcome the Christian Ulysses whose reappearance had the air of a return from the dead. Even the wonted calm of monastic life was broken by tales of marvelous exploits: how Brendan's ships laden with plants, seeds, and provisions had struggled against raging seas; of the islands seen and the wonders worked; of the monks' arrival and stay in the long-sought land, and of the angelic voice bidding them return. The heroic deeds thus related flew through the schools of Ireland, to Britain and the Continent until the name of Brendan became talismanic throughout Europe. It was inevitable that tales told with such impetus, and by nature of their very appeal, should develop into diverse and fantastic legends. Recited in Irish, sung in Norman-French, and read in an increasing number of languages during the eleventh century, Brendan's adventures fascinated the mediaeval mind and later influenced, among others, the poet Dante.

The Saint's fame brought religious thronging to his Rule. Providence was aiding him and he lost no time in turning to good account the material that lay at hand. He began with Kerry. In a sequence not determined he raised foundations at Kilmalchedar, Gallerus, and in the Blasket Islands, as though in response to that insistent call of the sea. Perhaps there was too in that choice a certain prescience of the trend of the later Gael. To Iveragh also it is thought he turned and built in the Glen Parish, near Caherciveen. With unabated zest he travelled constantly between the different communities, superintending, teaching, gathering neophytes, until Kerry was girdled with religious settlements and he was again seized with that divine unrest.

THE RULE THUS STRENGTHENED AND HIS SPIRITUAL SWAY AT HOME secured left Brendan still unsatisfied. He seemed hypnotized by conquest, he had an insatiable thirst for souls. Having appointed a successor, he left his native county and again his course is vague. The versatility of the man can be gathered from the fact that subsequently he occupied a chair at the school of Ross and founded a monastery at Inishdadrum, on the Shannon, where he worked several miracles. It is a matter of conjecture whether at this period he turned to Ireland's most famous school, Clonard. That he studied there at some time is certain, and the native love of learning in those days is sufficient to counter the possible objection of old age.

The fame of Clonard attracted crowds of students of all ages not only from Ireland but from abroad. Founded by Saint Finnian in 520, this college on the Boyne grew from a hermitage of wattles to an immense monastic establishment like a translated town of the Thebaid. There under the canopy of heaven, in those fields by the river, could be seen the amazing spectacle of three thousand scholars, freely fed and freely taught, acquiring the Classics, Philosophy, and Scriptures, and giving homage to God before Augustine had yet seen the heathen hordes of England.

It is impossible to determine how long Brendan remained at Clonard. When we next meet him, however, he is again trimming his sails for the sea. This second voyage is said to have been advised by Saint Ita and undertaken about the year 530 in penance for some rash act. But a more likely supposition is that his decision was influenced by the sojourn at Clonard. Finnian had labored for many years among the Britons in Wales and it is very probable he urged Brendan to a similar mission. So once more, impelled by the old impulse, Brendan spread sail and this time turned his prow to the east. There ensued a ten years' absence from Ireland which, despite the vagueness of his itinerary, stamps him as worthy of a place among the most indefatigable missionaries of our race.

Restless as the sea he loved or the winds he bent to his will, he followed his calling with the superb abandon of one who acknowledged it eternal and bounded only by the commandments of God. His was a sustained whirlwind campaign. One might light on his tracks anywhere from the Azores to the Arctic, or from Avilion to the littorals of the Holy Land. In Caledonia, considered unconquerable even by the Roman, he walked as if with royal license. There particularly he seems to have spent considerable time. Perhaps the secret of that protracted stay lies in the call of his exiled kin! At any rate his ubiquity there is commemorated by a variety of churches, shrines, and patrons, and by numerous hills, rivers, and sounds bearing his name. With the sea-roving Cormac he visited Iona and brought to the Orkneys and Shetland the light of faith. Nor is it unlikely that he voyaged at this time to St. Kilda, the Faroes, or even to the Ultima Thule of the north.

That these islands were visited by Irish monks in the early centuries of Christianity is undisputed history. Irish bells, books, and croziers were found in Iceland by Gardar the Dane in 863, and by Ingulf eleven years later when the Norwegians colonized it.

When he had spent three years in the north Brendan appeared in Wales, astonishing the people by his miracles. While there he visited that famous alumnus of Armagh—Gildas the Wise. We find Brendan with Saint Cadoc at the monastery of Lancarvan, and then building a hermitage, as might be expected, on the banks of the Severn. Still later he labored with his friend of the Atlantic voyage, Saint Malo, in Brittany. There he founded Alyth—Alectum—and lent his name to several spots along that shattered coast. A shrine to Saint Brendan in Teneriffe may not be unconnected with his voyage to Palestine.

Brendan's return about the year 540 is invested with the mystery that surrounded his departure. From the conflicting accounts there emerges, however, one fact: that he brought with him many disciples, one of whom bore princely rank. It is stated that Brendan visited Saint Brigid after his return, but as her death occurred twenty-five years earlier this chronology is manifestly wrong. Whatever the date of his visit, its purpose is interesting. During his travels abroad Brendan had heard Saint Brigid's help invoked with astonishing success. Greatly edified, he composed a hymn in her honor and on returning home he visited the Saint. Being asked the reason of her great power, she replied that never for a moment was her attention diverted from God. Whereupon Brendan, no doubt magnifying his peccadilloes, confessed his remissness and was sweetly reproved. The meeting is important because it shows the great humility which ran as a leitmotif through the lives of all the Irish Saints. Brendan's life was a prolonged striving after perfection; it is not wholly figurative to say he hid from ecclesiastical honors or knelt in penance before a nun.

It was probably after his return from this voyage that he built at Clonemery and carried on those labors that gave his name to a hill by the Nore. After this the ring of his evangel is heard once again in Connaught, but that thundering voice is on the wane. There on the Corrib, with his nephew, Moennen, he founded the monastery of Inchiquin—his first in the west—in the year 552. A little later and in the same vicinity he raised for his sister, Briga, and her community the nunnery of Anaghdown. That divine urge was still his driving force, but one has now the impression that he was fighting against time. He went northward to Mayo and established himself in the solitude of Inish-Gloria—an island off the coast. There he must have given himself up to contemplation. The years were crowding in upon him even as the billowing seas around his island home. Since his boyhood the world had grown larger, in the sphere of exploration he himself had played an honorable part. He recalled those voyages eastward and northward, the clamant heathen hosts. He looked to the west and remembered. There was challenge in what he saw: the infinite possibilities of the mission, the urgency of this warfare for souls. And relieved against all was the stark inadequacy of human endeavor.

Brendan's response was typical. He went south into Galway and there by the Shannon, in the year 560, founded the missionary school of Clonfert. He threw into the work all his remaining energy for it was the culmination of his labors and the last great venture of his life. Clonfert's rapid growth to the forefront of Ireland's numerous academies is a tribute to his influence and fame. Under the guidance of his nephew, Bishop Moennen, it attracted the intellect of Europe and had illustrious names on its roll. Renowned warriors become students might have been met there, or white-cowled mendicants who could have worn crowns. On the authority of Senan we have it that no less than six boat loads of foreign students, bound for the school, came up the Shannon on one day. Thus the school flourished for many centuries, fed on the produce of its own pastures, weaving its own wool, served by its own fleet, and numbering by the thousand those students whose heaven-fired enthusiasm sped the Faith to every land in Europe.

The organization of so important a settlement as Clonfert was heavy work for Brendan. But frequently, too, he was forced to absent himself. He responded to those urgent calls from his scattered communities, he attended Chapters, made visitations, arbitrated feuds. For about twenty years he toiled ceaselessly up and down the country, never slackening in his regard for the disciples of his Rule. But the work was wearing him and he was withering with the years. During those last visits to Kerry there was a longing in his heart and the brethren saw sadness in his looks at the sea.

In the year 577 he went to his sister's convent at Anaghdown. There, on Sunday the 16th May, having celebrated Mass, he turned to the community and told them that his end was near. An old Life, recording the dialogue between the Saint and his sister, recreates that pathetic scene and echoes, however faintly, their tremulous tones:

> BRENDAN: "Commend to God in your prayers my departure from this life."
>
> BRIGA: "Dear father, what have you to fear?"
>
> BRENDAN: "I fear as I pass away all alone, and as the journey is darksome, I fear the unknown region, the presence of the King, the sentence of the Judge."

Then Brendan, at the age of ninety-four, having given final directions for his burial, blessed the community and passed to his reward.

Great multitudes, hearing the news, flocked to the convent and clamored for the privilege of having his body buried in their midst. But the Saint had foreseen this difficulty and had provided. In the dead of night and by stratagem his remains were taken in a wagon from Anaghdown, on the three days' journey to the place of his choice—Clonfert. There, in all honor, Brendan—Saint and Navigator—was laid to rest while psalms were chanted, canticles sung, and maybe the winds and the waves were still.

SAINT COLUMCILLE (521–597)

by RAYMOND O'FLYNN

THERE IS A CHAPTER IN THE *IMITATION* ON THE "DIFferent motions of nature and of grace"; a complementary one might be added on their conformities. For it is not the effect of grace to destroy or to supersede nature, but to uphold and elevate it. Grace is essentially positive—an affirmation of all truth, a desire of all goodness, a delight in all loveliness; it is the assertion of the will-to-live.

No doubt, so long as the flesh lusts against the spirit, the negative aspects of asceticism will be prominent, and it is chiefly self-reproof and self-correction that are stressed by the older hagiology. But there is a newer, and perhaps a better way: which is, to exhibit the lives of the saints in accordance with their psychology; to show how this special character resulted in this special holiness.

In the case of the Irish saints this procedure is even obvious. For in no other people has the fusion of blood and religion been so natural or so complete. Some close affinities must have existed between the old Gaedhlic stock and the Gospel engrafted on it, when it burgeoned spontaneously into such luxuriant holiness. Already in the lifetime of their National Apostle, "the sons and daughters of the Scots were becoming monks and virgins of Christ" in numbers unprecedented. That vivid Celtic imagination which had peopled the countryside with preternatural agencies enabled them all but to visualize the unseen things of Faith. That dissatisfaction of soul which betrayed itself in wistful yearnings for the Land of the Ever-Young was readily transformed into Christian unworldliness. That ardent temperament—the *perfervidum ingenium Scotorum*, as it came to be called—speedily generated an army of intrepid apostles. That strange, almost mysterious influence, which made all who came into contact with them "more Irish than the Irish themselves," bade fair to fill Europe with their spirit. And generally the work of grace in them looked less like a new creation than a new direction.

But, among "the hosts of the Saints of Eire" there is one who represents in an eminent degree the national character sublimated by grace, and who, on that account, has been canonized in the supreme Triad of Ireland's sainthood by a people meticulous even as to the distinctions of sanctity. There were brave men, it has been said, before Agamemnon, and they were lost in oblivion, *sacro quia carent vate*—because they lacked an inspired bard. More fortunate in that respect than Patrick or Brigid, Columba was celebrated by the chief poet of his nation in a Song of Praise—the extant *Amhra Choluim Chille.* And fittingly. For it was he—himself a "harp without a base chord," as witness his Latin and Irish verses—who "stayed the poets," when they were threatened with banishment for their troublesomeness. But, what is of greater import still, he has been made the subject of a biography which Montalembert describes as "one of the most living, most attractive and most authentic monuments of Christian history."

According to its author's "Preface," based on "what was committed to writing before our time, or what we, diligently inquiring, have learned by hearing from certain experienced and faithful ancients," the "Life" by Adamnan, Abbot of Iona, is vivid and graceful portraiture indeed. To be sure, it is frank hagiography, and abounds in miracles and celestial apparitions which bespeak an age of greater Faith than ours. But why demur?—the modern world gapes even at the actualities of Lourdes; while we, who know how intimately interfused are nature and grace, feel as little misgiving when we read that the Saint changed water into wine for the Sacred Mysteries, or was visited by angels, as when we are told he transcribed the Psalter, or scaled the Grampians and urged his curragh through Loch Ness.

Whatever of the aura that surrounds the saint, even the unbeliever must acknowledge the greatness of the man and the splendor of his achievement. Columba has left no such literary monument as his younger contemporary Columbanus, nor did he occupy a like position in the ample field of Continental affairs. Yet has he made an impression on the imagination and exercised a spell over the heart more like the heroes of legend than the characters of history. To proud lineage, noble physique and fine culture, he united the lofty aspiration and splendid daring of the Ireland of his day; and fulfilled his vast enterprise in romantic conditions that would have enhanced the exploits of Cuchulain or Fionn. He was "the high saint and high sage, the archpresbyter of the island of the Gaedhal, the brand of battle set forth with the divers talents and gifts of the Holy Ghost." "There was not born of the Gaedhal," adds an old biographer, "a being more illustrious, or wise, or of better family than Columbkille, nor did there come of them another who was more modest, more humble, or more lowly."

Such the personality that forms the background to the prophecies, miracles, and visions which are the explicit theme of Adamnan. But it is a personality expressed with photographic distinctness. Certain events may be obscure; but the man himself, "angelic of aspect, clean in speech, holy in work, great in council"; the "Island-Soldier of Christ who could not pass the space even of a single hour without applying himself to prayer, or reading, or writing, or some manual labor"; the founder of churches and the friend of saints and kings, "dear to all, ever showing a pleasant, holy countenance," is more intimately known to us than any personage of his epoch.

"Noble in sooth," says the Life given in the *Leabhar Breac*, "was Columbkille's kindred, for of the kindred of Conaill son of Niall was he." The child was born on December 7th, 521, at Gartan, Co. Donegal, his father Fedhlimidh being Prince of Tyrconnel, and his mother Ethne eleventh in descent from Cathair Mor, progenitor of the Kings of Leinster. According to custom, he was given in fosterage to the priest who had baptised him Colum (Dove), and from a cell where he was used to pray he early gained the addition by which he has since been distinguished. "Has our little Colum," the children of the place would ask, "come today from the cell in Tir Lughdech in Cinnel Conaill?"

His education was continued in the Ecclesiastical School of St. Finnian at Moville, Co. Down, and after a further period of secular instruction by Gemman, an aged Bard of Leinster, he passed to the great institution of Clonard. There he had for preceptor another St. Finnian, "the Wise Tutor of Eire's Saints," and for associates the group who, with Ciaran the founder of Clonmacnoise and himself, were to become renowned as "the Twelve Apostles of Erin." Being ordained a priest by Bishop Etchen, he prosecuted his studies in the institute of St. Mobhi at Glasnevin near Dublin, where he remained until the students were dispersed by the Yellow Plague which devastated many parts of Europe in 544.

Incidentally, it is for those who talk of an "independent" Scottish Church to ask themselves if the pupil of St. Finnian, who had himself frequented Candida Casa (Whitherne) founded by the Papal Missionary St. Ninian, and who had stayed three months with Pope Pelagius learning "apostolical customs," was less likely to be a "Roman" Catholic than his master, even supposing Columbkille could have derived his Christianity from any other source than the "Roman" Church of St. Patrick.

Columbkille was only twenty-five, when he opened his first church and school amid the "Oak Trees of Calgaich," and in sight of "the salt main on which the sea-gulls cry"—"my Derry, my little Oak Grove," as he affectionately remembered it; and his subsequent career in Ireland was that of a monastic founder and scholar, until he "set up his everlasting rest in Iona" in 563. "A hundred churches which the wave frequents he has on the margin," says the *Leabhar Breac.* But there were others. Thirty-seven have been identified; and, significantly, two of them—Durrow and Kells—are associated with precious manuscripts. So richly and exquisitely illuminated is the Book of Kells, Cambrensis thought it must be the work of angels. Plausibly enough, tradition once ascribed it to Columbkille himself, for he was a lover of fine art and a tremendous bibliophile. The Lismore Life credits him with the writing of three hundred books; and though this may be merely a round number, no notice is so frequent in Adamnan as that which shows him engaged in writing. For instance: "On another day, about the same hour, a shout was raised on the other side of the strait; and the Saint, sitting in his little hut which rested on a wooden floor, says to Diarmuid: The man who is shouting beyond the strait is not a man of refined sentiment, for to-day he will upset and spill my ink-horn!"

In fact, according to an inveterate tradition, it was violation of the law of copyright that led to his exile. Was the original the Psalter of St. Jerome recently brought from Rome by St. Finnian? Was the copy, transcribed in a "neat but hurried hand," that known as 'the Cathach' or 'Battle,' which the O'Donnells carried before their array for more than a thousand years, and which is now in the Library of the Royal Irish Academy? Was Columbkille really responsible for mustering his kinsmen against the Ard Righ at Culdreimhne? Was he sentenced to perpetual exile for the bloodshed? (Ominously, his name is connected with two other battles—Coleraine in 577 and Culfedha near Clonard ten years later—and he was certainly a stout clansman.) Whatever be the truth of the matter, some crisis occurred, when he was at the height of his success, to induce him to quit the land he loved. Adamnan suggests that his venture was a voluntary *peregrinatio pro Christo.* And we can well believe that the spirit of high adventure which sped his victorious ancestor Niall through Britain to the Loire, and in pursuit of which King Dathi died at the foot of the Alps, was urgent in the blood of the Christian priest. At any rate, in company of twelve others (the Irish, as a rule, conformed to the Apostolic pattern) he directed his course to "Alba of the ravens"—the leader of that intrepid army of *peregrini* who, with staff and satchel of books, clad in white woolen tunic, and having strange frontal tonsure from ear to ear, and eyelids tinted blue, were to make Europe resound for five centuries to the *militiae Christi*—the warfare of Christ.

There is an old Celtic poem with the inscription *Columbkille fecit*, reminiscent of his Irish home—"the song of the wonderful birds the"; "level sparkling strand"; "the thunder of the crowding waves upon the rocks." But more often quoted are the lines from his "Song of Farewell":

> There is a grey eye
> That looks back upon Erin:
> It shall not see during life
> The men of Erin, nor their wives.
> My vision o'er the brine I stretch
> From the ample oaken planks;
> Large is the tear of my soft grey eye
> When I look back upon Erin.

In point of fact, he revisited Ireland more than once; certainly in 575 when he took part in the Convention of Druim Ceatt, and again before his death, when all Clonmacnoise, monks and populace, thronged to meet him, "as if," says Adamnan, "he were an angel of the Lord." Still, for thirty-four years the Islet of Iona was his permanent abode. There is a legend that he navigated from one island to another until he finally ran his curragh into the little bay since known as Port-na-Curraich. From the hill above—Cam-cul-ri-Erin, the Cairn of the Back turned to Ireland—he was satisfied he could no longer descry his native shores, and there amid the silence of the seas he built his monastery.

We can easily imagine it from Adamnan—the oaken church, where were celebrated the "Sacred Mysteries of the Eucharist"; the *monasterium rotundum*, probably a round tower; the guest-chamber with its fireplace and vessels of water; the wattled cells of the monks; the farmstead; the mill for grinding corn; and, not least remarkable, below in the harbor the fleets of boats with "sailyards in the form of a cross" plying to and fro with their cargoes of oak and pinewood. It was a veritable hive of industry, for the Columban rule, with its Penitential Discipline, suffered no drones and, apart from the short hours of sleep, the time not given to prayer was spent in a variety of manual industries and—a distinctive feature of Irish foundations—in the writing of books.

Unlike the homes of St. Benedict, an Irish monastery was never a mere asylum from the tumult of the world. Rather it was a citadel, a base of operations from which the "soldier of Christ" (Adamnan's expression) could conduct his campaign in the surrounding territory. According to this native conception, Iona was meant to be a strategic point to preserve the Faith among the Scots of Dalriada, and to carry it to the utmost confines of the Picts. Columbkille himself headed the expedition which had for objective King Brude in his northern fastness near Inverness. He pushed his way by land and water through the series of glens and lochs, now linked by the Caledonian Canal, but in those days presenting difficulties which had deterred the legionaries of Agricola. The effort met with success; and from that onwards we read of journeys of hundreds of miles on foot, and still more perilous voyages on uncharted seas, until not only the whole of Pictland, but the Hebrides, the Orkneys, the Shetlands, and even the Faroe Isles and Iceland were brought into the "obedience of Christ." So energetically, in fact, was the work carried on, that, already in the life-time of its founder, Iona was able to dispatch missionaries to Northumbria, and the Isle of Man, and Southern Britain.

With the incessant coming and going, the "watch" on Torr Abb must needs keep a strict lookout. When it was not some of the brethren rounding the northern side from a missionary outpost in the Isles, or strangers from distant Istria approaching on the south, it was a visitor from Ireland hailing across the Sound, or kindling the beacon-fire at night. Then must the little ferryboat put out and row him across the mile of water. For Irish hospitality was even a point of Rule at Iona; and "many," the Scriptures said, "doing hospitality, have entertained angels unawares." If it chanced to be a bishop, like Cronan from Munster, he was received with "the veneration due to him," and "bidden by the Saint to consecrate Christ's Body according to custom," and "in the episcopal rite." If it were an old friend and distinguished—Comgall of Bangor, or Caennech of Ossory, or Brendan of Clonfert—the ordinary fast was dispensed, and there was what Adamnan calls a "joyful day" in the community. When it was none of these, it was sure to be Cormac—a monkish Ulysses more in his element "seeking a solitude in the pathless sea" than poring over Greek manuscripts beneath the oak trees of Durrow. No one could tell when that restless adventurer might turn up. Columbkille expostulated with him: "Two years and a month to this night is the time thou hast been wandering from port to port, from wave to wave." Yet he loved the man—he was interesting, and could tell of a voyage of fourteen days and nights to the Arctic ice, and of encounters with strange monsters that threatened the vessel's side, and loathsome creatures "like frogs" that swarmed over the blades of the oars. The solicitous Abbot even used his influence with the Chieftain of the Orkneys to obtain for him safe conduct, and on one occasion summoned the brethren by bell to "pray with all fervor for Cormac; for voyaging too far he has ventured beyond the bounds of human enterprise."

But Columbkille was one of those whose sympathy extends to the meanest thing that breathes, and when the expected visitor was merely a crane—"a certain guest," he calls him—"who will arrive very weary and fatigued after the ninth hour of the day and, its strength almost exhausted, will fall on the shore"—even so, the sacred laws of hospitality were not to be neglected. "Thou must keep a lookout," he orders, "on the western part of the isle, sitting on the seashore; and thou shalt lift it up kindly, and carry it to a neighboring house, and attend it for three days and three nights." "At the end of three days" (the delicacy of sentiment is remarkable) "refreshed, and unwilling to sojourn longer with us, it will return to the pleasant region of Ireland whence it came. And I thus earnestly commend it to thee for that it came from the place of our own fatherland."

For such "minor occurrences" one may well be content to forgo a volume of historic lore. But there were episodes of greater social concern too, as when the Abbot "ordained" Aedhan king of the Scots of Dalriada, or journeyed with that monarch to Ireland, and secured political autonomy for the subject colony in Alba. It may be remarked by the way that the inauguration of the Scottish sovereign is the "earliest recorded instance of a royal coronation in Great Britain," and that part of the ceremonies then used survives in the corresponding service at Westminster. Normally, however, the life at Iona was that which has been outlined. It was a life of homely occupations, diversified by much land-faring and sea-faring, and hallowed by supernatural incidents more fit to be "a spectacle for angels than for men."

But "there remaineth a day of rest for the people of God." The time was to come when the "Soldier of Christ" should cease from his labors. No more should he embark in his coracle, or mount his chariot, or penetrate the dense forest with no other help than his staff, and no other defense than the "Prayer of God". No longer should he be seen "reciting the *Three Fifties* on the sand of the shore before sunrise," or "carrying his portion of corn on his back to the mill." No longer should he celebrate the "Mysteries of the Sacred Oblation," or lift up his voice praised for its "sweetness above all clerics." Even the period was to be affixed to the verse of the Psalm he was transcribing. "Here I must stop at the foot of this page," he said, "let Baithin write what follows."

Appropriately, it was on the *Die Sabbato* of the ecclesiastical week, he and the faithful Diarmuid went to inspect and bless the granary for the last time. "Greatly," he said, "do I congratulate the monies of my household that this year also you will have enough for the year without stint." And then: "This day is truly a Sabbath day for me, because it is for me the last day of this present laborious life, and at midnight, when begins the solemn Day of the Lord, I shall go the way of my fathers." Whereupon Diarmuid began to "weep bitterly." "And the saint tried to console him as well as he could."

Half way back to the monastery, being "weary with age" he sat down to rest by the roadside when "behold, the white horse, the one which used to carry the milk pails to and fro between the byre and the monastery, coming up to the Saint, lays his head against his breast, and began to whinny and shed copious tears, while foaming at the mouth." Seeing this, Diarmuid began to drive away the "weeping mourner." But the Saint forbade him—"Let him alone, let him alone, for he loves me. To this brute beast the Creator Himself has in some way revealed that his master is about to depart." And so saying, he "blessed his servant the horse as it sadly turned to go away from him."

True soldier to the end, he was in his place with the rest at the Vespers of the vigil of the Lord's Day and, "as soon as this is over, he returns to his cell and sits up through the night on his bed, where he had the bare rock for mattress and a stone for pillow." But when the bell rang for Matins, rising quickly, he hastened to the church before the others. Diarmuid, who followed close, saw the place flooded with heavenly brightness, but on his entering all was dark. "Where art thou, Father?" he called in a voice choked with tears; and "the lamps of the brethren not yet being brought, groping in the dark, he found the Saint lying before the altar. Sitting beside him, and raising him up a little, he lays the holy head on his bosom. Meanwhile the monks, running up with lights, began to weep at the sight of their dying Father. And, as we have learnt from some who were present, the Saint, with eyes upturned, looked round with wonderful cheerfulness and joy of countenance, seeing the holy Angels coming to meet him. Diarmuid then lifts up the holy right hand to bless the choir of monks. But the venerable Father himself moved his hand as much as he was able. And after thus signifying his holy benediction he breathed forth his spirit. The countenance remained so long gladdened by the vision of the Angels, that it seemed not to be that of one dead, but of one living and sleeping." It was Sunday the 9th of June, in the year 597.

So passed away one of the most majestic personalities in the history of the Christian Church. For three days after his death, "a great tempest without rain lashed the billowy waters," and prevented anyone crossing from the mainland, so that his obsequies were carried out with "melodious psalmody" by his spiritual children alone. The body "wrapped in a fair shroud" remained in the tomb at Iona until the Danish invasions; and it was then translated to Ireland, where it rests "under the flagstone under which are Patrick and Brigid."

Meet burial-ground for the man who loved the green hills, and the broad plains, and the winding shores, but most of all the churches of Holy Ireland. Three places, according to the *Leabhar Breac*, make up his "full habitation." To Iona from which he "preached the word of God to the men of Alba, and to the Britons, and to the Saxons" he gave his "grace without stain"; to Derry, "full of white angels from one end to the other" his soul; and where else should his body be bestowed but in that old Barn of Dichu at Saul in which Patrick said his first Mass on Irish soil?

Fisher-folk in the Hebrides still invoke Columbkille in their Shieling Hymn, and his name is engraved imperishably on the "fleshy tablets" of countless Irish hearts; but he is almost unknown in a land which owes its Christianity, and in great part its civilization, chiefly to him and his disciples. Even Catholics hear mention of him in England only in a prayer which enumerates "Our Fathers in the Faith." And yet, without his far-flung apostolate, there would hardly have been a Christian foundation among the Anglo-Saxons. After Augustine's death, the semi-converted tribes relapsed for the most part into heathenism, with little hope of recovery in the welter of barbarism and internecine warfare now dignified as the Heptarchy. But when the Hibernicised Oswald of Northumbria appealed to the monks of Iona, he introduced the force which definitely established Christianity through the whole extent of Anglo-Saxon occupation. Bishop Lightfoot summed up the situation when he wrote: "Augustine was the apostle of Kent, but Aidan was the apostle of England." Aidan was the spearhead of the Keltic invasion which was launched from Iona only thirty-eight years after the arrival of the Roman missionaries, and which continued supreme in the island until the coming of the Norman-French. Then another foreign influence began to mold the Anglo-Saxon races. But if they got their political organization and "Parliament" from the French, they got their Religion and Church from the Irish. It is true Columbkille was in his grave when a mission on a national scale was projected for England. But his memory was still recent in Iona, and it was his spirit that became the tradition of his successors. Courage, scholarship, humanism were vividly present in the monks of St. Columbkille, and no more pleasing amity ever sprang up between two peoples, nor one more prolific of the fruits of Religion and Culture than that which subsisted from first to last between the pupil Saxon and the tutelary Gaedhal.

It was the triumph of the "Irish Way" in the sphere of missionary enterprise. And that "Irish Way" had been pointed out by the greatest of their apostles—the devoted, affectionate, and scholarly Columba; the man who effected a more enduring conquest of Britain than Caesar, and brought a greater blessing than any comprised under the "Roman Peace." Iona is desolate, and Canterbury a mere simulacrum. But when Englishmen are recalled to a true sense of their past, it is of Iona they will think with affectionate reverence, as the cradle of their ancient Religion and the fount of their purest civilization.

SAINT COLUMBANUS (530?–615)

by VINCENT MCNABB, O.P.

> BANGOR...there had been a very celebrated monastery under the first Abbot Comgall which produced many thousands of monks, and was the head of many monasteries. A truly holy place it was, and prolific of saints... Into foreign lands these swarms of saints poured as though a flood had risen; of whom one, St. Columbanus, came to our Gallic parts and built the monastery of Luxeuil and there made a great people. Indeed so great a people was it, we are told, that the choirs succeeding one another in turn, the solemnities of the Divine Office went on unceasingly, so that not a day or night was empty of praise. (St. Bernard, *Life of St. Malachy*)

> The Abbey of Luxeuil was recognized as the monastic capital of all the countries under Frank Government. (Montalembert, *The Monks of the West*, Vol. II, book 7)

AFTER FOURTEEN CENTURIES THE MOST ILLUSTRIOUS Frenchmen are still grateful to the Irish Saint who once dwelt in their midst. Such *Laus perenmis* from the gratitude of France could be justified only by a character too great for the skill of any biographer. My readers will, therefore, understand that they are being offered not a complete life of one of Ireland's greatest sons and saints, but an outline sketch in charcoal which may serve to send them on a voyage of discovery amidst the manuscripts of monastic Ireland.

These manuscripts though outnumbering those of most of his contemporaries are hardly more than the droppings from a banquet table. Yet their scarcity has one compensation. Their very fewness leaves such gaps in the recorded doings of the saint that what is recorded tends to present a series of dramatic incidents which demand that indispensable element in all dramatic art—"the creative onlooker."

The only quite certain date in the Saint's life is the date of his death, 23 Nov., 615. Perhaps there is a touch of divine poetry in the fact that a soul so dedicated to the timeless principles of the spirit should enter history only by the day he entered eternity.

All historians agree that he came of a noble Leinster family. But they disagree about the year of his birth, some placing it as late as A.D. 543; some as early as A.D. 530. His people were of a noble Leinster stock—the aristocrats of Irish aristocracy!

According to the Abbot Jonas who wrote his life some thirty years after the Saint's death, Columbanus was trained in *Liberalium litterarum doctrinis et grammaticorum studiis.* In other words the young Leinster aristocrat received the highest classical education.

It would be natural for the Leinster youth to go to Clonard the great mother-school of Ireland which the Leinster Saint Finnian had founded with a rare Gaelic blending of sanctity and scholarship. No doubt Columbanus like the rest of the youth athirst for Greek and Latin culture built himself a wattle-hut.

We are in touch with the realities of his university life in listening to Abbot Jonas telling us how Columbanus was *formae elegantis praesertim corporis candore*—of handsome appearance, especially of fair complexion. The olive skinned southerner remembers the fair Gaelic "skin" of the Saint.

It was inevitable that a young Leinster aristocrat of no less talent than good looks should soon cross swords with the devil of the flesh. Jonas represents the matter as an attack made on the virtue of the youth by "*lascivae puellae.*" Light is thrown on the matter by the fact that somewhere about this time the king of Cualann sent his daughter to St. Finnian at Clonard to read her Psalter in Latin. It would hardly be beyond the evidence to say that Clonard housed some girl-students under conditions somewhat akin to our modern Universities.

A fundamental quality of the Saint's soul is shown in his way of meeting the battle now set up within him. But the Abbot Jonas must tell it in his own words.

> Whilst he was turning these things over within him he came to the cell of a religious woman dedicated to God. After having greeted her with lowly voice, he made as bold as he could to seek her counsel with the forwardness of youth.
>
> When she saw him in the budding strength of youth, she said: "I going forward with all my strength began the battle. For twelve years have I had no home. Since I sought this place of exile—Christ being my leader—I have never followed the world; having set my hand to the plough I have never looked back. Had I not been of the weaker sex I would have crossed the seas and sought an even more hidden place of pilgrimage.
>
> "You are aflame with the fires of youth, yet you dwell in the land of your birth. You lend your ear willy nilly to weak voices, your own weakness bending you. Yet you think you can freely avoid women. Do you remember Eve coaxing, Adam yielding, Samson weakened by Delilah, David lured from his old righteousness by Bethsabee's beauty, Samson the Wise deceived by the love of women?
>
> "Go," she said, "go, child, and turn aside from the ruin into which so many have fallen. Leave the path that leads to the gates of hell." Affrighted by these words and—beyond what you would believe of a youth terror-stricken—he returns thanks to his chastener, and bidding farewell to his companions he sets out. His mother

> beseeches him not to leave her... Casting herself on the ground she refuses him leave to go. But he crossing the threshold and his mother, implores her not to be broken with grief, saying that she shall see him no more in this life, but that whither soever lies the path of holiness, there will he go.

Leaving aside from this moving story what may or may not be due to the imagination of the historian we find the Columbanus who never once went back but always went on and on. We miss the hot-headed somewhat self-opinionated Celt so dear to modern historians. We have the picture of a handsome clever aristocrat at issue with his first battle, yet so self-mistrustful that he timidly seeks counsel where counsel can best be had. This religious woman, dedicated to God, is no doubt one of those noble women of the world who in Ireland and England withdrew in such numbers from the temptations of their high state of life. Only gradually did her shy visitor unlock his soul to this holy woman. Historians have not noticed the very human quality in this lad's search for help. There were many wise priests in the Ireland of his day, and especially at Clonard, if we are here dealing with Clonard. But there are shy lads that can hardly muster courage to unlock their souls to a priest even in confession. They seem to be able to say what they want to say at first only to a cloistered nun. Every cloister of contemplative nuns from this nameless counsellor of Columbanus down to the Little Flower of Lisieux is the authentic proof of the shyness of the stronger sex.

Later on when he had left his beloved land of birth and was the spiritual father of a family of monks he wrote a Rule, which is almost a spiritual autobiography. In it we find a chapter with the now misleading title "*On Mortification.*" It speaks of taking counsel and of obeying counsel taken. How far are we from the headstrong Celt in words like these: "Nothing is sweeter than calm of conscience, nothing safer than purity of soul, which yet no one can bestow on himself because it is properly the gift of another."

The words of this religious woman meant that Columbanus is next to be found with a holy man, once a student at Clonard, who dwelt on one of the hundred islands of Loch Erne. The young Leinster lad had withdrawn from the field of battle. But his withdrawal, far from being accepted defeat was accepted battle. The counsel he had received from the holy woman did not mean that he should decline battle with his enemy but that he should decline to do battle on the enemy's own battlefield. Like his Master he accepted battle on the field chosen for him by the spirit of God.

One only fact of this quiet sojourn on the island has come down to history. We are told that he became so versed in the Sacred Scriptures that he wrote an explanation of David's Psalter. Imagination compels us to wonder if he had been one of a class at Clonard, including the daughter of the King of Cualann whom St. Finnen instructed in the Psalter. No doubt the sob of self-conscious though repented sin vibrating everywhere in these psalms of Sion seemed the fit prayer of this young fugitive from himself.

Our next sight of Columbanus is amidst the wattle huts of the newly founded monastery at Bangor on the southern shores of Belfast Lough. About the time when Columbanus was with Sinnel on the island of Cluan, another saint, Comgall, was preparing for his life's work by the life of an anchorite on one of the neighboring islands. Whether the two saints met is a matter of surmise. But the surmise strengthens on learning that soon after Comgall began the monastic life at Bangor one of his first monks was his former neighbor amidst the islands of Loch Erne.

A phrase of Abbot Jonas covers the life of Columbanus amidst the brethren whom he loved, and in a spot as romantically beautiful as any to be found on the coast-line of his beloved country.

> The cycles of many years being now fulfilled in the monastery he began yearning to be a pilgrim, mindful of the divine word to Abraham. "Go forth from thy birth-land, and from thy kindred,

and from thy father's house and go into the land I will show thee." [Genesis 12.]

His old self-mistrust and his duty of obedience made him broach his desire to his Abbot St. Comgall. No doubt it was a willing obedience that heard his Abbot's refusal. He obeyed the human authority even against what seemed a divine impulse until at last the human authority recognized in this obedience the mark of a divine call.

Bangor could hardly help pricking his soul to pilgrimage. Once or twice during his stay at Bangor he must have seen a boat coming southward from Iona to Bangor Bay, with his fellow countryman St. Columba.

Again, Bangor was within that part of Ireland so hallowed by the coming, and labors and death and burial of Ireland's apostle, as to be called "St. Patrick's Country." Downpatrick where St. Patrick lay buried was some twenty miles to the south.

Saints touch history at its vital points. When Columbanus, remembering the nun's challenge to pilgrimage, saw the place where the runaway slave lay buried far from his homeland and amidst his old slave-masters, even a monastery by one of his country's fairest coasts became unendurable.

A letter which the Saint sent from exile to his monks at Luxeuil will suggest that other motives may have driven him from the consolations of Bangor. He there speaks to the one whom he had left in charge, of the dangers of being loved too much. Columbanus was not a soul that revealed himself easily even to himself. Yet for this reason amongst others he drew men to his love. But when affection was given him—and it rarely failed to be given—he fled from it; not as if it, but as if he, was sinful.

When the day came for Columbanus to leave his birthland forever it was a group of thirteen monks that embarked at Bangor. A few years earlier another group of thirteen, monks under Columba had embarked perhaps at the same monastic jetty on Belfast Lough. The traditions Columbanus had learned at Clonard and Bangor led him to Wales where his teaching masters had sought sound learning from the Britons, David, Gildas, and Cadoc. The Celtic Saint in flight from the love of his own birthland so won upon the monks of Wales that some of them went with him into willing exile. This slender fact sets us wondering what might have happened if later missionaries to the Anglo-Saxons had found the Columbanus-way into the hearts of these Britons of the West.

If Columbanus was born in 530 and his flight from Ireland was 590 he was then in his sixtieth year. According to some historians it was the age of St. Patrick when he came back as Apostle to Ireland. We note these resemblances because more lies within them than secular history may detect. It is undeniable that St. Patrick became, as indeed he has still remained, not only the national apostle but equally the national hero of Ireland. The very details of his life were an inspiration to the Island of Saints.

We do not know and cannot guess the motives why the group of Irish monks asked and found a place of exile in Burgundy then ruled by King Gontran, a grandson of Clovis. We only know that it offered the Saint the two things he sought above all else—quiet contemplation of God and work among souls. The dark mountain forests with their darker caves gave him constant isolation from the world which God's love was teaching him to fly. The simple, untaught pagans or clansmen of these forests, needed his teaching of the faith.

For some time, we are not told how long, the band of monks dwelt in a ruined castle-hamlet at Annegray in Haute-Saone. He and his monks seem to have been content to bivouac amongst the ruins. Yet even in these uninviting conditions the Saint's personality had gathered round him such a throng of Burgundians athirst for the monastic life that a new home had to be sought some miles distant at Luxeuil. There was built from the stones of a ruined Roman bath and temple a monastery which has made Luxeuil a place-name famous not only in France but throughout the Church and the world.

Though classically-minded Abbot Jonas has a charming verbosity in recording the seemingly miraculous everyday life of the Saint, yet he lets us see that life in its sometimes stark reality. He tells us how the holy Father Abbot and the community prayed for the wife of a man and she was instantly cured though she had been ill over a year. But he incidentally tells us how this man had brought a wagon of bread and vegetables most opportunely because the community were so poor that they could give a brother stricken with fever nothing but roots and bark!

There is a wonderful story of what befell the Saint as he was one day walking in the dark woods of Haute-Saone. A phrase of Jonas is almost untranslatable: *Librum humero ferens de Scripturis Sacris secum disputaret.* "Bearing" [no doubt in a Celtic leathern satchel] "the Holy Scriptures and discussing with himself." A saint's dialogues with himself are seldom wanting in interest. St. Columbanus, no doubt stimulated by the wisdom borne on his shoulders, was thinking whether he would prefer to fall in with wild beasts or wicked men. He answered his own question by going forward into the forest where he might meet with the beasts, who, unlike men, had never sinned.[1] The story ends dramatically by his meeting a pack of twelve wolves whom he drove off with a prayer—of how the wolves were followed by a band of Suevi robbers who though close to him did not see him—and how diving further into a forest he saw to his ascetic delight a dark cave which he made his own only by instantly taming a fierce bear to whom it belonged.

This bear-cave plays a major part in the drama of the Saint whom history has, perhaps, largely misrepresented.

1. An Irish Innocent whom I had the honor to tend in Leicester Jail once said to me: "St. Patrick druv the sarpents out of Ireland. But what was the good of drivin' out the sarpents when he left men—worse than sarpents!"

The authentic sources of his life give no reason for representing him as what we might fairly call "the stage Celt"—a man of violent and somewhat uncontrolled zeal. Everywhere he is shown us as a shy blending of scholar and saint whose chief and difficult concern is to find out the will of God and do it. When the love he always enkindled by his gifts of soul and even of body was obvious even to himself he fled to his bear-cave to be *solus cum Solo.*

There is a charming story of how through divine revelation given him in his cave he knew that many of his beloved monks were ill. At once he hastened home. He bade the sick brethren rise and thrash the corn in the thrashing-floor. Needless to say, our beloved Jonas tells us that the obedient brethren were instantly cured; the disobedient stayed ill for the best part of a year and came near dying. The story reminds us of another who said to a man with a withered hand: "Stretch it forth;" and it was at once cured.

Another story throws light not only on the soul of Columbanus but on the soul of monasticism at its best. Lest we spoil it in the telling, we must let Jonas do the telling. "At length the time came when the harvest should be gathered into the barns; yet so strong were the winds that they ceased not to gather clouds. Assuredly there was great need, lest the ripe heads of corn beginning to shoot might be lost.

"The man of God was at Fountains monastery" [an offshoot of Luxeuil] "where some fallow land had yielded a heavy harvest. But the storm gusts beat down in such unceasing showers that the clouds ceased not to flood the earth with rain. The man of God thought anxiously in his heart what he should do—faith armed his heart and bid him beseech what was fitting. He summoned them all and bade them reap the grain. All wondered at the father's command; none told the father of his wonder. All come and cut the corn amidst the falling showers; whilst watching what the father might do. At the four corners of the field he sets as leaders four men full of holiness, Cominius and Eunous and Equanacus of the Irish race, and the fourth Gurganus by race a Briton. These being so placed he, in the middle, with the rest reaped the harvest. O wondrous power! the showers fly from the grain; everywhere the rains cease; the middle reapers are burned with the sun's rays, and a great heat lasts till the harvest is reaped."

The present writer can hardly allow his pen to desecrate with comment this perfect scene. But in his heart he prays that the emptying wheat fields of our islands may soon witness a kindred sight which will give immortality as Jonas has given immortality to the names of one British and three Irish monk-harvesters in a wheat field.

Another story tells us of Columbanus and some of the brethren splitting oak-trunks in the forest and how a wedge—leaping as wedges will—from the log deeply wounded the brow of Winnucus, a monk. But the Saint laid his lips to the wound, which instantly healed.

Another story reminds us of the brewer who has found honorable mention amongst the "company" of St. Patrick. One day before the monks' dinner the cellarer was drawing beer from the hogshead into the large tankard when he was summoned elsewhere by Columbanus. In the hurry of the moment he forgot to put the cork back in the hogshead. It is needless to say that on his return to the cellar the cellarer found not one drop spilled! Whereupon the Abbot Jonas writes: "O how great was the merit of him who commanded; and how great the obedience of him who did as he was bid."

Another story tells of a dead stag found in the forest by the Saint. A bear was drinking the stag's blood; but had not yet wounded its skin. The provident Father Abbot saw at once in the skin of the dead stag the leather to make shoes for his monks! He forbade the bear to injure the skin; and—the monks had a fresh supply of leather!

Tales like these even when garnished by the religious imagination of a home-historian make two things clear—how lovable was the monk whom they idealize; and how realistic were the monks whose life was not only in their house of prayer but in the fields and in the forests. In making these two things clear cloistered chroniclers have created an atmosphere as romantic as the West gave us in Robinson Crusoe or the East in the Arabian Nights.

The growth of the monastery at Luxeuil is witnessed by the foundation of a second monastery at Fountains. With this growth in numbers and influence there came inevitable opposition. As this opposition ended by King Theoderic exiling Columbanus and all monks not of French blood, the matter is seen to be a quarrel between the new religious revival centered in the monasteries and the half-savage, half-Roman imperialism of the Merovingian monarchs.

The short account of the quarrel given us by Jonas has the merit of being substantially verified by authentic history. The young king of Burgundy, Theoderic (Thierry) II, had given shelter to his grandmother Queen Brunhilda when she was driven out of her own kingdom of Austrasia by the Austrasian nobles. This expulsion from her own kingdom by a very decisive ballot on her character, is corroboration of Jonas.

Inevitably the Abbot of Luxeuil began to attract the confidence of the young king. But a king, with Merovingian ideas of morality, and an Abbot, who was in self-exile for chastity's sake, could be related only on condition that either the king or the Saint uprooted his soul. There was another alternative: that the relationship should end violently as indeed it did.

Pope Gregory's letters to Queen Brunhilda and her grandsons on the need of stamping out simony especially from the episcopate allow us to think that the bishops of the two kingdoms of Burgundy and Austrasia were not the men to correct Merovingian morals. If things came to breaking point between Luxeuil and loose-living Theoderic these prelates might be expected to find their conscience coincide with the king's.

The account given by Jonas of the inevitable collision between the Court and Luxeuil seems true to human nature. Theoderic, though unmarried, was already the father of four children. There is nothing incompatible with the moral atmosphere of a Merovingian court that one day Queen Brunhilda asked Columbanus to bless these four royal children. It may not have surprised but it angered Brunhilda that this foreign Abbot of Luxeuil refused to bless the spurious offspring. When Columbanus the foreigner proved himself more Burgundian than this Spanish Queen by boldly asking for a legitimate offspring to inherit the throne, the break between the monastery and the Court became inevitable.

But the break with such a man as the widely reverenced Columbanus demanded diplomacy. A favorable opening seemed to be in the question of the keeping of Easter. It was and still is a question so obscure that some writers have accused the British and Irish Churches of being "Quartodecimans," by keeping Easter as the Jews keep their Pasch, on a day determined by the full moon, even if that day were not a Sunday.

Yet little is known of how the British and Irish Churches computed their Easter. Only one thing is quite certain, that they kept the Easter as first taught them by Rome. For a loyal obedient monk like Columbanus it was somewhat perplexing to be asked to give up chronological customs authenticated for him by Rome itself. It was for him as for St. Paul when St. Peter refused to eat with gentile converts. St. Paul's astonishment was great when a policy towards the gentiles inaugurated by St. Peter seemed to be set aside by—St. Peter. For both Saints it was a crisis of bewildered loyalty. No wonder that in the letters wrung from each by the crisis their bewilderment seems to express itself in phrases almost overshadowing their loyalty.

A Synod of Merovingian Bishops was summoned, as it would seem, on the advice of Pope Gregory, but by order of the Merovingian King, Theoderic. Pope Gregory's reiterated demands that the King [or Queen Brunhilda] should summon a Synod, made mention of several matters needing reform; but there was no mention of the Easter difficulty. When, then, the Episcopal Synod made it their chief concern to indict Luxeuil for its Easter observance the Abbot did two things: (1) he wrote a plain letter to the Synod, and (2) he wrote an equally plain letter to Pope Gregory. In other words he followed his national Saint and hero St. Patrick, who met a kindred difficulty by appealing to the Pope.

Both letters have been unfortunate in their commentators. Few if any of these commentators have been capable of judging the letters *in vacuo* as the pleading of an Abbot for retaining in his monastery a chronological observance initiated by Rome. They have seemed to think that the nationality of this self-exiled Irishman was the determining factor in the letters. Yet the present writer has sought in vain to find in these letters any trace of the stage-Irishman so beloved by even the Catholic historians of the incident.

In the letter to "My Lord and Fathers and Brothers in Christ, Bishops, Priests and other orders of the Church," Columban the sinner and the scholar (and the Leinster aristocrat) never forgot his courteousness of sanctity, even when Celtic humor might easily have soured into gall. He most humbly thanks God that they, who should have assembled twice a year to correct public morals which were so corrupt, should at last assemble on his account to deliberate on the matter of Easter which has been so often discussed. There is a tone of weariness but not of anger when he deals with this matter; as if Bishops who were contentedly living under a king ruled by concubines might well discuss something more vital than the Calendar!

The old master of classical phrases has a passage which ranks him with even the Latin masters of eloquence. He beseeches but one thing from them that in their holiness they would have peace with him and charity and would "let him be quiet in these woods[2] and live near the dust of our seventeen dead brethren as indeed you have let us live in your midst these twelve years so that we might pray for you as we have prayed—and, indeed, as was our duty."

2. *Ut mihi liceat cum vestra pace et charitate in his silvis silere*—a phrase so perfect with its wealth of sibilants that we can almost overhear the rustling of the forest leaves.

He even pleads—alas! unsuccessfully—for his ageing fellow-exiles with these court-clerics: "Take heed, O holy Fathers, to these poor veterans and aged exiles, whom to my mind you should console rather than disturb."

The saintly Abbot had gauged the situation with the realism of a contemplative. This Synod was not an assembly of delicately orthodox Bishops who could not bear a different ritual or even a different Calendar: they were a group of perhaps court-cowed prelates who were made the cat's-paw of a Merovingian Court, enraged at Columbanus and his monks sitting in silent Mardochai condemnation at their gates. The result of the Synod's and the Court's deliberations was inevitable. Columbanus the exile who had proved himself a more patriotic Burgundian than their hierarchy or their king was driven from the silence of the woods, and the seventeen graves of his dead brothers, into exile.

A LETTER OF THE SAINT TO THE REIGNING POPE ST. GREGORY THE Great has found immortality amongst the topics of controversy. It must always be borne in mind that if St. Columbanus has left us more written remains than most of his contemporaries there is not one line of merely self-defense; but many precious lines in defense of others. To himself he was always Columbanus the sinner, who since his exile from his birth-place and then from his birthland had never slackened his flight from himself. But as often happens to men of God, these souls who are so shrinking and voiceless in self-praise or self-defense, these lambs of self-diffidence become lions when they have to defend some old *veterani* against the fury of a king.

We do not know whether this letter from St. Columbanus to St. Gregory was written before or after the Synod. But it seems certain that it sprang from the circumstances that called the Synod together. That the Abbot of Luxeuil addresses the Bishop of Rome to end a controversy, not on a matter of faith or even of ritual but only of observance, is a sign of that instinct for Rome which St. Patrick had implanted in the Church of his apostolate. Those who see in the letter a proof that St. Columbanus was in effect a pre-protestant of the seventh century lay stress on words that would make a pre-protestant of St. Paul for his letter to the Galatians and of St. Irenaeus for his letter [on the Easter question] to St. Victor.

A picturesque pun has done much service to this theory of Columbanus, the pre-protestant. Those who differed from the Luxeuil monks on the Easter date quoted St. Leo the Great. But St. Columbanus with whimsical childlikeness suggests that in this matter St. Leo's decision could be set aside by Gregory—for "is not a live dog better than a dead lion [Leo]." Far from depreciating the great "Chair of Peter," as he styles it, the man who uses this phrase is making a profession of faith that the present occupant of this chair can reverse the disciplinary enactments of a former occupant whose name still resounded through West and East as the Defender of the Faith in Jesus Christ.

It is regrettable that this letter and another sent to St. Gregory seem never to have reached their destination. Perhaps it was asking too much of Merovingian broadmindedness to permit such letters to pass out of the country. Had the letter reached St. Gregory the difficulty felt by Columbanus in giving up, on the authority of the Gallic Church, what he and his fathers had received from the authority of Rome, would have been met by all the broadmindedness of St. Gregory's letters to St. Augustine on the difficulties in England.

In the end St. Columbanus seems to have recognized that Rome of the Popes had spoken and the matter was ended, save for his obedience. As all mention of the difficulty passes from his correspondence and from the further annals of Luxeuil he and his monks seem to have been obedient.

In order to appreciate the state of things against which the peace-loving Saint and scholar Columbanus battled, only to find himself in exile, we must realize the following plain facts about the Merovingian sovereigns.

1. Chilperic, king of Neustria, at the instigation of his concubine Fredegonde, murders his wife Galeswinde.

2. Chilperic's brother, King Sigebert of Austrasia, is murdered by Chilperic and Fredegonde, concubine of Chilperic.

3. Queen Brunhilda, sister of the murdered Queen Galeswinde and wife of the murdered King Sigebert immediately marries Merovee, son of King Chilperic the murderer.

4. The day after Merovee's marriage with Queen Brunhilda, King Chilperic imprisons his son Merovee. Soon afterwards it is given out that Merovee has committed suicide!

5. Chilperic is murdered presumably by either Fredegonde his concubine or Brunhilda his sister-in-law. This murder leaves Fredegonde acting queen at Neustria, during the minority of her son Clotaire.

6. King Childebert, son of Queen Brunhilda, dies a sudden and apparently natural death. This death leaves Brunhilda acting queen of Burgundy and Austrasia during the minority of her sons Theoderic and Theodebert.

7. Theoderic becomes king of Burgundy—is notoriously profligate—is advised to marry by St. Didier, Bp. of Vienne—marries Queen Brunehault—within a year divorces his wife and murders St. Didier.

8. King Theodebert, brother of Theoderic and grandson of Queen Brunhilda, marries Bilichild; and then murders her.

9. Theodebert is murdered by his brother Theoderic or by his grandmother Brunhilda.

10. King Clotaire of Neustria murders his cousin Theoderic, and the five illegitimate sons of Theoderic and his aunt Queen Brunhilda. This brings a lull of peace to France.

This is a plain unvarnished statement of some of the authentic facts about the atmosphere in which the quiet peace-loving contemplatives of Luxeuil found themselves. Yet some Catholic historians are so concerned to justify Queen Brunhilda as to sacrifice St.

Columbanus. Lovers of their fellow men on being tempted to look with despair upon these centuries called the Dark Ages are lifted up to hope when out of the offal of these royal adulteries and fratricides they see rising like a white lily the quiet God-soaring sanctity of Luxeuil.

It is therefore to the credit of Luxeuil and its monks that their Abbot and all the monks that were not Franks were forced to leave the kingdom ruled over by Theoderic.

The spirit in which this champion of justice met exile is summed up in one incident.

On the day when Theoderic defeated and captured Theodebert at Tolbiac, Columbanus, exiled at Bregentz, was seated on a fallen trunk with a noble young French monk Cagnoald whose father was in high position under Theodebert. In a vision he saw the battle, and the bloodshed. He awoke in grief. Cagnoald having found out the cause of his master's grief besought him to pray for Theodebert and against Theoderic. But the old Saint, incapable of personal hatred, answered: "Your counsel is foolish and unholy. Nor is it the will of God, who bade us pray for our enemies."

THE LITTLE GROUP OF MONKS WITH COLUMBANUS AT THEIR HEAD were escorted down the Loire through Orleans and Tours to the port at Nantes. Whilst awaiting the hour of his forced departure for Ireland the heart of the Saint, the man, the father, dictated a letter of which another noble soul has said: "it contains some of the finest and noblest words that Christian genius has ever produced."[3] But as we deem it almost sacrilege to mutilate a masterpiece we must leave the reading of it, and the finding of it, to those Catholics and Celts who still have a thirst for the best.

One thing only must be said, in defense of a Saint who sometimes needs defending against his fellow Catholics.

3. Montalembert, *The Monks of the West*, book 7.

From its first word of peace to its last anguish-laden word of fatherly love and prophecy there is not even a shadow's shadow of anger. Indeed the Saint contrives to suggest that instead of being soldier-driven from the delights of Luxeuil he is flying from its burden, "*Ego fugio.*" Yet true to himself, he implies that the burden he is flying is only the burden and danger of their too great love.

There are certain noble words of this half-willing exile which must be given to our readers as the faithful Jonas has given them to us. One day when the king's messengers, Bertarius and Bedulius, found Columbanus in choir they asked him in the king's name to leave the kingdom and go back whence he came. The undaunted follower of St. Patrick replied: *Non enim reor placere Conditori, semel natali solo relicto, denuo repetere.* ("I do not count it pleasing to the Creator that having once left my birth-land, I should again return.")

In the face of such supreme desire for exile we are not surprised to read that the Irish bark which was to make Columbanus break his troth was driven upon the rocks where it lay stranded for three days. How far this was due to the Saint's prayers with God or with the captain we have no means of knowing. This much we know, that if the stranding of the bark was not a supernatural doing of God's love for the Saint it was a deliberate doing of the Saint's supernatural love for God. In all these obscure matters one thing is clear. The Saint had his way. He did not go back whence he came!

But the old Saint did not mean to stay out of his birthland only to "be quiet in the woods." In a delicately-tuned mood of self-accusation he confessed that his desire of "preaching the Gospel" had somewhat cooled. He determined to go eastwards where there were still many pagans. Theodebert of Austrasia was able to give him a place of prayer and preaching at Bregentz on Lake Constance amidst the ruins of a Roman town. Some three years were spent amidst dangers from famine and men. The pagans were so hostile to these Westerns that two of the monks were slain. Yet the little group of monks left their ruins only when their old enemy Theodoric by defeating and murdering

Theodebert had become King of Austrasia. The King's hatred could not spare the Saint; and Columbanus with only one companion was again driven forth to his place of exile and death.

Some years before in the quiet woods of Luxeuil he had penned these immortal words of a soul homesick for heaven:

> *And thou, O Life, how many hast thou played false; how many misled; how many made blind?*
>
> *Nought thou art in thy flight; a shadow to our sight; cloud-smoke in thy height.*
>
> *Daily thou contest; and daily goest—one in thy beginning; many in thine end—sweet to the foolish; bitter to the wise.*
>
> *Who love thee, know thee not; who look down on thee, understand thee. Thus art thou not truthful but deceitful—thou makest thyself true; and showest thyself false.*
>
> *What then art thou, O life of man? Man's life thou art not; but a way to life.*
>
> *Sin is thy beginning; death, thy end. Thou wouldst have been true had not man's sinful trespass maimed thee; now thou art faltering and mortal since all who go thy way are appointed unto death.*
>
> *A way unto life thou art, not life; for thou art not true—a way, but not straight—to some long, to some short—to some broad, to some narrow—to some glad, to some sad—to all alike, swiftly passing and beyond recall.*
>
> *Thus art thou to be questioned; not trusted, not defended—traversed, not dwelt in, O unhappy life of man! since on the way a man dwelleth not but walketh; and he who in the way walketh in the homeland dwelleth.*

It was an old man of three score years and ten—or, according to others, it was an old man of four score—who set out to cross the Alps in his last pilgrimage. His mind, which had always been to him a kingdom peopled by the nobility of thought, was more than ever filled with the thoughts of life's swift passage to the *patria* of his soul. If ever his own song on "Life but the way to life" reflected his outer circumstances it was when he turned his exile face southwards towards death.

Something like a reward of peace was given to this peace-lover in this short nightfall of his life. The province of Lombardy, which he entered when he had crossed the Alps, was ruled by Agilulph, an Arian. His wife was the wise, noble, saintly Theodolinda, to whom St. Gregory had dedicated his *Dialogues*. The fame of Columbanus seems to have already reached the Lombard court. King Agilulph, who a few years before was besieging Rome and creating the desert of the Campagna, welcomed the exiled saint almost as a national asset. Within the Apennines, at a spot now famous under the name of Bobbio, there was a ruined basilica dedicated to St. Peter. If, as is not unlikely, the ruins were the handiwork of these ruthless Arian Lombards, there was a quality of penance and restitution in Agilulph, the Arian's gift to Columbanus.

An incident, clothed by Jonas with his wonted garb of miracle, throws a last light on the undaunted worker so soon to be called into the night where no man can work. To restore the basilica the little group of monks cut and dragged timber from the neighbouring wood. Sometimes the great trees were felled where no timber-wain could go. The monks were forced to carry the great beams on their shoulders. Yet God seemed so manifestly to help these men to help themselves that heavy logs which, on the word of Jonas, thirty or forty men could barely have carried over level ground, were carried over rocks on the shoulders of Columbanus and two or three monks. With a touch of poetry Jonas adds that the Abbot and his two or three monks carried their load "with such unfaltering feet as if moving in play and with joy."

For the last time we ask our readers of a century which has heard the heresy of the "Leisure State" to watch the old monk of some four score years helping to carry great beams on his shoulders. This man and his little group of monk-woodmen are, for the moment, the most vital center of education in the West. But what further conclusion should be drawn from this Nazareth poverty our readers themselves must draw.

Queen Theodolinda's prayer and plan for the conversion of her Arian husband and the Lombards received sudden reinforcement by the illustrious exile from Luxeuil. The anger of one Queen—Brunhilda—was the opportunity for a greater. Although ten years had elapsed since Agilulph had begun a friendship with St. Gregory which might soon have fruited in the King's conversion, Gregory's death had withdrawn the main clerical influence over the King's Arian mind. With the coming of Columbanus Theodolinda saw the possibility of Gregory's influence being renewed.

But in Lombardy Columbanus met for the first time the subtle atmosphere of the two great Eastern heresies: the King and most of his Lombard subjects were Arians. Of the rest of his subjects many, even amongst the clergy, were Nestorians, enmeshed in the famous controversy of the *Three Chapters*. Columbanus could find his peace-nurtured believing mind only bewildered by these Oriental disputations and phrase-weavings. His age and all his past training were towards peace. Historians wrong both him and the original sources of his history when they see descending the slopes of the Alps only a dogmatic sleuth-hound yearning for controversial blood.

But Queen Theodolinda saw that this undaunted lover of truth and peace was God-sent to bring peace to her King and people through the truth. Though his life was now measured only by months he could not stint himself when from the Lombard court itself came a royal request for help in bringing Arian and Nestorian Lombardy to faith guaranteed by the See of Rome, "the Chair of Peter."

A letter written by the Saint to the reigning Pope Boniface IV on the need of summoning a Synod to bring dogmatic peace throws a last ray of light upon the soul of the Saint. We will set down some of its main features.

1. He writes this letter to the Pope: "I am asked by the King that I should put before your kindly ears in detail the matter that is grieving him; for the schism of the people is a grief to him on account of the Queen and her son and perhaps for his own sake too; seeing that he is believed to have said that if he knew the truth he would believe...."

Again: "a pagan Lombard King requests a dull-witted Irish stranger to write..."

Again: "The King asks you, the Queen asks you, all ask you, that all things may become one as soon as possible, so that as there is peace in the father-land there may be peace in the *faith* and the whole flock of Christ may henceforth be one. *Rex regum! tu Petrum, te tota sequetur ecclesia.* (O King of Kings, follow thou Peter, and the whole Church will follow thee)."

2. An attempt was made to separate him from Communion with Rome: "Almost the first moment of my crossing the frontiers of the country a certain person gave me a letter giving me to understand that you were to be shunned as having fallen into the sect of the Nestorians."

This anonymous "certain person" was probably a Bishop of some importance in Northern Italy.

3. Thereupon he wrote a defence of Rome and of the orthodox faith: "Thereupon I made such reply as I could...for I believe that the Pillar of the Church is always unmoved in Rome."

The Abbot Jonas assures us that, no doubt by the wish of King Agilulph and Queen Theodolinda, he took up his abode near Milan, and that "by the weapon of the Scriptures he might rend and destroy the deceits of the heretics, that is, of the Arian heresy, against whom he wrote a book of fine scholarship."

4. His loyalty to Rome is so great that he sends this book to the Pope for approval or condemnation. It is the same Columbanus who appealed to Pope Gregory for a ruling on the Easter question: "This (book) I have sent to you that you may read it and correct it where it is contrary to the truth; for I dare not count myself to be beyond correction."

5. He witnesses that the Irish Church acknowledges the authority of the Roman Pontiff, not because of Rome but because of St. Peter: "All we Irish dwelling on the edge of the world are disciples of Saints Peter and Paul and of the disciples who, under the Holy Ghost, wrote the Sacred Canon. We accept nothing outside this evangelical and apostolic teaching. There was no heretic, no Jew, no schismatic, but the Catholic Faith, as first delivered to us by you, the successor of the apostles, is kept unshaken... We, indeed, are, as I have said, chained to the Chair of St. Peter; for although Rome is great and known afar, it is great and honored with us only by this Chair."

In writing this last witness of an Irish Saint, Columbanus was refuting beforehand the argument current since the 16th century, that the See of Rome set up by St. Peter obtained its supremacy not because of Peter but because of Rome. Two Churches, Persia and Ireland, by their witness to the Chair of Peter, are the refutation of this argument; because Persia in the East and Ireland in the West were unconquered by Rome.

The sequel of this effort of the Saint to further the designs of Agilulph and Theodolinda was the conversion not only of Agilulph, who had but a few months to live, but of the Lombard people. In founding Bobbio so near Milan, the emporium of so many Eastern heresies, this exile from the furthest West had set up a blockhouse of the faith where it was most effective. For centuries it was a citadel of scientific defence which owed its existence to the man who united culture and sanctity in one mind and heart. When ruin overtook it after centuries of life the gathered treasures of its library enriched the libraries that still enrich the scholarship of the world.

Before we part from our patient readers, we would remind them that the Church has to thank St. Columbanus for two contributions of great worth—his Rule and his Penitential.

In his Rule he does not seem to have set down much that was original, but merely to have embodied the stern asceticism of his fellow-countrymen and especially of his fellow monks at Bangor. In the end it was found that the less exacting Rule of St. Benedict was more acceptable to the would-be monks of the West. Yet although the sterner rule everywhere yielded to the milder, every movement towards a reform of the Rule of St. Benedict has been a movement towards the ideal, and even the toil-ideal of St. Columbanus.

But the Rule of St. Columbanus has not rendered to the Church a greater service than his *Penitential.* A recent writer has said:

> The fact of outstanding importance with respect to the *Penitential* of Columbanus is that while it corresponds to no existing practice to be found anywhere in force from former times on the continent of Europe, it reproduces all the main features of the peculiar system which has been seen at work in the Keltic Churches... As in the British and Irish systems, the penance and the reconciliation are alike private.[4]

> It is not a little remarkable that by the end of the seventh century the Rule of St. Columbanus, for whatsoever reason, practically disappears, and the Rule of St. Benedict becomes supreme. But his Penitential system not only survived in the monasteries which were now being founded, but was destined in time, after the later English influence, to become the general penitential system of Western Europe.[5]

Few customs are so characteristic of "the Latin Church" which is officially distinguished from "the Eastern Church" as the very frequent and humble practice of Confession. It is to the credit of sinful human nature that this Sacrament, which our Redeemer made not so much an obligation as a privilege, should yet be frequented almost as an obligation. Perhaps we are close to the motive of this

4. Oscar D. Watkins, *A History of Penance* (Longmans, Green & Co., 1920), p. 615.
5. Ibid., p. 124.

humble practice in thinking of its connection, by way of cleansing, with the great Banquet of the Body and the Blood. One of the chief glories of the fellow-countrymen of Columbanus will be that to him more than to any other individual in the Church this lowly practice seems due.

The last literary testament left by St. Columbanus during his few months at Bobbio is this letter to Pope Boniface IV. Were it the only clue to the soul of the Saint during his approach to death, we might so misread it as to look upon its writer as a born and unwearied warrior for the faith—the Tertullian of his age. But we have other clues to his character. When three score years and more—and as he says: *morbis oppressus acerbis* ("bowed with heavy ailments")—he wrote to his young friend Fedolius a charming poem in Adonic verse. Its student touch, its wealth of classical allusion, its preciosity, if proof of anything, are proof that its writer, far from being the Tertullian, was the Nazianzen and the Prudentius of his war-distraught age.

It would be a shallow even if true criticism of this Irishman who died an exile in Italy, that he fled and fled again from temptation. The deeper truth would be that Columbanus the self-conscious never fled save from Columbanus. He had the same attitude towards himself as another heroic exile whose constant cry was, "who shall deliver me from the body of this death?" Columbanus was too undeniably a lover of men and the haunts of men to leave his kindred of the hearth or the heart in any mood of hate or self-seeking. He was not one of those sad lovers of health or haters of discomfort who quit their northern mists and go southwards for the sun. Columbanus was ever flying from Columbanus; or truer still the self-conscious sinner was ever wayfaring towards the sinless coasts of heaven, the hunted stag was ever yearning for the water-brooks.

We are not told how, but only when he died. It is the one certain date in his life; for on that day, the twenty-first day of November, the year of Our Lord six hundred and fifteen, Columbanus the exile was welcomed home by his Father Who is in heaven.

And the heavenly Father has been so generous towards the tireless fugitive from himself that throughout the centuries that have scattered holy things to the winds the body of Columbanus has been untouched in its last resting-place in the heart of the Apennines.

SAINT MALACHY (1095–1148)

by VINCENT MCNABB, O.P.

A SAINT WHOSE LIFE WAS PASSED BETWEEN THE YEARS 1095 and 1148, and in Ireland, could hardly fail to provide matter for picturesque and even dramatic biography. It is to the credit of St. Malachy's contemporaries that one of them, perhaps the most illustrious of them, St. Bernard, saw in his son of a wild western island a man worthy to be a model even to saints.

Some notion of the Ireland of St. Malachy is needed by anyone who wishes to have a true notion of the Saint. Yet, even for men and women born within its borders the Ireland of St. Patrick is almost as elusive as a will-o'-the-wisp. If we took at its face-value St. Bernard's Gallic judgment on our people, they would appear as a race of partly-Christianized barbarians whose very language was hardly a betterment of animal cries. But we shrewdly suspect that the Malachy whom Bernard loved at first sight had his own scholarly and silent opinion about Bernard's Gallic culture.

A visit to the Hall of the Collars of Gold, by one who remembers that the runaway slave Patrick took ship with a crew who were taking Irish wolfhounds to Italy, may convince the ordinary reader that the problem of Irish culture is not to be decided by the rhetoric of neighbouring writers. Ireland of the Brehon laws, the bards, the metal-craftsmen, the foreign-going seamen, is a problem that may have only an ascetical solution. If something that St. Bernard and the Latins looked upon as culture had never found a footing—as the Roman legions never found a footing—in Ireland, it may have been that the Irish either by necessity or choice had anticipated the first of the Beatitudes: "Blessed are the poor in spirit for theirs is the Kingdom of heaven."

Co. Down, which may have been the birthplace and was largely the life-place of St. Malachy, introduced the Saint to all the strong currents of contemporary Irish life. The hamlet of Saul had seen the first as well as the last Mass of St. Patrick. At Downpatrick lay the bodies of St. Patrick, St. Brigid and St. Columbkille. A few miles from the grave of these Saints on Island Magee could be seen the handiwork of Danish invaders in the fire-blackened ruins of the school of St. Nendrum founded, perhaps, before St. Patrick's School at Armagh. At the head of Loch Cuan—called Strang-fiord by the Danes!—the school of Moville was another proof that Danish warcraft had as its war-cry, "Destroy! Destroy!" Again a few miles north of Moville, on the south-eastern shores of Belfast Lough, was all that successive Danish raids had left of the world-famous monastic school of Bangor. Light is thrown on the strange Irish world of our Saint's day by the fact that in his twenty-eighth year the young priest Malachy found himself Abbot of Bangor with its vast possessions, by the will and resignation of his uncle—a layman!

The latest biographer of St. Malachy sketches the state of things into which the Saint was born. After stating that Armagh had been plundered and burned nine times by the Danes before their final defeat at Clontarf on Good Friday, 1014, he writes:

> The victory brought, no doubt, freedom from foreign oppression, but it did not bring peace. The period separating the defeat of the Danes from the advent of the Normans (1168) was occupied by a fierce contest between three families, the O'Briens of Munster, the

> MacLoughlins of Ulster and the O'Connors of Connacht—for the dignity of Ard Ri. This war of Gael against Gael was marked by sacrileges and atrocities quite equal to the worst attributed to the Norsemen... The great wonder was that anything survived of the old Christianity and culture.[1]

If the Ireland of St. Malachy's troubled days is too elusive for even the insight of those who love it, the dim historic figure of the Saint himself is an equal problem of elusiveness. A key to this problem may be found, perhaps, in his love for the great apostle who gave up the dignity of the See of Armagh for the hidden life and death at Saul. The two Saints separated from each other by some seven centuries are brothers in their unslaked desire to be hidden, and in their irresistible power of enkindling even a human love which has given them a human immortality.

Malachy O'More (Maolmhadhog Ua Morgair), was the son of Mugron O'More.

His mother's name is unknown. Both parents gave him noble blood. By his father he was given the traditions of Donegal; by his mother he was a child of Down. No better blending of blood could be given even in the Island of Saints.

His father, who died when Malachy was only seven years old, could have bestowed on the child little beyond his nobility of rank and his gifts of mind and soul. Mugron O'More, like so many of the Irish nobility, was a scholar of such distinction that at the school of Armagh, the most famous in Ireland, he held the most important professor's chair.

Perhaps some matter of scholarship had summoned him from Armagh when death overtook him at Mungret, Limerick, in 1102. The coming of death, perhaps sudden death, into the little family could not fail to influence the sensitive soul of the young Malachy.

---

1. Ailbe J. Luddy, O.Cist., *Life of St. Malachy* (M. H. Gill & Son, 1930), pp. xv, xvi.

Even at such an age the sight of a mother's weeping for the death of her children's father can give a new insight into the true value of human life. Indeed sorrow of such weight at an age of such tenderness may end by overshadowing the young mind.

St. Bernard is probably introducing us into the reality of the Saint's next few years by his praise of this nameless woman who was the Saint's mother. A widow with a child-saint in her keeping has done her work well to deserve from the Abbot of Clairvaux such praise as the following:

> His parents, however, were great both by descent and in power, *like unto the name of the great men that are in the earth.* (2 Sam. 7:9). Moreover his mother, more noble in mind than in blood, took pains at the very beginning of his way to show her child the ways of life; esteeming this knowledge of more value to him than the empty knowledge of the learning of this world. For both, however, he had aptitude in proportion to his age.
>
> In the schools he was taught learning; at home, the fear of the Lord. By daily progress he duly responded to teacher and mother.
>
> For indeed he was endowed from the first with a good spirit in virtue, of which he was a docile boy, and very lovable and gracious to all in all things.[2]

St. Bernard's praise of the "good spirit" or high intelligence of the son of Mugron O'More, Armagh's chief professor, is authentication of the dominating intelligence of the twelfth century.

But St. Bernard is revealing the secret of his own conquest by one whom he looked on as the child of a semi-barbarous people when he speaks of Malachy as "very lovable and gracious to all in all things." These words of the First Saint of the twelfth century were an unofficial canonization which the official Church had only to ratify. But

2. St. Bernard of Clairvaux, *Life of St. Malachy*, trans. H. J. Lawlor (S.P.C.K., 1920), p. 7.

written about a dead friend within a few days or weeks of their parted fellowship, they are as much an open door into the heart of the living as of the dead.

St. Malachy's childhood was thus passed at Armagh, where a boy's schooling was easily to be had. St. Bernard has given us two incidents which unveil the dramatic energy of boyish holiness.

It would seem that one of his teachers, as so often happens, took delight in the companionship of his boy pupil. Often he would make the boy his companion in those walks which every home of learning treasures as a tradition. The boy's studies were so exacting that, in default of praying in church, he had taught himself to mingle prayer with his work; and even with his country walks. But when he was walking with his own teacher, who may not have been a priest, the boy could find his prayer only by something like a boyish prank. Like the average boy sauntering along a country road he would seem to lag behind. Then when he knew he was not seen he would stretch out his arms and send a dart of prayer to be seen and heard not by his teacher on the road but by his Father in heaven.

Something of the struggle which gave the quiet, meek, lovable boy the victory over himself is in the remaining incident which we must give in St. Bernard's own words.

> Roused once on a time by the reputation of a certain teacher, famous in the studies that are called liberal, he went to him desiring to learn. For indeed he was now grasping after the last opportunities of boyhood, and was longing eagerly for such learning.
>
> But when he went into the house he saw the man playing with an awl and with rapid strokes making furrows in the wall in some strange fashion: And shocked at the bare sight, because it smacked of levity, the serious boy dashed away from him and did not care even to see him from that day forward.

It needs little imagination to realize the dramatic quality of this incident which appealed so strongly to the master artist, Bernard of Clairvaux. A widow's son, eager to follow the ways of a scholarly father, yet conscious that the opportunities of boyhood are fast slipping away, will grasp impetuously at a chance of learning. This gentle, lovable boy of noble blood had charms of character that might easily lead him into danger. An atmosphere of university learning and literary culture can provide temptations of a subtle, refined and therefore perverted character which make even the relation of pupil to master one of danger. St. Bernard's account of this incident shows us how a boy still in his teens—but a boy whom death-sorrow had led to God—could meet perhaps the most bewildering temptation of student life.

Somewhere about this time death again came under his roof to take away the one who had given him consolation on death's first visit. At the Saint's age the passing away of an only parent would seem like the passing away of a world. For Malachy, his brother Gillachrist (Christian) and their sister it must have meant the end of their family life.

If ever Malachy had hesitated about his career in life the death of his mother would be the end of these hesitations. His beloved country needed nothing quite so urgently as good priests who might shepherd the people. Everything in Malachy's soul and life—his strength and weakness—urged him to the priesthood.

A step of seeming unwontedness was taken when Malachy placed himself under the spiritual direction of a man whose influence over Malachy was probably the most decisive of his future career. This was Imar O'Hagan, once an Abbot of a Culdee (?) monastery, and now an anchoret in a cell near the great Church of Armagh. St. Bernard's account of the matter is full of the suggestion that St. Malachy's withdrawal from the world was not just an enthusiasm of youth for the ideal, but was opening manhood's strategy of defence against the enemy called the flesh. A family without father and mother *is* open to attack on all sides. St. Malachy's experience of what might befall him in the company of a renowned professor had given him the experience which ripens to wisdom. Perhaps at the time when, in his teens, he disappointed his family by withdrawing from the world he was withdrawing from a tangle of temptations which soon caught and held his beloved sister. St. Bernard's words are a drama in the making. "The Saint abhorred her carnal life, and with such intensity that he vowed he would never see her again." The dramatic element in this meagre outline is not the strong words from the pen of the French orator but the still stronger action from the man whom this biographer has described almost as the meekest of men. The vow never to see his sister must have meant, what was all too common in those wild ages, some adulterous relation of the powerful, shamelessly maintained, to the scandal of the simple and against the laws of God.

As so often happens, the lead given by a nobleman found followers. Soon around the cells of Imor O'Hagan and his young follower were seen a group of Irish youth adventuring all for God.

Some years of this quiet life with God have left only silence with his biographers. But when next these biographers show him to us—as an ordained deacon of some two and twenty years—the quiet life of God is seen to have wrought a work in his soul. No doubt when preparing for this sacred order, which was itself an immediate preparation for the priesthood, he had dwelt on the reason and work of the first deacons who had given the Church its first martyr, St. Stephen. Armagh now saw one of its fairest sights, a young man of noble blood, proving himself of nobler soul by serving the poor in life and in death. His devotion to the poor which aroused the anger and reproaches of his sister must have touched the grateful hearts of the people who could not forget what was remembered three and thirty years afterward when the great St. Bernard told the world how this young Irish nobleman would himself bury the dead poor.

It was not nobility of blood but fitness of learning and holiness of soul that moved Archbishop Cellach of Armagh to ordain St. Malachy to the priesthood in his twenty-fifth year.

This Archbishop Cellach is a man to be studied. Like St. Charles Borromeo he is a proof that an evil state of things, even of ecclesiastical things, need not be all evil. At the age of six and twenty Cellach found himself—we can hardly use a fitter expression—found himself Lord Abbot and Archbishop of Armagh, by right of blood.

But the blood within Cellach's veins was so generous that the young Archbishop, from the first moment of his consecration, was on the side of the Saints. His whole policy from that day till the day of his death was to strengthen the bond between Ireland and its Mother-in-God, the See of Rome.

Cellach was but nine and thirty years old when he saw the Saint so clearly in the young deacon Malachy that overlooking his want of years, he ordained him priest. Within a few months the newly ordained priest was governing the See of Armagh whilst its Archbishop was carrying out the duties of Metropolitan of Ireland in other parts of Ireland. All that we read of this young priest, now acting head of the chief See of Ireland, is a proof that he was a true priest of the people. Amongst the people he restored the great sacramental life of the Church—Confession, Holy Communion, Confirmation, and Marriage according to the rites of the Church. Amongst his brother priests he introduced the saying of the Divine Office according to the Roman use. We are told that he had learned singing—St. Bernard, no mean judge of Church song, is explicit on the fact—and that he spread the love of sacred song—the Gregorian plain-song (?)—amongst his brother priests.

Hardly sufficient notice has been given by Irish historians to these two Irish noblemen, whom the Church honors as Saints. The *Annals of Ulster* says of the elder:

> Cellach, successor of Patrick—son of purity—and eminent Bishop of the West of Europe—the one Head who was obeyed by Gaels and foreigners, laics and clerics—after ordaining Bishops and priests

> and persons of every ecclesiastical rank—after the consecration of many churches and cemeteries—after bestowing treasures and wealth—after enjoining discipline and good conduct on everyone—after a life spent in celebrating Masses, in fasting and in prayer—after Holy Unction and extraordinary penance—sent forth his spirit into the embrace of angels and archangels in Ard Patraic in Munster on the Kalends of April in the twenty-fourth year of his episcopate and in the fiftieth of his age.

As Rome has placed his name in the Martyrology we have no hesitation in calling him Saint Cellach.

The two Saints seem to have understood and loved each other without a shadow of misunderstanding or mistrust till death came to part them for a few years. They shared a great love of their motherland, once the Island of Saints and Scholars. But their love was not blind to the fact that neither sanctity nor scholarship is transmitted by birth; even by gentle birth. It was therefore their common desire to study these two qualities of heart and mind that prompted St. Cellach, on his return to Armagh, to send St. Malachy to Malchus, Bishop of Waterford and Lismore. Malchus, then in his seventy-fourth year, was well qualified to introduce the young priest of Armagh to the sources of the best scholarship and highest sanctity of his age. He had left his Irish home in youth to be a monk in the monastery at Winchester, where the new continental movements in asceticism were fostered. When St. Anselm consecrated Malchus Bishop in 1096 the Irish monk of Winchester came into vital relation with one of the most acute intellects not only of Italy, his native land, but of the Church, not only of his century, but of all time. For three years, under Malchus, the young priest Malachy completed that training of his mind and heart that was fitting him to be looked upon by some historians as St. Patrick's most illustrious successor.

St. Bernard has recalled but one incident of these three years of quiet study with Malchus on the wooded banks of the Blackwater at

Lismore. So sinful a life was his sister living that, as we have seen, this young priest, who was all gentleness and mercy, had made a vow never to visit her whilst she lived in sin. Death came to her whilst her brother was at Lismore. St. Bernard's words are in that master of words' most poignant manner.

> For the Saint indeed abhorred her carnal life; and with such intensity that he vowed he would never see her alive in the flesh.
>
> But now that her flesh was destroyed his vow was also destroyed; and he began to see in spirit her whom in the body he would not see.

On hearing of her death he had offered up the Holy Mass for her. Some thirty days after having ceased to offer up the Holy Sacrifice for her:

> He heard in a dream by night the voice of one saying to him that his sister was standing outside in the courtyard, having tasted nothing for thirty days. On awaking he soon realized the kind of food for want of which she was pining away.

His prayers and Masses for her soul continued. Soon he saw her at the threshold of the church; but clad in black. Later on he saw her clad in grey; within the church, but not allowed to the altar. At last she was seen a third time, with the throng of the white-robed and in apparel that shone.

This public sin of his sister, with his vow never to see her whilst her sin lasted, may have helped him to quit Armagh for Lismore. At any rate her death, with seemingly her known repentance, made it easier for him to return in a position of authority.

The summons to return came to him in 1123, when his mother's brother, a layman, had been elected, by the law of Tanistry, to be Abbot of Bangor. This layman, determined to break the unhappy tradition of centuries, resigned the Abbey with its rich lands to his priest nephew, Malachy. But the same Nazareth spirit of poverty was alike in nephew and uncle.

St. Bernard's account of what took place throws light on the soul of the young Abbot of Bangor.

> Vast were the possessions of that place. But Malachy, contented with the holy place alone, resigned all the possessions and lands to another... And though many urged him not to alienate the possessions but to keep them all for himself, this lover of poverty did not consent, but caused one to be elected, according to custom, to hold them; the place itself being kept for Malachy and his followers.

For the moment, dear reader, note St. Bernard's praise of his fellow-saint's poverty. We shall return to it again.

St. Bernard's praise of Bangor, of which an excerpt has already been quoted, is couched in noble prose.

> Bangor.... There indeed had been formerly a very celebrated Abbey; its first father being Comgall. It brought forth many saints and was the head of many monasteries. Truly was it a holy place, bringing forth most abundant fruit in God, so that one of the sons of that holy brotherhood, Lugaid by name, is said to have been himself alone the founder of a hundred monasteries. This I narrate that those who read may know from this one instance what a countless number of others there were. Indeed, its shoots did so fill Ireland and Scotland, that these verses of David seem to have sung beforehand especially of these times:
>
> Thou visitest the earth and blessest it,
>   Thou makest it very plenteous.
> The river of God is full of water.
>   Thou preparest their corn;

> For so Thou providest for the earth.
>   Blessing its rivers,
> Multiplying its shoots,
>   With its drops of rain shall it rejoice while it groweth.

> Nor was it only into the regions just named but also into foreign lands that these swarms of saints poured as though a flood had risen. Of these, one, St. Columbanus, came to our Gallic lands and built a monastery at Luxeuil, and was made there a great people. So great a people was it, they say, that, choir following after choir, the Divine Office went on unceasingly and not a moment of day or night was empty of praise.

With ten brethren from St. Imar's monastery at Armagh, St. Malachy began to rebuild the abbey and the monastic life at Bangor. Three miracles which the Saint wrought during the rebuilding of the monastery throw light on the Saint's inward soul. St. Bernard, accustomed to the noble stone buildings of France, says: "The church was finished in a few days. It was made of smoothed planks, but closely and strongly fastened together—a Scotia work, not devoid of beauty."

It would seem that the young Abbot, a lover of plenty of work, took his place amongst the workers, who were smoothing the planks. No doubt the Saint was using the great broad-edged hatchet which was used in these islands well into the nineteenth century. One of the Saint's fellow workmen put himself in the place of the young Abbot's stroke and was felled to the ground. St. Bernard quaintly records that the man's tunic was "rent from the top to the bottom" (Matthew 27:51), but that the man himself was unhurt. Again, dear reader, take notice how Malachy is being prepared to succeed St. Patrick at Armagh by working as a carpenter at Bangor.

The second miracle shows the fearless apostle. A young man dying told those round about him that if Malachy came to his house he would kill him. On hearing the young man's mind those round about him came to warn Malachy. But the Saint having heard the warning took notice of it as saints usually do. He prayed. Then he boldly went to the place of danger—and in St. Bernard's phrase "put to flight both the disease and the demon." Again take notice of the zealous apostle who visits the sick in their homes, and at the risk of his life. Such are the Soggarths of Ireland! No wonder they are near and very dear to Irish hearts.

The third miracle was wrought when he cured a young monk by sending him something from his own table! A fatherly act which went straight to the heart of the Father in heaven.

It is to the credit of those who controlled the Irish Church in those days that a priest so fit to be Bishop was soon appointed to the Bishopric at Down and Connor (Antrim).

It was in 1124, when the Saint was not quite thirty years old, that the same great soul, St. Cellach of Armagh, who had made him deacon and priest, crowned these orders and his own long-standing desires by consecrating St. Malachy Bishop. It is the last time that history records the meeting of these two great men. And though the elder Saint did not know how soon the younger was to succeed him at Armagh, he had even then, no doubt, fixed upon him as his successor.

It was to no place of ease that St. Cellach's consecration sent the young Bishop of Down and Connor. St. Bernard's dark picture of the state of Christianity that met St. Malachy has stimulated countless attempts at defence. Perhaps the most dexterous defence against the French Saint's denunciation of this Irish diocese is a kindred and almost equally dark denunciation of the Church in Southern France and in Rome. But we venture to suggest that the context of St. Bernard's words might well refer to Connor alone, which St. Malachy had not yet visited; and not to Down, which he had known from childhood.

Of far more importance and perhaps accuracy than St. Bernard's denunciation of the good folk of Connor (and Down?) whom he calls "not men but beasts," is his description of the young Bishop's way of dealing with them. Fortunately St. Malachy recognized that in the people of Down and Connor he had to deal with men, of a rugged stamp, perhaps, but men who knew and would follow a good leader when they found one. That they had found one in their new Bishop—a sapling of their own soil—is clear from St. Bernard's words:

> He recognized that he was a shepherd and not a hireling. [That was the straight way to the heart of the Down and Connor folk!] He made up his mind to stand and not to flee; and even to give his life for his sheep… He chid in public, he argued in secret, he wept now with one and now with another. To some he spoke sharply; to some, gently; as he saw what befitted each. And when all these stratagems failed he offered for them a "broken and bruised heart." How often did he spend whole nights in a wake, holding out his hands in prayer. And when they would not come to the church he went to meet the unwilling ones in the ways, and going round about the city he eagerly sought whom he might gain for Christ. Often did he go into country parts and villages with that holy band of disciples who never left his side.
>
> Nor did he ride on a horse, but went on foot, thus showing himself an apostolic man. How often was he faint with hunger, how often afflicted with cold and nakedness.… At last, all things were so changed for the better that to-day the word which the Lord speaks by the prophet may be spoken of this nation: Those who before were not my people, are now my people.

There can hardly be a doubt that when St. Bernard in his cell at Clairvaux wrote this description of the Irish Archbishop whose tomb in the Lady Chapel was hardly finished, he was setting before the Church of his age the model of a Catholic Bishop. No doubt Bernard of the human heart was grieving for and remembering a dead friend. But Bernard, the untiring champion of the Church, was recalling for all time how in a land overrun by wolves a good Shepherd, by name Malachy, had changed wolves into sheep.

In 1128, some northern king, perhaps Conor O'Loughlin, invaded Connor and Down. St. Bernard's dark description of St. Malachy's fellow-countrymen receives corroboration when we read that this northern king destroyed the monastery of Bangor and drove off the monks. But their Abbot and Bishop Malachy knowing that his diocese needed these, his fellow-laborers, found a home for his hundred and twenty monks at Iveragh in Kerry. The site was the gift of Cormac Mac Carthy, King of Desmond, whom St. Malachy had befriended when King Cormac was a fugitive at Lismore. St. Malachy's genius for friendship was again seen when the king not only gave him the site and means to build the monastery but gave his hands and shoulders to the work of building. Once again the Abbot of Clairvaux becomes lyrical as he praises his friend the dead Archbishop:

> And these as it were beginning anew, the burden of law and discipline which he laid on others he bore with greater zeal himself, their bishop and teacher. He himself in the order of his course, did duty as cook; he himself served the brethren whilst they took their food. Amongst the brethren who succeeded one another in chanting or reading in church he would not be passed over, but strenuously took his part as one of them. And in the life of holy poverty, he not only shared but took the lead; being zealous for it more than they all.

On the 1st of April, 1129, St. Cellach, then in his fiftieth year died at Ardpatrick in the county of Limerick. If the same ruthless invasion by Conor O'Loughlin drove St. Cellach and St. Malachy from their Sees, we can understand how a man of Cellach's sensitiveness broke down in exile.

His death was another landmark in the life of his friend Malachy. Students of psychical research will find it of interest to read in

St. Bernard's life how in a vision St. Malachy saw a woman of great stature and reverent mien who, on being asked, said she was the Bride of Cellach. Then she gave to Malachy a bishop's staff and disappeared. A few days later St. Malachy received from the dying Cellach a letter naming him Archbishop of Armagh and sending the bishop's staff which St. Malachy recognized as the staff given to him in the vision. One can hardly imagine that on 5th April when St. Cellach was laid to rest at Lismore, far from his See at Armagh, his lifelong friend and successor was not by the graveside.

In the Ireland of those days the Staff of St. Patrick and the nomination by a successor of St. Patrick did not make a *de facto* Archbishop of Armagh.

The kinsmen of the dead Archbishop used their hereditary right to name as successor his first cousin, Murtough. There was nothing glaringly wrong or even illegal in this application of the clan system to the ecclesiastical hierarchy. Even later centuries have seen royal nomination to bishoprics tolerated by the Church.

As Malachy, who was already a Bishop, held out for three years in his refusal to accept the Archbishopric it is evident that Archbishop Murtough was hardly the wicked intruder of St. Bernard's Gallic invective. Unless, indeed, we are to deny the validity of Archbishop Cellach's election we must hesitate to deny the election of his cousin Murtough. When St. Bernard, true to his portrait of Murtough, paints his death as that of the unrepentant, his rhetoric must be contrasted with the words of the Four Masters: "On 17th of September, A.D. 1134, he died after the victory of martyrdom and penance."

It was only in 1132 that St. Malachy allowed himself to be nominated to the See of Armagh. It is significant that the two Bishops who finally broke down his opposition were Malchus of Lismore, and Gilbert of Limerick, the Papal Legate. It would almost seem that the final authority to compel obedience was the Holy See of which Gilbert was Legate. Three years would give time to lay the matter before the successor of St. Peter. Unfortunately the successor of St. Peter,

Innocent II, found the See of Rome, like the See of Armagh, claimed by another—Anacletus—who, after being elected by a group of Cardinals, had been crowned in St. Peter's on the same day that Innocent II was crowned in another church in Rome. Something of the still more distracted state of the Church at large may have been reflected in the Church of Ireland. If it was five years before St. Malachy took possession of his archiepiscopal chair in Armagh, it was eight years before Pope Innocent II took possession of his Papal Chair in Rome. In each case the final step was taken by the help of the secular arm. Yet for two years preceding the death of Murtough, St. Malachy "did not enter the city" of Armagh, "lest by such an act it should happen that any of those should die to whom he came rather to administer life."

Even the death of Murtough was not the end of the troubles. Murtough had followed the precedent of his cousin, Archbishop Cellach, by appointing his successor. The choice of Niall, brother of Cellach, was an adroit move to secure local loyalty.

Fr. Luddy's account of the circumstances leading up to St. Malachy's entry into his cathedral city is a striking commentary on the state of things:

> Niall could count perhaps on the support of Conor O'Loughlin, the most powerful ruler in Ulster. But at this time—September, 1134—the allied kings of Munster, Mac Carthy and O'Brien, having fought their way through Connacht, were actually in the neighborhood of Armagh, near enough to control the situation.

St. Malachy's determination to avoid bloodshed, even in seeking his right, seems to have kept the fighting men apart—no small miracle in an Irish atmosphere. Indeed, the miracle is attributed by an expert, no less than St. Bernard, to the Saint's prayer, which brought down such a thunderstorm that the ringleader and three of his confederates were first killed by lightning and then blown by the storm into the branches of a tree, where they were found charred and corrupted.

Light is thrown on the state of things in Armagh by St. Bernard's naive remark: "For though there was no one now who would harm him openly, yet the bishop had no place that was safe from plotters, and no time when he could be at ease. Armed men were appointed to guard him day and night; though he rather trusted in the Lord." An Archbishop of Armagh who can fulfil his duties only by a trust in God made effective by the help of a posse of police is not riding comfortably in the saddle! But he presents little difficulty to the Celtic mind.

St. Malachy's dealings with Niall can only be surmised from the documents. It would be perhaps unjust even to St. Malachy to take St. Bernard's words at their face value.

The facts are:

1. Niall on leaving Armagh took with him the Staff of Jesus (*Bachall Iosa*), which seems to have been St. Patrick's crozier; and the Book of Armagh (*Canoin Phadruig*).

2. Shortly afterwards (7th July, 1135), according to the Four Masters, St. Malachy bought the Bachall, perhaps from Niall.

3. At the same time St. Malachy obtained the Book of Armagh. St. Bernard says that both were handed over to St. Malachy by Niall.

4. St. Bernard adds that "Niall was henceforth quiet in all subjection." The Four Masters say "he yielded place to Gelasius" (whom St. Malachy named to succeed him), and that "he died in 1139 after great penance."

5. St. Malachy before resigning the Archbishopric appointed to be his successor Gelasius (Gilla Macliag), Abbot of Derry, coarb of Columbkille. Though this appointment broke for ever the bad tradition of the clan-archbishops of Armagh, Gelasius occupied the See till his death in 1174. During his long reign of thirty-seven years there is no mention of any anti-bishop. It was a peaceful settlement which might have been the envy of the City of Rome.

6. The quiet humility of St. Malachy was so successful that St. Bernard, in writing an account of it, seems to have offered it as a model to the bishops of the Church at large.

When St. Malachy finally agreed to accept the Archbishopric of Armagh, St. Bernard reports him as saying:

> You are leading me to death, but I obey in the hope of martyrdom; yet on this condition that if the enterprise succeeds and God frees His heritage from those who are destroying it—all being then completed, and the Church at peace, I may be allowed to go back to my former bride and friend, poverty, and to put another in my place!

It is hardly possible that St. Malachy was not thinking of the beloved apostle of his country, whose memory was in every townland of Down! St. Patrick, the boy who ran away from slavery, was never greater than when in his old age he became a run-away from honor. Saints are often pursued by the example of brother saints. All the holy men who had such an influence on St. Malachy copied St. Patrick's masterstroke of resigning honors. Imar O'Hagan resigned the Abbotship of St. Peter and St. Paul at Armagh to become a hermit and to die in Rome, 1134. Malchus had resigned the Archbishopric of Cashel to return to his first diocese of Lismore and Waterford. Gilbert, the Papal Legate, in 1139 resigned his legatine commission and his Bishopric. It was two years after St. Malachy had resigned Armagh for the quiet and poverty of Down. We question whether any Church in Christendom was setting a higher example of flight from ecclesiastical honors than the Church in Ireland.

Once back in his beloved Down, St. Malachy began again to organize a community of men amidst the charred ruins of Bangor. Death had been so usual amongst those he loved that his thoughts, never set on the world, were more and more fixed on God. His brother, Christian, Bishop of Clogher, had gone to God on 12th of June, 1138, with such repute of holiness that St. Bernard wrote of him: "He was a good man, full of grace and virtue. In the mind of the people he ranked second only to his brother, whom he perhaps equalled in zeal for justice and in sanctity of life."

Another death by its suddenness and its mode must have wrung the heart of St. Malachy. In 1127, when St. Malachy found at Lismore the exiled King Cormac Mac Carthy of Desmond, the two men had been knit in friendship. It was Cormac to whom he fled when driven from Bangor in 1128. It was from Cormac, now restored to his kingdom, that he received the gift of Iveragh. It was Cormac, with his wife's uncle, Conor O'Brien, who had over-awed the supporters of Niall in 1134. But in 1138, shortly after marrying Conor's niece, he was assassinated by his own father-in-law.

When a man who is a saint, like Malachy, sees his life's work nearing completion, he redoubles his energy lest death overtake him, and the night come in which no man can work. One greater than any saint, after spending thirty years in silence and thirty months in daily preaching, at length when His work was nearing its close, set His face and hastened towards Jerusalem. None of the great men—Cellach, Imar, Malchus, Gilbert, Malachy—may have known that, under the guidance of God, they were organizing a spiritual building in their beloved country that was to take the stress of eight centuries of political subjugation and four centuries of religious persecution. It was not foresight but insight that guided these men when they built better than they knew. They only knew that no building of theirs would stand when Satan's storms buffeted it, unless they built upon the successor of the man who was made a Rock. St. Patrick had left them the command "to be Christians, be Romans." That word, faithfully kept, has been the keeping of Ireland's faith.

Instinctively, then, St. Malachy felt that the organization of the Irish Church, so patiently made by Cellach and his friends, would not stand or last if it had not the knowledge and approval of the Pope. It was a Catholic's homing instinct, therefore, that sent St. Malachy to Rome late in 1139 or early in 1140. This instinct was all the more praiseworthy because for some nine years Rome had welcomed an anti-Pope, Anacletus, and had made the rightful Pope, Innocent II, little less than a wanderer in Germany and France.

The Saint's way of travelling was on foot, with only three packhorses to carry the baggage. Allowing for a month in Rome, the party covered some 3,000 miles in nine months!

Their route took them through Scotland to York. St. Bernard records that at York a priest named Sycarus (Sighere) pointed out St. Malachy as a holy man about whom he had been given revelations. York also brought him in touch with another holy man, St. Waltheof, Prior of the Canons Regular of St. Augustine, at Kirkham. Although St. Waltheof was stepson of King David of Scotland, he went about in such poverty that his only mount was a black packhorse, very rough to ride. Such as it was, he offered it to St. Malachy, who was, perhaps, even then beginning to show signs of the failure of his strength. The Burgundian nobleman, Bernard, is at pains to give the courteous speech of the Saint who gave and the Saint who received the cross-tempered black packhorse. But he is at equal pains to tell how once made the go-between of Saints the sorry beast changed both its character and its color; from cross-tempered it became docile; from black it became white. Indeed, in St. Bernard's own words—and he had often seen it at Clairvaux—"there was scarcely a whiter horse to be seen." Nor did it fail its new master till he died. Perhaps, like the mule that used to carry the Dumb Ox of Aquino, it died of grief at its master's death. Perhaps, again, it is a beast-of-kin to another Saint's companion, the White Swan of St. Hugh.

The most important incident in the Saint's journey to Rome was his going aside from his direct route to visit St. Bernard at Clairvaux. No doubt, during his stay at York, he had heard of, perhaps visited, the Cistercian monastery of Rievaulx, founded by monks of Clairvaux itself. If so, he would see a state of things recalling his own beloved country—a sparsely peopled, largely untilled countryside being gradually tilled and peopled by groups of peasant families that clustered round an agricultural community of contemplative monks. When St. Stephen Harding, and later on St. Bernard, used the Rule of

St. Benedict to form communities of contemplative monks working on the land, they may not have foreseen how this challenge to the Catholic youth of Europe-in-ruins would be romantically accepted. Even the enthusiasm that met the mendicant challenge of Francis and Dominic was hardly greater. In England alone, between the years 1128 and 1152, the Cistercian houses numbered fifty. The community at Rievaulx, shortly after St. Malachy's visit, numbered three hundred, and included the young monk St. Aelred.

It was thus that even on his way to the city of his desire, and to the authority of his obedience, St. Malachy caught sight of what seemed to him the necessary supplement of all ecclesiastical organization. Throughout his life he had sought it without knowing clearly what he sought. He had sought it as a lad when he put himself under the roof and the care of Imar O'Hagan. Even as a young Bishop of Down and Connor, he had sought it at Bangor. Driven from Bangor he had not been driven from his desire, but had sought it again at Iveragh. Driven from Iveragh to be the successor of St. Patrick at Armagh he sought it with such increasing keenness that he resigned his Metropolitan See to seek it again as Bishop of Down, in his beloved home at Bangor.

It would be an oversight not to detect in St. Malachy a rare genius for what is most practical. He had the even rarer genius to know that practical matters are best taught, not by lessons, but by practice. He never asked others to undertake a burden that he himself had not already undertaken, or was preparing to undertake. The stones and timbers of his monasteries were authentic witness.

When, therefore, he saw Cistercian monasticism civilizing the countryside's of France and Northern Italy he determined to ask his superior, Pope Innocent II, for leave to become a Cistercian. Yet he was not drawn to this merely or primarily by the desire of his heart for contemplative union with God. Knowing that he could not love God, Whom he did not see, if he did not love his neighbor whom he did see, he desired to lead others into the Cistercian life by himself preceding them. But his desire to see himself and them working in Cistercian fields or chanting in Cistercian choirs, included a desire to give to his beloved Irish people something of the life that redeemed the world in the highland hamlet of Nazareth.

It is to the credit of Pope Innocent II that he gave St. Malachy every desire of his heart except one. Yet—to use a fine epigram of St. Augustine—"in refusing the desire of his heart he did not refuse the heart of his desire." While sanctioning the creation of the new Archbishopric of Cashel, making Armagh Metropolitan of Ireland, and consenting to give the pall to the two Sees of Armagh and Cashel, Innocent II refused to let St. Malachy become a monk at Clairvaux. In the end this refusal meant that, instead of Clairvaux receiving there and then one Irish monk, Ireland received later on a community of monks firmly settled at Mellifont by the authority of St. Malachy, the legate of the Pope!

Pope Innocent had been for too many years a fugitive from his See not to feel grateful to this Saint and Bishop, who brought him reverence and obedience from the Island of Saints. He showed his insight into character and his gratitude for loyal obedience by making St. Malachy his legate in Ireland. St. Bernard records details of a personal kind that show how St. Malachy's invincible charm had won the Bishop of Rome as it had won the Abbot of Clairvaux.

> Then the Pope took his mitre from his own head and placed it on Malachy's head; nay more, he gave him the stole and maniple he was wont to wear at Mass. Then he gave him the kiss of peace and bade him farewell strengthened with the Apostolic Blessing and authority.

When St. Malachy revisited Clairvaux on his way home he left four of his companions with St. Bernard to be his proxies in the monastic life. In time they came back to him when he founded the first Cistercian abbey in Ireland.

Miracles marked his way home. He raised from deadly illness to health Henry, the son of his friend, King David of Scotland. At Cruggleton, a hamlet on Wigtown Bay, he cured a dumb girl. At St. Michael's Church a poor lunatic woman bound with cords was brought to him by a crowd of people. He blessed her and reason was given to her.

Another incident throwing great light on the Saint's characteristic zeal has not escaped the eye or pen of the indefatigable Abbot of Clairvaux. Whilst waiting for fine weather at Cairngarroch, the time of delay did not pass idly. In the meanwhile a chapel of wattle was built, he himself directing and working. He surrounded it with a wall and blessed the enclosed space for a cemetery. He never forgot his old Gaelic devotion to the dead. No wonder the simple folk of the neighborhood brought their sick to be cured in the hallowed garth with the wattle church built by a saint whilst waiting for fine weather to cross the channel!

The eight years of life now remaining to St. Malachy have left little record in his biographies. Three activities may sum up his last years: (1) His foundation of the Cistercian Abbey at Mellifont in Co. Louth; (2) His journeyings throughout Ireland as Papal Legate; (3) His presiding over a National Council.

Four Irish monks and some eight French monks began the first Cistercian Abbey at Mellifont in 1142. The name *Honey-well* recalls that St. Malachy who had chosen the spot had not forgotten his desire to see contemplatives tilling the rich soil of Ireland.

Fr. Luddy, speaking with the authoritativeness of a Cistercian, suggests that the disagreement between the Irish and French monks may have been partly occasioned by the French monks' building plans! *Sit omen.* The Irish monastic tradition of extreme architectural poverty did not easily fit in with Gallic views. In the end the French views prevailed. Fr. Luddy adds: "All the buildings, of course, were of stone; and of such proportions as must have astonished the simple-minded Celts." Abbeys were founded in the little island so thickly that there were some forty-six at the time of the Dissolution when the population of the country was not so great as London or New York. But it is still a moot point whether the Gallic or the Gaelic view of architectural poverty should have prevailed.

An itinerary of St. Malachy's legatine journeys in Ireland would probably give us the names of every considerable town in the island. Of greater importance than this geographical aspect of the Saint's journeyings is St. Bernard's account of the legate's manner of life as he journeyed.

> From the first day of his conversion to the last of his life he lived without personal possessions.
>
> He had neither manservants nor maidservants; nor villages nor hamlets; nor, in fact, any revenues, ecclesiastical or secular, even when he was a bishop.
>
> There was nothing whatever assigned for his episcopal upkeep, for he had not a house of his own. But he was always going about all the parishes, preaching the Gospel and living by the Gospel... When he went out to preach he was accompanied by others on foot; bishop and legate that he was he too went on foot. That was the apostolic rule; and it is the more to be admired in Malachy because it is too rare in others. The true successor of the apostles assuredly is he who does such things. But it is to be observed how he divides his inheritance with his brothers, who are equally descendants of the apostles.
>
> They lord it over the clergy—he made himself the servant of all.
>
> They either do not preach the Gospel and yet eat; or preach the Gospel in order to eat—Malachy, imitating Paul, eats that he may preach the Gospel.
>
> They suppose that arrogance and gain are godliness—Malachy claims for himself by right only toil and a burden.
>
> They count themselves happy if they enlarge their borders—Malachy glories in enlarging charity.

> They gather into barns and fill the wine-jars that they may load their tables—Malachy forgathers men into deserts and solitudes that he may fill heaven.
>
> They though they receive tithes and first-fruits and oblations besides customs and tribute by the gift of Caesar and countless other revenues, nevertheless take counsel as to what they may eat and drink—Malachy having nothing enriches many out of the store-houses of faith.
>
> Of their desire and anxiety there is no end—Malachy, desiring nothing, knows not how to be solicitous for to-morrow.
>
> They exact from the poor that they may give to the rich—Malachy implores the rich to provide for the poor.
>
> They empty the purses of their subjects—he for their sins loads altars with vows and peace-offerings.
>
> They build lofty palaces, raise towers and ramparts to the skies—Malachy, not having whereon to lay his head, does the work of an evangelist.
>
> They ride on horses with a throng of men who eat bread for naught, and that is not theirs—Malachy girt around by a throng of holy brethren goes on foot bearing the bread of angels.
>
> They do not even know their congregations—he instructs them.
>
> They honor powerful men and tyrants—he punishes them.
>
> O apostolic man whom so many and such striking signs of apostleship adorn. What wonder that he has wrought such wonder, being so great a wonder himself.

When the first Cistercian Pope, Eugenius III, asked his old Abbot St. Bernard for guidance as the Supreme Bishop of the Visible Church, the holy Doctor answered in effect: "Study the life and follow the example of St. Malachy; and all will be well." Had St. Bernard's words been more widely read and more faithfully copied all would not be ill as it is today.

Some of the wonders wrought by St. Malachy are narrated by

St. Bernard. We are not sure that the evidence for their supernatural character would be accepted by a modern Congregation of Rites. But the narrative is almost a substitute for the Legate's wide itinerary. At *Coleraine* he drove the demon first out of one woman and then out of a second into whom he had entered; in *Ulster* a sick man was at once cured by lying in the Saint's bed; at *Lismore* a demoniac was cured; in *Leinster* he instantly cured a sick babe; in *Saul, Co. Down*, a woman, whose madness was so great that she was tearing her limbs with her teeth, was cured when he prayed and laid his hands on her; at *Antrim* a dying man recovered the use of his tongue and his speech on receiving the Holy Viaticum; at *Cloyne* when a nobleman besought his aid for his wife, in danger of death through child-birth, the Saint sent her a cup he had blessed and her child was happily born; at *Cashel* he cured a paralyzed boy; on the borders of *Munster* a cripple boy was cured; at *Cork* he raised from a sick bed one whom he named bishop of the city; in another unnamed place a notorious scold was cured when she made her first confession to the Saint (here St. Bernard not, perhaps, very chivalrously observes that this is a greater miracle than raising the dead!); an *island (Rathlin?)* long famous for fishermen had suffered from lack of fish which came back when the Saint knelt down on the shore and prayed.

The witnesses to these wonders have passed beyond their power to authenticate. Yet if not one of these recorded wonders happened as recorded, their litany of Irish place-names would record the untiring apostolic zeal of Ireland's greatest apostle since the days of St. Patrick.

The following incident deserves a place of honor in a biography of the Saint, inspired by the first Eucharistic Congress held in the Saint's native land. It must be told in St. Bernard's own words.

> In Lismore there was a cleric of better life (it was said) than faith. A scholar in his own eyes he dared to say that in the Eucharist there was only the sacrament and not the reality of the sacrament; in other words, only the hallowing and not the truth of the Body.

On this matter, having been often summoned by Malachy secretly but in vain, he was bidden to a council, yet apart from the laity, so that, if possible, he might be healed without being put to shame. In this council, therefore, there was given the man opportunity of explaining his opinion.

When, with all his cleverness, which was not a little, he had explained and defended his opinion, Malachy himself took up the discussion and answered him. Whereupon being condemned by a unanimous judgment he went out of the meeting, ashamed but not convinced. He said he had not been overcome by argument but compelled by the authority of the Bishop. He added: "And you," Malachy, "have this day put me to shame, speaking against the truth and your own conscience."

Malachy saddened by the hardness of the man, but grieving still more for the hurt to faith and dreading the danger, summons the church, publicly corrects the erring one, publicly warns him to retract. When he would not agree to this, even after the bishops and clergy had urged him, they pronounce anathema upon him as contumacious and declare him a heretic.

Yet did he not awake, but said: "It is the man you all seek; and not the truth. But I will not follow the man and leave the truth." At this word the saint being deeply moved said: "May the Lord make you confess the truth of necessity." To which the other said "Amen." Then the council was brought to an end.

Branded with this mark, he planned to flee, being unable to be accounted disgraced and dishonored. Gathering his belongings together he soon set out. But lo! seized with sudden illness, he stood still, and in sheer weakness threw himself down on the ground breathless and weak.

By chance a wandering simpleton coming to the spot stumbled upon the man and asked him where he was going. He answered that he was taken with weakness and could neither go on nor go back. Whereupon the other said: "Your weakness is nothing else but

> death!" This he did not say of himself; for the Lord very fitly corrected by a simpleton one who would not hearken to the same counsels of the wise. Then he added: "Go back home. I will help you."
>
> Thereupon with his help to went back to the town; indeed he went back to his heart and to the mercy of the Lord. At once the Bishop is summoned, the truth is acknowledged, the error is rejected. He confesses his sin and is absolved—he asks for Viaticum—is reconciled, and almost at the same moment his unfaith is disowned by his mouth and dissolved by his death.

St. Bernard's pen has here given us a very finished picture not only of an Irish Saint, but of the Irish Church and people. Lismore, where this *sciolus* was spreading false doctrine about the Blessed Sacrament, might well be called the Maynooth of its day. It held so high a place in the ecclesiastical world that the priest Malachy, although trained in the school of Armagh, had sought further learning from the school of Lismore.

So many cherished memories linked Lismore with St. Malachy that it must have been a heartbreak to find its hallowed schools darkened by heresy. Yet truth, and especially the truth of faith, was always more to the Saint than the most hallowed memory.

It cut him to the quick to realize that some eddies of the heresy of Berengarius were finding defenders in his beloved country, and even in his twice beloved mother-school. Yet he did not let his feelings stifle his wonted kindness of soul. We are grateful to St. Bernard for recording how this Legate of the Holy See had such compassion for a brother-priest that often and in secret he sought to win him back to truth. No good shepherd could have done less or more. Only when these secret frequent talks were unavailing did he take steps publicly to counter an evil which was publicly endangering the faith of the Irish Church. Thank God that faith of the Irish Church in the Holy Eucharist was not to be measured by the teachings of one misguided professor. It was with full trust in the orthodoxy of his people that

St. Malachy summoned Bishops and clergy to hear the facts of the case. Biographers of the Saint have not yet, perhaps, seen the full significance of this first council summoned by the papal legate. At that council the Bishops and priests of Ireland uttered their traditional faith in the Real Presence of Jesus in the Holy Eucharist.

There is something of Bethlehem homeliness in the description of the one whom St. Bernard calls *vagabundus insanus*, the "wandering simpleton" or "innocent." This is perhaps one of the earliest references to a very important mediaeval institution—the fool. In those days of faith the fool was often the only one willing or allowed to utter the platitudes of wisdom, and to point out disagreeable or dangerous facts. This harmless necessary heirloom from the Ages of Faith survived in the Ireland of our childhood and was held in honor. No doubt St. Bernard's artistic eye saw the dramatic quality of a *sciolus* being helped to complete wisdom by a "fool." When heresy seeks to find a footing in Ireland *solvuntur risu tabulae*—the people are kept from it by a saving sense of humor.

Let us here bestow on our readers a spray of Irish Fioretti as fair and fragrant as any of its Tuscan kindred. St. Bernard must say it in his own way:

> A man who in the world's sight was honorable, and in God's sight holy, came to Malachy. He sorrowed concerning the barrenness of his soul; and besought him to obtain from Almighty God the grace of tears.
>
> Then Malachy smiling because he was pleased there should be spiritual desire in a man of the world laid his own cheek on the cheek of the other as though caressing him and said: "Be it done unto you as you have besought."
>
> From that time rivers of water ran down his eyes, so full and so almost unceasing that the word of Holy Writ might seem applicable to him: A garden fount—a well of living waters.

Once on being asked where he would choose to die, he replied: "If I die here, I should do so nowhere more gladly than whence I may rise together with our apostle" (St. Patrick); "but if I must go abroad, then with God's leave I have chosen Clairvaux." On being further asked the day, he named All Souls'.

The man and the saint spoke in these desires. St. Patrick had been from childhood the hero by whose deeds he had shaped his life. He was shaping even his death and burial place after the manner of Ireland's apostle, for whom the grave in Downpatrick is burial in a foreign land.

Clairvaux, with its band of contemplative monks redeeming the soil and thereby redeeming their souls by divinely appointed toil, had appealed to him with the power of a crusade. His own ideal of Nazareth poverty—which anticipated the Poverello of Assisi—saw in Clairvaux something like realization.

And All Souls' Day—the Day of the Dead—bespoke the Western Gael who even as a young deacon had loved the dead with the lowly services of the burial spade!

Nothing was now left for the Saint but to set in order a few things of duty, and then answer his Master's summons of death.

Early in 1148 St. Malachy summoned a National Council at Patrick's Island, Skerries. Innocent II had promised that if such a Council asked for the palls to be given to the Sees of Armagh and Cashel they would be given. Although the Roman See was now occupied by Eugenius III, the promise of Innocent II was not likely to be unfulfilled. Eugenius III, a Cistercian and pupil of St. Bernard, had to flee from Rome and dwell in France, where he presided over a General Chapter of Cistercians at Clairvaux itself.

St. Malachy set out with the request of the National Council that the Sees of Armagh and Cashel should receive the archiepiscopal pall.

As he was setting out from Bangor some of the monks came to the water's edge. Amongst them was a young monk who for some years was subject to epileptic fits. He was in tears at the thought of the loss he was suffering. At the Saint's blessing he was cured; and in St. Bernard's words: "he has suffered no new attack."

Two of the brethren were mouthpieces of the Bangor monks in making the Bishop promise he would once more return to Ireland. Though the promise was wrung from his affectionate heart under compulsion, God gave him to keep it. The boat he embarked in for Scotland was driven by wind and current to Blackcauseway, Strangford Lough. Close by was the chapel of Ballyculter, belonging to the monastery at Saul. It was holy ground. St. Patrick had landed there some seven centuries before; and there had died. God had arranged that the Saint of Down's last night in his beloved Ireland was spent where his mind was filled with hallowed memories of the apostle he loved in life and death. That night the two Saints were nearer than men knew.

Through delays in England, where King Stephen was forbidding communications with France, St. Malachy was some months in reaching Clairvaux, where with God's courteous leave he had chosen to die.

St. Bernard's account of how St. Malachy came into their midst and died belongs to the classics not only of divine but of human love! Some day, perhaps in the near future, the scholars in the schools of Down will know it by heart in the sweetness of its original Burgundian Latin:

> Though coming from the West he was received by us as the Day Star from on high that visited us. O how greatly did that shining sun fill our Clairvaux with added splendor. How gladsome was the festal day that opened upon us at his coming.
>
> How swiftly and lightly I at once ran to him, though trembling and weak. How joyfully I showered kisses.[3] With what glad arms I embraced this dear one sent from God! With what eager look and

3. Catullus has hardly a more daring phrase: "*Quant laetus in oscula rui.*"

> soul, O my father, did I lead thee to the home of my mother and into the room of her that bore me!
>
> What happy days I spent with thee, though few I and he with us? To all of us our guest showed himself always gay, always kindly; yea lovable to all beyond belief....
>
> Four or five days of this our feast had gone by when on the solemn day of St. Luke, Evangelist [October 18, 1148], he had celebrated the Holy Mass before the community with great devotion, being taken with a fever he laid himself down; and we were with him.

Though the fever seemed to the brethren but light, the Saint told them smilingly that it was the beginning of the end!

He asked to be anointed. But when the brethren proposed to bring the Last Sacraments he rose from his sick bed in a far-off cell at the top of the house and walked unhelped to the church. Then having received the Last Sacraments he again walked back unhelped. It was the last journey of one who had worn himself out on foot in the service of his Master.

> He assured us that death was at the threshold. Who would believe him a dying man? Only himself and God could have known it. His face seemed no paler nor thinner, his brow unfurrowed, his eyes not sunken, his nostrils not sharpened, his lips not contracted. Such was his fair body and his gracious countenance which even death did not destroy.

Towards evening on All Saints' Day all are around the bedside of the dying Saint. He thanks God Who has heard his request to die where he is dying.

Then he sweetly consoled us, saying: "Bear me in mind; I, if allowed, will not forget you. It will be allowed. I have believed God, and all is possible to him who believes. I have loved God; I have loved you; and charity never falleth away."

Then laying his hands on the head of each, he blessed them and bade them rest, "for his hour was not yet come." It was the ritual of death in Christ.

His hour came at midnight when All Saints' Day passes into All Souls'; and a shaft of light passes from the Church in bliss to the Church in pain.

> The house was filled—all the brethren—many Abbots who come hither. With psalms and hymns and spiritual canticles we bear our friend company on his homeward way.[4]
>
> In the fifty-fourth year of his age, at the time and place he had forechosen and foretold, Malachy, Bishop and Legate of the Holy Apostolic See, as if an angel snatched from our hands, blissfully slept in the Lord.

And in truth it was sleep. His peaceful brow was a token of his peaceful going forth.... His cheeks had the same flush, the same serenity as in one asleep. You would say that none of these things had been lessened but heightened by death.

St. Bernard's love for his dead friend expressed itself in his own poetic way. Whilst the monks were washing the sacred body he changed St. Malachy's tunic for one of his own. Later on he wore this tunic of his dead friend whenever he chanted Mass on great feasts.

He himself sang the *Requiem* for St. Malachy. But for some reason which no question ever succeeded in unveiling he changed the Post-communion prayer for the dead into the prayer for a Confessor Bishop: "O God, Who hast made the blessed Bishop Malachy equal in merits to Thy saints, grant, we beseech Thee, that we who celebrate the feast of his holy death may copy the example of his life. Amen." When he had finished the Mass, he went and kissed the feet of his dead friend! It was the canonization of a saint by a saint!

4. "*Prosequimur amicum repatriantem.*" The Doctor Mellifluus has a store of such phrases.

Another slender incident may well find a place amongst the Fioretti of St. Malachy. At some distance from the body of St. Malachy St. Bernard noticed a boy whose arm hung dead by his side. "I beckoned him to draw near. The dead hand I applied to the hand of the Bishop, and he gave life to it. The boy had come from afar, and the arm he brought hanging he took back sound to his home-land." Between two Saints the boy's chance of cure was not a minimum!

A glimpse of St. Malachy's Celtic love of Our Lady is given in St. Bernard's simple words: "And now when all had been rightly done Malachy was given unto burial in the chapel of the holy Mother of God, Mary, wherein he took such joy; the year of the Incarnation of the Lord, one thousand, one hundred and forty-eight, the second day of November."

Five years later St. Bernard, clad in the habit of his dead friend, was laid to rest in the same chapel of their beloved Mother. Thus by God's good will, not only are the names of Bernard and Malachy one for all time, but through the befalling's of time their very dust is indistinguishably one in a common tomb.

SAINT LAURENCE O'TOOLE (1128–1180)

by C. P. CURRAN

In 1128 when Lorcan O Tuathail was born scarcely more than a day's march from Dublin, the seat of his future See was to him and his people an almost foreign city. It had been a Norse town for nearly three hundred years. It had grown to be the convenient center of a maritime Norse state which stretched from the Orkneys to Waterford exercising sovereignty at times over Northumbria and Man. Olafs and Sitrics minted their own coins there with the title "High King of the Northmen of Ireland and England." The eleventh century city of "gold, silver, hangings and all precious things" grew steadily in wealth during the twelfth century but was shrinking in political importance. Its dream of a Norse hegemony was over; its kings had dwindled to ruling jarls who were beginning to adopt Gaelic patronymics and to own the real or nominal overlordship of Ard Ri, or Leinster King as the central sovereignty waxed or waned. In this seesaw of power where also the fortunes of the saint's family fluctuated, the city was gradually falling into the national rhythm but in many essentials its people were still a Norse and not an Irish community; a seafaring, trading folk living within walls with their ships lying up along the Stein, meeting in assembly at the Thing-mote, ruled by bishops who looked to Canterbury and not to Armagh, worshipping in Christ Church founded by Sitric beside which Hasculf the Jarl had his stone mansion, or in churches dedicated to over-sea saints, St. Mary's of the Ostmen, St. Olaf's or St. Michan's.

The bishops, as we have said, looked to Lanfranc, Anselm or Ralph rather than to the successors of St. Patrick. The Norse of Dublin owed their Christianity to the Anglo-Saxons. They saw England a great Christian and Danish Monarchy under Canute. When the Conqueror landed they recognized the Northman cousinship and so grew up an orientation of which Lanfranc and his successors were not slow to take advantage in the interest of Church reform and enlarged jurisdiction.

Thirty miles south of this city of conflicting tendencies Glendalough lay in the heart of the Wicklow mountains, the "quiet habitation of sanctity and literature" to use Dr. Johnson's phrase, though in truth it had been plundered and burnt by Norse or by accident already some thirteen times. Across the hills to the west lay the plains of Kildare where—probably near Castledermot—Lorcan was born. His mother was an O'Byrne, his father O Tuathail, on both sides a princely stock. To be the descendant of kings is in Ireland to be in the way of humorous commonplace. None the less the vitality of some of these old stocks is worth observing. The Ui Neill, for example, maintained an independent principality for fifteen hundred years down to the flight of the Great Earl in 1607 throwing out repeatedly and indeed in our own day foremost men in the State. So also we find a recurring outcrop of notable names in the family of St. Lorcan to the present occupant of his See. It is not to be supposed that the vigor of such a stock counted for nothing in the shaping of a saint.

When he was born his family had been ousted from their ancient throne and Dermot MacMurrough was the representative of the usurping line. Giraldus has painted the portrait of this great-limbed, violent man whose voice was hoarse with much shouting in battle, an enemy of his own people and hated by strangers, whose hand was against every man and every man's hand against his. Between

Dermot and Lorcan's father there was that brooding hostility which seeks guarantees. The king's hand fell heavy on the son who was sent to him, a ten year old hostage, to Ferns. Less ill-used than his sister who was later given to the king in marriage, Lorcan was sent in bonds away from the king's house to a "stony and barren region" where first he practiced by necessity those austerities which were later his by choice. There he passed two years in sordid misery until rescued from the king's hands by his father's threats of speedy reprisals. The Bishop of Glendalough was the mediator and the young Lorcan was sent across the hills to him who first introduced him in St. Kevin's sanctuary to the quiet recollectedness of Christian life and studies. His father arriving in a few days and, proposing to dedicate one of his sons to the service of God and St. Kevin, the saint's biographer relates how he desired the Bishop to cast lots between his sons to this end. *Laurentius risisse fertur*, the only laugh recorded in his dolorous life, *non opus est, pater, sortium jactatione.* He himself would most willingly choose God as his inheritance. And accordingly he enters the novices' school where he is invested by his biographer with the student's proper virtues: eager to hear, careful in repetition, prudent in judgment, solicitous to hold tenaciously what he has heard. In Glendalough he remains, novice, monk and abbot for the next twenty-two years, shaping himself in what its great school, the austere beauty of the mountains and lakes, and the needs of the people about them would teach him of the spiritual life, of Christian learning and the handling of men.

The Valley of Glendalough is the deep reservoir which fed St. Lorcan's actions. This man who spent the rest of his life in cities, passing between armed camps, arranging between contending kings and living amongst strangers the external life of negotiation had as his *point d'appui* a rock overhanging a dark mountain lake. In the sixth century a narrow cavern set in this rock and difficult of access drew St. Kevin to Glendalough with its promise of solitude and anchoretic severities. The anchorite's cell multiplied into the monastic hive. The valley became a university settlement, an ecclesiastical city, the seat of a diocese, made splendid with a cathedral, towers and churches which still constitute one of the remarkable ecclesiastical groups of Western Europe. In the twelfth century, when Lorcan went there, it still guarded an unimpaired tradition. The spirit of the cell still animated it and became his own. Lorcan's character was annealed in the ascetic training of the early Irish Church whose austerities would seem fabulous if they were not well authenticated. He stood in the direct line of descent from St. Kevin and the early anchorites. When, therefore, in his later years as Archbishop of Dublin he returned, as his habit was, to spend Lent in St. Kevin's bed—the *spelunca de deserto*—and on the rocky shelf beneath it where still stand the ruins of Teampull na Sceilg, he was only adding the joys of lonely contemplation—*contemplativas delicias*—to austerities which had become part of his normal life.

The typical Irish monastery was a school of asceticism, of psalmody and of ecclesiastical science. But it was also, in a degree peculiar to early Ireland where the Abbot overshadowed the Bishop, the spiritual center of the countryside. The monastery was not the monk's refuge from a wicked world but his sally-port. The abbot stood in as close relationship as the chief to the population outside the monastic community and on his special plane had need of all the qualities of leadership. Coming of a ruling stock it is not surprising that Lorcan rose so quickly to the Abbotship to which *clero et populo id postulantibus* he was elected in 1153 when only twenty-five years of age. His tenure of office gave him the widest exercise in the art of ruling men. Within the household he had to reckon with the envy and malice provided by his early elevation; without the enclosure he had distress to alleviate in the mountainy lands, south, west and north, which gave precarious support to the population and he had to ensure peace and order along roads harassed by robbers. The ecclesiastical city was in his charge whose temporalities were richer than the Bishop's. His unbounded charity first becomes known during a famine which marked the beginning of his office. Into its relief he flung, not only the monastic resources of the monastery, but also his father's fortune, ministering to the poor, the Latin text notes, as a servant rather than as a prelate. He spent freely on Church building and from this period dates the beautiful priory of St. Saviour's at the eastern end of the valley. After four years of office his spiritual stature was so plainly evident that men sought to make him Bishop of Glendalough. He put the proposal aside not as the historian Lanigan maliciously suggests on the ground that holy men do not ambition bishoprics but pleading his non-canonical age. For ten years the administration of the monastery engaged his zeal and charity; he was in touch with the great reform synod of Kells in 1152 and one finds his name subscribed in 1161 to the Charter of the new Augustinian foundation at Ferns where years later the fugitive king Dermot, its founder, sought a monk's disguise when deserted by his kinsmen and friends. In the same year Gregory, the Archbishop of Dublin, died and Lorcan was elected in his place and was consecrated in 1162 in Christ Church in Dublin by Gelasius of Armagh, the Primate, in the presence of his suffragan Bishops.

The consecration was as significant in the history of the Irish Church as it was in his personal life. The predecessors of the new Archbishop, two of them schooled in Canterbury and St. Alban's, had in many cases received their consecration from Canterbury and professed obedience to that see. The vicissitudes of his immediate predecessor are evidence of the racial and ecclesiastical jealousies which his election allayed and the manner of his consecration is signal testimony to that new consolidation of the National Hierarchy which was a principal object of the Irish Reform movement of the twelfth century.

Reform had been urgent for two reasons. The Norse had raided and plundered the Abbeys for nearly two hundred years. Under their blows the monastic system had given way over great portions of the country and in spite of a growing concentration in certain centers, Armagh, Derry, Kells, Clonmacnoise and Kildare, Christian morale had weakened. In the monasteries the Abbot or *comarba* who ruled as heir of the saintly founder was commonly a layman. Ireland in the eleventh century was as the Continent in the tenth. Rome inspired by Cluniac ideals, as Dr. Kenney observes, had struggled successfully against the absorption of the Church into the feudal system. In Ireland the reformers had to struggle against its absorption into the Irish system. The vices of laicization were rampant. The temporalities of even the primatial see of Armagh remained for generations in lay hands. There was a collateral necessity to organize according to the hierarchic rule of Christendom a Church which had forgotten diocesan organization and episcopal control. The authority of bishop, archbishop, and primate had to be defined and established upon a territorial basis. The Norse wars being over, Irishmen resumed their close contact with Rome and a Europe afire with the spirit of Gregorian reform, and to their eyes these abuses and anachronisms with other canonical and liturgical backslidings became intolerable. In this matter, as Dr. Kenney states, inspiration, advice, example may have come from abroad, but the driving force which effected the ecclesiastical revolution was from within the Irish Church. Behind every reform movement there stands a saint. In Ireland, as the preceding paper has shown, the saint was Malachy, having as precursors Cellach of Armagh and Gilbert of Limerick. Their movement, carried on from synod to synod beginning with Rath Bresail in 1111, achieved its main purpose in the Synod of Kells in 1152, when amongst other decisions the sees of Dublin and Tuam were erected to Archbishoprics and the number and limits of the present dioceses were substantially fixed. Minor outstanding disciplinary reforms were completed in subsequent synods held in 1162, 1167, and 1172, all of which were attended by our Archbishop.

In this movement which had come to a head when Lorcan was still in Glendalough, Dublin played only a subordinate if not indeed a passive part. But as a Norse town, standing apart like Norse Waterford and Limerick, it presented the useful example of an already clearly defined diocese with a diocesan administration independent of monastery or comarb. Unlike, however, Gilbert of Limerick, who owed no allegiance to Canterbury, and Malchus of Waterford who quickly shifted his to Armagh, some of its Bishops had professed obedience to Lanfranc, Anselm and Ralph who were nothing loath to use the town as the bridge head of an assumed jurisdiction. With the gradual assimilation of Dublin to Ireland this assumption of authority could not fail to be questioned. Already in 1121 Cellach of Armagh had gone into possession of the see of Dublin "by the choice of the Foreigners and the Gael" and when Gregory was set up by a rival party and consecrated by Ralph of Canterbury, Gregory was unable immediately to occupy his See and had to return to England to be maintained there during the rest of Ralph's life.

This is, therefore, the significance of Lorcan's consecration by the Primate in Dublin. He was the first Irishman to be so consecrated and the last for many centuries. For it was his tragic destiny to have been the pledge of Norse-Irish union under the national monarchy and to witness the dissolution of both under a new invasion.

So, at any rate, Lorcan came from the inland valley of the two lakes to the metropolis with its crowded harbor. He whose frontiers were mountains was now penned within a walled town, exchanging the cloister for its chattering streets where he must have heard as much Norse, Norman-French and English spoken amongst its merchant folk as his own Irish. The integrity of his outer life is split. He moves henceforward perpetually between opposites, between Gael and Gall, Norse and Norman, King Ruaidri and King Henry. The other-worldly man must put on the man of affairs, the monk-bishop become a politician, almost a soldier. He might lament like St. Bernard: "I am become the chimaera of my century, neither cleric nor layman." We know the hot vehemence with which St. Bernard fused these contradictions and we are similarly still aware *post annorum multa curricula* of the saintly charm with which Lorcan drew the exigencies of his outer and inner life into harmony. In the few sentences of his biographer, confirmed by the less ornate surviving testimony of his bones, we perceive a man *elegantis staturae*, of tall stature and graceful bearing, carrying with seemly dignity the Bishop's pontificals. Beneath them a hair-shirt. He dispenses hospitality to rich and poor in his home beside his Cathedral where the present Synod-house stands, a hospitality discreetly liberal, in his first biographer's phrase, amongst rich foods choosing for himself the plainest and coloring water with wine for courtesy and company's sake. Each day at his table he dines thirty to sixty of the poor that his other guests may be encouraged in well-doing. From the day he put on the white robe of the Augustinian Canon he took no meat, and on Fridays only bread and water. Three times daily he used the discipline; his nights were lonely vigils or spent in choir. Assiduous in attendance at the Divine Office, when at dawn the canons left the choir for their cells he remained in solitary prayer and when day came he passed out to the cemetery to chant the office of the dead. His life was what the old Irish homily calls the "white martyrdom" of abnegation and labor. The Bull of his canonization recites his constancy in prayer and his austere mortification. These were the secret springs of his energy and profuse charity. *Austeritas, benignitas.* This white-robed figure of whose speech hardly four sentences remain is seen always in the gracious gesture of giving and with the gravity of silence about him. Crowds depend upon him, recognizing in him a source of supernatural power and the records of his canonization attest his miracles. He lived through two famines and two sieges and saw the city of his adoption once sacked. He moves through them with the equilibrium of the saint and a saint's equal mind. But also with a saint's energy. He has hardly taken his seat in his Cathedral when his zeal turns to the reform of his clergy. His predecessors had been trained in a milder climate and under a more lax monastic rule. The service of the Cathedral had suffered. Looking abroad for a model he persuaded his secular canons to join him in community life as Augustinian regulars of the Arroasian rule and converted the Cathedral Church of the Holy

Trinity into a Priory. His community became a school for bishops, Albin of Ferns, Marianus of Cork, Malachy of Louth who were subsequent witnesses to his sanctity.

In the Irish monasteries psalmody occupied a great space in the monk's life. Lorcan raised the Gregorian chant, still so little heard in Irish churches, to its proper place about the Altar and restored its appropriate splendor to the Divine Office. He commenced the rebuilding of his Cathedral and added to the number of the parish churches which for a city of small size were already numerous—a deed of St. Lorcan is witnessed by the priests of seven churches and four or five others appear to have existed at this time. During a famine which afflicted the city the destitute flocked about his doors. He exerted himself in the public relief not merely by prodigally multiplying his personal charities but by organized assistance, quartering the city poor upon the abbey lands of his Cathedral—Swords, Lusk and Finglas. When these were filled and the famine still continued he sent others further afield through Ireland recommending them to the popular charity and chartering a vessel at no small cost to convey others to England. Then came the scourge of war throwing city and country into confusion. When he is in the very act of negotiating terms with the Normans the city is seized by a sudden, treacherous irruption and the peacemaker turns to save the wounded, to bury his dead, to guard the ecclesiastical property from spoliation and to recover the looted Church vessels and books. Henceforward he must double the parts of a Mercier and a Vincent de Paul. Resistance becomes a duty of patriotism. Fronting the unjust aggression he becomes for a moment the center of the national resistance, serving the irresolute Ard Ri with steadfast loyalty. No contemporary Irish record of the Archbishop's doings exists, but Giraldus, a little pained perhaps to find a saint amongst his adversaries, says with an *ut ferebatur* that the princes of Ireland were moved to action by the patriotic zeal of the Archbishop who joined with Ruaidri in rallying the country and its allies, sending missives abroad to Gottred of Man and to the other Lords of the Isles.

The confederacy which he formed seemed for a moment like achieving its purpose and Strongbow, reduced to the sorest straits, used the Archbishop as the mediator of his offer to do homage to Ruaidri in return for the lordship of Leinster. The Ard Ri refused the terms, but taken unawares by a sortie of the now desperate Normans saw his far-drawn forces scattered.

The rest of his political life is busied with embassies of peace. When Henry II holds his state in Dublin to receive the submission of the Irish princes, Lorcan journeys to Connacht on his behalf on a fruitless errand to induce the Ard Ri "to go into the King's house." In 1175 the situation is reversed; Lorcan is Ruaidri's envoy to the King, negotiating the Treaty of Windsor, a mission requiring high qualities of skill and statesmanship where the contracting parties represented the feudal system opposed to Brehon law and Irish custom. The task was not made easier by a mischance which came to him at this time. For, visiting the shrine of St. Thomas at Canterbury, a madman who had heard of the visitor's reputation for sanctity, thought that he would meritoriously make another martyr and felled the saint to the ground before the high Altar. The traces of this blow on the head were verified by the Cardinal Archbishop of Rouen in 1876.

Meanwhile synods had been held at Armagh, Cashel and Dublin which the Archbishop attended in his subordinate place. None of them shows any trace of his leading or statesmanship. The first was held in 1170 in the shadow of the invasion, Gelasius, almost a nonagenarian, presiding. It expressed the pious opinion that the national calamity was a divine judgment upon the sins of the people who bought as slaves the children whom their Anglo-Saxon parents sold to them contrary to natural law and to the 28th Canon of Anselm's Council of London of 1102. The second, convened by Henry within twelve months under the Cistercian Bishop of Lismore, was Henry's quittance for Adrian's Bull. It gathered up some of the loose ends of the reforms initiated by Cellach a generation before, redressed certain surviving irregularities in discipline and made provision for special treatment of the clergy. Its decrees were confirmed at a Dublin synod in 1177 with Cardinal Vivian as Legate. The final decree of the Cashel synod provides that "all divine matters should be conducted agreeably to the practice of the most holy Church and according to their observance in the English Church." Giraldus is our chief authority for these decrees, which he sets out verbatim. By unaccountably omitting from his text the words *ad instar sacrisanctae Ecclesiae* his English translator infuses a wholly unjustified Anglican flavor into the decree. This omission has misled later writers. Accepting it and representing as a synodal finding what is more probably merely the comment of Giraldus, a recent scholarly and sympathetic historian has been constrained to a mild criticism of St. Lorcan's share in that synod. Following the definition of this decree Giraldus' text proceeds: "It is right and just that, as by Divine Providence Ireland has received her Lord and King from England, she should also accept reform from the same source," with much else to the same effect. Upon which this writer passes the natural judgment that "it is strange that Archbishop Laurence, a truly Irish-hearted man, should have 'concurred' in this claim." I suggest, following Dr. Lanigan and the form in Wilkins' *Concilia*, that the language of the preceding decrees makes it reasonable to detach these subsequent sentences from the definition of the decree, and when one restores to the English translation the omitted words of the original text which identify English observance with the recognized practice of Western Christendom Lorcan's concurrence is not open to criticism. The fact that English observance was at this time in accord with the practice of the universal Church could not prejudice Lorcan's view of the matter.

Lorcan presided in his Cathedral at the obsequies in 1176 of Strongbow, whom a singular fate had united to his own family. The Cathedral in which the Earl was buried was then rising from the ground in something of its present dimensions, and the Earl's name is associated, second to the Archbishop's, in the building of the tower, the choir and two chapels. His confirmatory grant to the Cathedral of churches and termon lands is dated 1178, when he was probably watching the erection of the transepts. In the following year he left for Rome to attend the Third General Lateran Council with five other Irish bishops. On their passage through England Henry compelled them to take an oath that they would seek nothing at the Council prejudicial to the king or his kingdom. Some three hundred bishops were present at the Council and from that great assembly Lorcan passed into the closest confidence of the Holy See. He obtained from Alexander III a Bull confirming the rights and privileges of the See of Dublin. Jurisdiction is conferred over five suffragan Sees and the Pope takes the Archbishop's church in Dublin and all its possessions under St. Peter's protection and his own, defining and confirming its possessions and ensuring it and the property of his suffragans by strictest penalties against any interference, ecclesiastical or lay. Finally on his return home Alexander gives him the supreme mark of his confidence in naming him Papal Legate.

In the brief space of life that was left to him Lorcan exercised his new powers with exemplary decision. With the invaders new abuses had crept amongst his clergy, abuses in the minor and even major orders, peculiarly hateful to the Archbishop, *castitatis et honestatis zelator.* He is said to have refused his absolution to these offenders and to have dispatched no fewer than one hundred and forty to Rome. In the steps he had taken in Rome to protect the rights of his See and perhaps in the resolute purge of his clergy, which must have included many newcomers, the King was offended. A new Thomas à Becket touched his authority. And, therefore, when on a final peace mission for Ruaidri Lorcan crossed the Irish Sea, bringing with him the king's son as hostage to Henry, he finds the Channel ports closed against his return by royal edict. Following the King to Normandy and landing near Treport at a cove which still bears his name the saint falls ill. He sees the Abbey towers of Eu and asks some shepherds what they might be. The Abbey belongs to the monks of St. Victor. *Haec requies mea in saeculum saeculi*, replies the saint, and the dying man is received amongst the monks whose Abbey Church he will hallow with his bones. Two sentences are recorded of his dying hours. Asked by the Abbot to make his will: "God knows," says he, "I have not a penny under the sun." And again, but in his native tongue, thinking of his own people: "*Heu popule stulte et insipiens, quid modo facias? Quis sanabit adversiones tuas? Quis medebitur tui?*" He knew himself the pastor and defender of his people, who would find themselves without such a defender for many years—for seven centuries.

A good and just man, Giraldus calls him; he died in exile—an exile and fugitive, the Abbot Hugues wrote to Innocent III, *pro libertate ecclesiae*—an exile as well, he might have written, of charity and patriotism. His life was written and re-written at Eu from information eagerly gathered by the canons from the saint's disciples and other pilgrims from Ireland who journeyed to his shrine, from his nephew Thomas, Abbot of Glendalough, his intimates Albin, Bishop of Ferns, Marianus of Cork and Malachy of Louth, and from Jean Cornyn, who succeeded him in the See of Dublin. In 1225, forty-five years after his death, he was canonized by Honorius III, and thereupon became patron of the Archdiocese of Dublin.[1]

1. For further reading, see:
   Vie et Miracles de St. Laurent. (Anal. Boll. ed. Ch. Plummer).
   Vita S. Laurentii. (Messingham's *Florilegium).*
   Life of St. Laurence O'Toole, by O'Hanlon (1857).
   Vie de St. Laurent O'Toole, by Legris (1914).
   Sources for the Early History of Ireland (Eccles.), by Kenney (1929).

DERMOT O'HURLEY (1520?–1584)

by MYLES V. RONAN, C.C.

DERMOT O'HURLEY WAS BORN AT LYCADOON, A FEW miles outside Limerick, between the years 1520 and 1530. By the time he was growing up, Henry VIII, having broken with the Pope, had an Act passed in the Irish Parliament for the suppression of the Irish monasteries, and, as a consequence, of schools for the education of priests. Few schools of any kind could continue to function without grave risk. Henceforward, the southern ports as being considered the safest were to see many young aspirants to the priesthood set out in merchant vessels bound for France, Portugal, and Flanders. The day soon came when Dermot O'Hurley went that way. He had received his early education at the house of his parents William O'Hurley and Honora O'Brien (a descendant of the O'Briens who held princely sway in Thomond) who were tenants of an extensive tract of land.

Dermot's first preparation for the priesthood was made at Paris, but Louvain appealed to his studious mind. Thither he went and having graduated in 1551 and taken his doctorate degrees in Letters, Theology, and Canon and Civil Law, taught philosophy for about twenty-five years. These points are worth stressing as they show his studious habit of mind and his love for academic life; he had no thought of returning to his native diocese, even in Mary's reign (1553–1558), to take up missionary work or to teach. They are evidence also of the high esteem in which he was held by the famous university.

His fame had spread beyond the little University town, and Archbishop de Guise of Rheims, who had recently founded a university there, requested him to come and teach Canon and Civil Law. His four years there added new luster to his reputation for learning and sanctity, of which the Vatican was well aware. He was then approaching his sixtieth year, content to spend the few remaining years of his life at his congenial work in the university and in the peace of prayer. This quiet life was, however, not to last.

During those peaceful academic years many grave disturbances had taken place in his native land. The first half of Elizabeth's reign had seen laws for the Queen's Supremacy, and Uniformity of Protestant Worship, passed in the Parliament of Dublin, and the Pope's Spiritual Claim made treasonable. In that period Irish bishops and lords had sent a declaration of fidelity to the Holy See and had sent agents to Paris, Madrid, and Rome to ask for help to carry on a religious war to recover their churches, then mostly in ruins, their church temporalities, and their liberty of worship. The attempt culminated in 1579 in the disastrous expedition of James Fitzmaurice, one of the noblest Irishmen of any period.

Fitzmaurice had come out from Smerwick harbor (Co. Kerry), towards Dingle, with a procession of bishops, friars, and soldiers—a small band—led by a cross-bearer, with the papal ensign blessed by his Holiness. They sang the Litanies as they marched and called on the Catholic chiefs to rally to the papal standard in the name of the Pope for faith and fatherland. It was a veritable crusade for which the Pope had issued the usual Indulgences. It failed, however, through the want of cooperation from the Catholic chiefs, who would risk nothing to join such a small force. Fitzmaurice was wrong in believing that the papal standard would be sufficient to rally them. The failure made the position of the Irish bishops then in Ireland more difficult and made the return of those who were on the continent more dangerous.

MacGibbon, Archbishop of Cashel, one of those who had been active agents abroad for material help for the crusade, died after many toils at Oporto in 1578.

For three years the See of Cashel had been vacant, the Queen's spies and ships being particularly busy watching for arrivals from abroad in the shape of "Rome-runners." A bishop entering the country with his Papal Bulls of appointment was guilty of high treason to her Majesty as Governor of the Church in Ireland. All this was well known in Rome, for the Pope had already absolved Elizabeth's subjects from fealty to her. The war for spirituals and temporals against the Queen was thus aided and abetted by the Vicar of Christ. But when he appointed a new archbishop to Cashel he was preparing a victim for the sacrifice for the faith, for there was then no thought of renewing secular warfare.

The victim was Dermot O'Hurley, who was called to Rome, consecrated on 11th September, 1581, and given the pallium on 27th November. The spiritual warfare had to be carried on, dangerous though it was, and bishops had to be provided for the faithful Irish flock. To escape detection in the exercise of their ministry was morally impossible, and sooner or later they would be apprehended and cast into prison. In spite of all this the aged prelate, who had spent over forty years at his books, took upon himself this heroic task. He had never mixed himself up with politics, intrigues, or preparations for war. At the bidding of the Holy Father he was returning to his native land, a Catholic bishop, to minister to the people of his diocese, to preach, to offer Mass, to confer the Sacraments, and then—He was almost an old man—sixty years was very old in those days—and he waited for the return of Spring before setting out on a trying journey through Italy and France. Rheims was calling him to revisit the scene of his scholastic labors. There he fell gravely ill. The strain was telling on him, and it was many months before he was fit to continue his journey. His greatest perils lay still ahead of him, turbulent seas infested with pirates and Government frigates on the watch for such as he.

To sail straight for a southern port would have been to court disaster, as all merchant ships from abroad were well watched and searched. O'Hurley wisely decided to take ship for Drogheda, along with a priest, John Dillon, who was a brother of Luke Dillon, Chancellor of the Exchequer. Disguised, probably as seamen, they embarked at a French port and reached Skerries in North Dublin safely. In company with a trusted sailor they proceeded by land to Drogheda for lodging, in order to size up the situation and to take the safest means of reaching Cashel.

Before doing so O'Hurley had to dispose of his box of belongings—episcopal robes, vestments, pallium, chalice, holy oils, pyxes, books, and Papal Bulls of appointment. These Papal letters were the only ones he had from abroad. He had no desire to mix himself up with the affairs of the lay lords. He was simply a Catholic bishop on his way to his diocese. His box he consigned to a Wexford merchant bound for Waterford where he expected to pick it up in the shortest possible time. Unfortunately, the merchant ship fell in with enemy vessels, and boat and bishop's belongings were confiscated. The chance of any vessel running the gauntlet was infinitesimal, yet it had to be taken.

Meanwhile, O'Hurley, Dillon, and the faithful seamen reached Drogheda about 8th September, 1583, and put up at the house of someone "of good account." His "gesture and behavior" did not escape observation, especially on the part of one Walter Baal or Ball, a pervert of a well-known Dublin family, who brought the intelligence of the distinguished stranger's arrival to Dublin Castle. The Lords Justices—Archbishop Adam Loftus of Dublin and Sir Henry Wallop—having received particulars of the capture of O'Hurley's belongings, including his Consecration papers, concluded that the distinguished stranger was no other than the Archbishop of Cashel. Immediately, they caused a "narrow search" to be made in the vicinity of Drogheda and set the hue and cry throughout the County Meath.

O'Hurley, apprehensive of danger, set out at once for the Castle of Slane where, he learned, an old acquaintance of his, Piers Butler, base son of the Black Earl of Ormond, was staying with his father-in-law, Thomas Fleming, the Baron, who was a Catholic. Here he expected to be befriended, and he was not disappointed. For twenty days he lay hidden in a secret room, the Baron and his wife, Catherine Preston, ministering to his comforts. The noise of the hue and cry having died down, the Baron fell back on his usual hospitality and had guests at the Castle board at which the unknown guest appeared and talked learnedly.

It chanced that Robert Dillon, Chief Justice of the Common Pleas, appeared at table one evening, and, astonished at the stranger's speech, concluded that he was no ordinary person. Shortly afterwards, Dillon advised the Baron to lay hands on the stranger, otherwise the Lords Justices would call him to strict account and fine him severely. The Baron was exceedingly angry with Dillon for his breach of etiquette, and feeling that it would be contrary to the privileges of hospitality to apprehend a stranger who was never in his house before, did nothing in the matter and left the castle.

Meanwhile, Robert Dillon, to acquit himself, being a Privy Councilor, acquainted the Lords Justices that a distinguished stranger had come to Ireland, and that he had warned the Baron to beware of him and to apprehend him. Thereupon, the Lords Justices sent post-haste for the Baron and examined him about the stranger, but the Baron answered him that he knew him neither to be a priest nor bishop, and that if Robert Dillon knew him to be so dangerous a member, it was rather his fault, being a Privy Councilor, not to have laid hands on him. But no excuse could avail; either the Baron must search and find the Bishop or suffer the consequences of having given hospitality to one guilty of treason to her Majesty.

When the Baron left the castle after Dillon's threat, O'Hurley in company with Piers Butler journeyed into O'Reilly's country (Longford) to see some clerical friends, and then southwards, skirting the Pale, and making for Thurles, and then Holy Cross and Cashel. The few days he spent among his flock were indeed days of bliss for which he had been yearning, and into them he crowded a great deal of work, preaching to his flock and administering the Sacrament of Confirmation to the young. But he had to push on towards Waterford where he expected to pick up his belongings.

Having reached Carrick-on-Suir, where the Earl of Ormond was then in residence, O'Hurley felt sure of the Earl's protection although he was a Protestant, and tarried in a house in the town. But the appearance of the Baron of Slane soon put an end to his security as the Baron had come with a warrant for his arrest. The Baron was sorely grieved to come on such a service and told O'Hurley of the dangers likely to befall his own house if he did not return to Dublin with him for the purpose of examination.

To this O'Hurley replied, in the presence of the Earl:

> My good Lord, rather than your Honor should take any harm or lose the least part of anything which you do esteem in this world for me or in my default, I would not rest until I came in person to your Lordship with the simplest boy that followeth your Lordship, and am ready to sacrifice my life to discharge your Lordship of any danger that may befall you on my behalf.

O'Hurley and the Baron reached Dublin on the 7th of October, the Baron being committed to safe custody in St. Sepulchre's, the palace of Archbishop Loftus, whilst O'Hurley was thrown into a dark and filthy dungeon in the Castle. Here he was to spend the remaining nine months of his life only to see the light of day when he was led out to undergo examination before the Lords Justices.

O'Hurley knew Loftus to be a crafty, cowardly time-server who had succeeded in inducing Elizabeth to remove him from the unpleasant See of Armagh to the comfortable living of Dublin. The pleadings and the sophisms of such a man must have sounded particularly futile to one who had spent his manhood teaching Catholic doctrine.

In vain did Loftus confront him with the "Confessions" of Charles Barnewell, a renegade of the Catholic Barnewells or Barnwalls of north county Dublin. These "Confessions" were to the effect that, at a meeting at Cardinal Como the Papal Secretary's palace in Rome, at which the Cardinal, O'Hurley, Richard Eustace (brother of Viscount Baltinglass), and he (Barnewell) were present, the question of sending aid to the Earl of Desmond was discussed. O'Hurley denied that he had heard any matter of such importance raised.

He admitted one thing, however, namely, that he had brought letters from Cardinal Sens, the Protector of Ireland, addressed to Desmond, but asserted that he left them in France as he had no desire to meddle in politics. For the rest, his only crime was that he was a Catholic bishop returning to his native land and to his diocese to minister to his people. He denied all knowledge of "foreign practices" (Roman intrigues) against her Majesty. Loftus and Wallop were so overwhelmed with the denial that they asked Secretary Walsingham if he wished the case against O'Hurley to be dropped or pursued. If it were to be pursued it would be advisable to submit him to torture and force him to admit the Queen's Supremacy.

Though it was illegal to submit any prisoner to torture, yet the Lords Justices were informed that it was her Majesty's pleasure that they should do so. But there was neither rack nor other instrument of torture in the country for the purpose of terrifying O'Hurley. Accordingly, Loftus and Wallop thought it better that he should be removed to the Tower of London. Besides, he was held in great esteem by the Irish people and had many "patrons" and "favorers" even amongst the Queen's officials. It would be clearly impossible to get a verdict against him in Dublin as no charge could be sustained against him. Moreover, they had to think of their own safety if he was put to death in Dublin. It would be better, they reported, to send Barnewell secretly to London to justify his "Confessions."

Three months passed but the Queen made no move to have O'Hurley transferred to London; such matters were not working smoothly for Elizabeth in the Tower at the time, so she preferred to let Loftus and Wallop do the work in Dublin. More examinations as to the foreign intrigues followed but they, too, were a failure as O'Hurley both demanded proof that they had intercepted the letters directed to the Earls of Desmond and Baltinglass, and denied that he had had anything to do with them. Loftus and Wallop, seeing the futility of the examinations, ordered O'Hurley to be put to the torture as advised by her Majesty, namely, "to toast his feet against the fire with hot boots." Early in March, 1584, he was brought out from his close confinement into the Castle yard to where the stocks, the mediaeval cross for common malefactors, were set up. Head, arms, and legs were thrust through the openings, and the legs up to the knees were immersed in a mixture of oil and tallow in raw-leather boots. A red-hot fire was brought near, and the boiling mixture playing on flesh and muscles soon gnawed at his very bones causing "an unusual and exquisite torment."

The torture having at last come to end, with no admission or recantation from the Archbishop, being unable to walk, he was bundled back to his dark dungeon. The Lords Justices were fearful lest they had gone too far with the torture and might miss the supreme pleasure of seeing him hang on the gibbet. A Jesuit priest, one Charles Mac Morris (Lea), a friend of O'Hurley, and one versed in the art of restoratives, was discreetly allowed to visit him and to apply his art, with the result that the Archbishop was able to leave his bed after fourteen days.

Loftus and Wallop again repeated their blandishments, promising O'Hurley the highest promotion in the Church and the Queen's favor if he would accept her as the Governor of the Church in Ireland. Submission of O'Hurley, the greatest prelate in the Catholic Church in Ireland, and the most revered, would be a great personal success for themselves, and the most potent weapon to wield against the Faith of the Irish people. But his only response was:

> I have made up my mind never to abandon for any temporal reward the Catholic Church, the Vicar of Christ, and the True Faith.

That reply establishes for all time O'Hurley's cause.

Loftus had still a card up his sleeve. Like a cunning conjurer he introduced a veiled figure into O'Hurley's dungeon. It was Dermot's own sister Honora. Schooled by Loftus she begged Dermot to think of his safety, renounce the Pope, and obey the Queen in matters of religion. Summing up all his strength, in indignant tones Dermot ordered her to fall on her knees, beg his pardon and absolution from God for her horrible crime. Repenting of her folly, she was led away from the prison.

There was only one way left to satisfy the Privy Council of O'Hurley's guilt, and that was to send the examinations of the Baron of Slane, John Dillon, who had been also captured, and others. This they took. Loftus refers to the documents as showing that O'Hurley was guilty of treason "in his own person," namely, as a Catholic bishop. This indeed was a rare admission, as the authorities always strove to cover up their hatred for the Catholic Faith by ascribing political motives to their victims. "He had come," the Lords Justices said, "to poison the minds of the people with disobedience to her Majesty." The only disobedience even hinted at was that of refusing to recognize Elizabeth as Governor of the Church in Ireland of which he was an Archbishop.

A usual trick of the Elizabethan Government was to make an example of a bishop or a Mass-priest to strike terror into others. If the Queen will attend to their safety, Loftus and Wallop see nothing for it but to put O'Hurley to death by martial law. It will strike terror into those who are ready to come from Rome and enter into their ministries in Ireland and England; a public trial would do harm because of his "impudent and clamorous denial," and the "no small admiration of him"; the lawyers will not arraign him because his alleged treason was in foreign parts, and there is no statute to punish such in Ireland. The whole case against him was a ghastly failure, and incompetent and irresponsible officers were to be ordered to condemn him to death.

The weeks dragged along, and still no reply from the Queen's Secretary. Loftus and Wallop wrote that it was dangerous to leave things as they were. They do not know whether they are to stay their hand

and "not further to stir those coals to scorch ourselves, knowing how dangerous it is for us to busy ourselves in this sort with setting these matters abroach here...in lieu of backing and good countenance from thence our doings shall be discovered." In this dangerous position and in this state of mind they remained for weeks, wondering if they had not gone too far and fearful of the fickleness of the Queen.

At last they were reassured; it was the Queen's pleasure that they proceed with "so notorious and ill a subject to execution by ordinary trial of him," or else because "of affection of the jury," or because of no trial for treason for deeds abroad, they should "take a shorter way with him by martial law." The royal advice was tortuous, but it gave Loftus and Wallop the sanction they required for expediting the long-drawn-out business with the inevitable result that O'Hurley was sentenced to be hanged on the gallows outside the city.

The term of office of the Lords Justices was rapidly drawing to a close; only two days were left, and then Sir John Perrott would be installed as Viceroy. The Earl of Ormond, whose friendship for O'Hurley was well-known, was on his way to Dublin for the installation on Trinity Sunday. Delay was extremely dangerous; they would not be cheated of the pleasure of putting O'Hurley out of the way. They took their final step late on Friday night and ordered the marshal of the Castle to have O'Hurley brought out before dawn on the morrow to Gallows Green.

The 20th of June, 1584, had not yet dawned when the aged prelate was awakened to his fate and bundled into a cart in the Castle yard. Surrounded by soldiers in mail, with halberds erect, the cart was drawn through the postern gate and over the rough road that led through the Castle street, Werburgh street, across the bridge at the Pole gate, through Sheep street and St. Stephen's street, out through the fields to Gallows Green (at the junction of Merrion Row and Ely Place, overlooking the present Government buildings and the site of the new cathedral). Few were astir at such an early hour, only some friends of O'Hurley who had gained knowledge of the crime about to be perpetrated.

These were city merchants who pretended that they were going forth to the fields with their bows to shoot a match agreed between them the night before. Seeing them, O'Hurley was greatly rejoiced, and, being upon the ladder, called them to draw near and desired the soldiers to "respite his life a little until he did utter a few words in the presence of these honest men, whom it pleased God to send to witness his innocent death." Which request being granted, he stood upon the ladder, and with great humility and patience uttered these few words following:

> Gentlemen, first I thank my Lord and Savior Jesus Christ because it hath pleased His divine providence to send you hither to bear testimony of my innocent death, being it was meant I should die obscurely, as may be seen by sending me to this place of execution so early. Be it, therefore, known unto you, good Christians, that I am a priest anointed and also a Bishop, although unworthy of so sacred dignities, and no cause could they find against me that might in the least degree deserve the pains of death, but merely for my function of priesthood wherein they have proceeded against me in all points cruelly contrary to their own laws, which doth privilege any man that is worth ten pound in goods not to die by Martial Law, which I leave between them and the Majesty of the Almighty, and I do enjoin you, dear Christian Brethren, to manifest the same unto the world and also to bear witness at the day of Judgment of my innocent death which I endure for my function and profession of the Holy Catholic Faith.

It is said that one of the "honest men," bolder than the rest, approached the ladder and was rewarded for his fidelity with the Sign of the Cross impressed on his palm by the Archbishop.

Desiring them all to join with him in prayer, and recommending his soul to God, his Maker and Redeemer, Dermot O'Hurley most patiently ended his life.

He was hanged with the rod and not with the rope; why, does not appear. It is hardly conceivable that they had not a rope with the gallows. Hanging with the gad, or twisted osiers, was the Irish method. It would appear that the soldiers cut down the branches from adjacent hedges, twisted them rope-wise, and hanged their victim to the cross-beam.

O'Hurley was not so much martyred as murdered. Having thrown the body into a hole dug in the field nearby, as they did not wish to arouse the curiosity of the passers-by, the soldiers, with their empty cart, entered the Castle yard with the dawn.

The few faithful friends who had watched the execution waited for the evening shadows to fall, and removing the loose earth, placed the saintly body in a rude wooden box and consigned it to devout women of the city who quietly removed it to the nearest graveyard. On the little hill close to St. Patrick's Cathedral and St. Sepulchre's, the palace of Archbishop Loftus, stood the ancient church dedicated to the founder of Glendalough, St. Kevin, and inside its ruins they deposited their sacred charge. Having taken with them portions of his clothes as relics of his martyrdom, they departed in the night to their homes in the quiet city. "The realm," as Loftus and Wallop described the final act of their administration, "was rid of a pestilent member."

Soon the faithful came to pray beside the mound of earth that sheltered O'Hurley's remains, and pilgrimages became frequent, for many miracles were related as having been performed through the intercession of the martyr. To make the sanctuary more worthy of the saintly remains, the faithful built up the walls of the half-demolished church, set up a decent enclosure, and cleared an entrance for the faithful from the highway.

Alas! the graveyard today is known to the few, but the exact place of his burial should not be difficult to ascertain. Perhaps, during the year of Ireland's Eucharistic Congress, due honor will be at last done to one of Ireland's most remarkable champions of the Faith.

THOMAS FIHILLY, S.J. (1549–1625)

by AUBREY GWYNN, S.J.

THE FIRST IRISH JESUIT WAS A NATIVE OF LIMERICK CITY, Father David Woulfe, received into the Society of Jesus by Saint Ignatius himself. For five or six years Father Woulfe was kept in Italy. Then, in 1561, he was sent to Ireland with plenary powers from the Pope, and with a special commission to found Catholic schools, even a Catholic University, in Ireland. Six years were spent in the effort to fulfil that mission, and in the end, when Father Woulfe was arrested by the English in 1567, there was little enough to show in the way of permanent results: his mission had been one long endeavor to escape from the Government spies. But one result at least had been achieved. In Father Woulfe's own city of Limerick a school was opened which escaped suppression for two or three years. The priest in charge was an English Jesuit, Father William Good, who was assisted by an Irish scholastic, Edmund Daniel or O'Donnell, also a native of Limerick. We have no details beyond the bare mention of the names, but it seems certain that one of the young Limerick boys who attended this first Jesuit school in Ireland was Thomas Fihilly, destined to be one of the founders of the great Jesuit mission in Paraguay.

Thomas Fihilly was born in 1549, the son of a Catholic doctor of the city, William Fihilly. Six years after the child's birth, his father obtained "English liberty" for himself and his family, getting thus the rights of citizenship in exchange for an English status and an English name, William Field. His son was to be known in later life as Felie or Field or Fildio. What he learned at the Jesuit school, we do not know; but it was there, if anywhere, that the seeds of his vocation were sown. In 1568, Thomas Fihilly left Limerick at the age of nineteen, never to see the city again. We hear of him as a student on the Continent, first in Paris, then in Douai, finally in Louvain, where he spent three years (1571–1574) as a student of philosophy, at a time when St. Robert Bellarmine, then a young Jesuit priest, was stirring the University by his weekly Latin sermons. Father Good, who had been driven from Ireland in 1569, was also at work among the English and Irish Catholics in Flanders; and in 1572, Thomas Fihilly must have got news of the death of his other Jesuit teacher, Edmund O'Donnell, who was captured in Limerick in that year and hanged in Cork—a tale of martyrdom which may have decided his own vocation. In 1574, Thomas Fihilly, now a Master of Arts, left Louvain for Italy, and entered the Jesuit novitiate in Rome on October 7th of that year. With him there went from Louvain an English student, John Yates, who, like Fihilly, had been a spiritual child of Father Good, and who was now to be his companion on their first missionary journeys.

Those were the epic days of Jesuit missions; and it is small wonder that the two young students should have turned their thoughts to the New World that was opening out before them as a vast harvest in need of workers. Spain's Empire of the Indies had only been opened to Jesuit priests ten years before this time; but the Kings of Portugal had been from the first generous patrons of the Society's work. It was from Lisbon that Francis Xavier had sailed for the East, and Brazil had been open to the Jesuits since 1549. To Brazil then our two young students resolved, under God's guidance, to go. Six months had barely passed since their admission to the Roman novitiate, and again we find them on the road—this time begging their way across Italy, France, Spain and Portugal, from Rome to Coimbra. At Coimbra they spent the best part of two years, completing their noviceship and beginning their studies in theology. In the summer of 1577, the two friends received orders to sail for Brazil "with many Fathers and brethren of our Society."

The record of Jesuit missionary labors in Brazil has not yet been critically studied, and there is an air of legend about the little that has been published. One name stands out: Father Joseph Anchieta, reputed worker of countless miracles, and esteemed by his contemporaries as the Xavier of Brazil. Young Brother Fihilly (for he was not yet ordained) had the good fortune to learn his first lessons in missionary tactics from the great apostle. Brother Yates remained in Bahia, where he was ordained some three years later. Thomas Fihilly, or Fildio as he is now always called, went south to the town of St. Vincent, near the modern Sao Paulo. St. Vincent had been for many years the scene of Father Anchieta's heroic labors, and every year the apostle came south for a season (he was now Provincial of the Province of Brazil) to renew contact with his favorite mission-field. Young Brother Fihilly seems to have accompanied the holy priest on his missionary tours, for the *History of Paraguay* tells us that *Padre Fildio* had been Father Anchieta's travelling companion, and a witness of his miracles. A letter from John Yates gives us a more intimate glimpse. Writing to Father Good, he tells of the dangers to which the missionaries were then exposed: "many dangers of death, hunger and thirst for lack of victuals and water, making peace with the ignorant and beastly people for to pass more safely…and lying every night in the fields and woods, passing also the rivers upon rotten trees and not in boats." Of Fihilly, his former companion, he writes. "To turn now to Father Thomas Felie I do give you this knowledge of him, that he was very unapt to learn this Brazil's speech; but he did always edify with his virtuous life and obedience all those with whom he was conversant." Brother Fihilly, as he still was, spent eight years in St. Vincent, and for most of that time he was probably engaged in the work of teaching the Portuguese and native children of the town;

he also studied moral theology for two years. Then yet another call came. Paraguay, as we now use the word, is the name for an inland state of South America. In the sixteenth century the name was used loosely for a vast ill-defined territory, now divided between Argentina, Paraguay, and the southern provinces of Brazil. Little or nothing had been done for the evangelization of these countries. Missionary priests from the three orders of the Dominicans, Franciscans and Augustinians had been at work here and there, but their efforts had mainly been directed to the instruction and salvation of the Spanish settlers and soldiers who held these lands for Spain. Two Bishops, both Dominicans, governed the vast territory: one as Bishop of Paraguay, resident in Asuncion; the other as Bishop of Tucuman, resident at Cordoba. Both were in urgent need of men, but it was the Bishop of Tucuman who first appealed for help to the Jesuits. In the year 1585, he wrote two letters, one to the Jesuit Provincial of Peru, the other to Father Anchieta, the Provincial of Brazil. The letter to Peru was the first to reach its destination, and two Spanish Jesuits were sent at once. The letter to Brazil had a longer route to follow, and the messenger was delayed for a time at St. Vincent in the middle of November. Brother Fihilly would thus have had time to hear the news of this appeal. What action he took, we do not know; but eight months later he was one of a party of six who sailed from Bahia for Buenos Aires in answer to the appeal. He seems to have been ordained a priest just before leaving Brazil.

The voyage was not without its adventures. Since the party would have to journey up the river La Plata from Buenos Aires to Cordoba, they set sail in an ocean-vessel accompanied by a small riverboat, specially constructed for them at Bahia. The boats were heavily laden with supplies as well as ploughshares, spades and so forth; the crew numbered a hundred and twenty. All went well as they coasted down from Bahia, past St. Vincent to Buenos Aires. The estuary of La Plata was reached in January, 1587, but here their adventures began. At dawn three English corsairs were sighted, commanded by Captain

Robert Widdrington. Resistance was impossible, for the two Spanish vessels were poorly armed. The English boarded their prey, and soon found that they had captured a party of Spanish priests. A scene of wild brutality followed. The Jesuits were "*evil* handled" and kicked; their relics and *Agnus Deis*, which they were carrying with them for the mission, were trampled on before their eyes; their statues were melted to make shot for the English. One of them, Father Ortega, a Portuguese, was thrown overboard, and Father Fihilly was then set upon as an Irish Papist. For a moment it looked as though all would be hanged or drowned, but the sailors changed their minds. Better maroon them, and leave them to die of starvation. So the Spaniards were towed out to sea again for twenty eight days, and then abandoned "at forty-one and a half degrees south." Here the two ships were plundered of all their cargo, and the crew, including the Fathers, were stripped of all their clothing except their red shirts; they were then set adrift with no more than five barrels of water. But God can make the winds blow as He wills, and eighteen days later this strange red-shirted crew drifted into the harbor of Buenos Aires, where the inhabitants received them "with many tears of compassion."

As it happened, the Bishop of Paraguay was just then on a visit to Buenos Aires. He it was who told the newcomers that Jesuits from Peru had already reached Paraguay from overland; and he urged the party to alter their plans and come to his diocese at Asuncion. It was a tempting offer, and the Bishop backed it with a solid argument. Paraguay was near Brazil, and the natives of his diocese spoke Guarani, the language which Father Fihilly had been learning with such difficulty. In Tucuman the dialects of the Gran Chaco were spoken, all of them reported to be very difficult. Was all the work done in Brazil to be thrown away? And there was the added difficulty that the Jesuit Province of Peru was distinct from the Province of Brazil. To organize a mission from both Provinces would lead inevitably to confusion. It was a nice case of conscience, and three of the party decided to return to Brazil; but the three remaining priests pushed on to Cordoba in accordance with their instructions. They were a mixed party: Father Ortega, a Portuguese; Father Saloni, an Italian; and Father Fihilly. At Cordoba they were welcomed by the two Spaniards from Peru, and a division was then made. The three priests from Brazil, having soon learned by experience that they were helpless in a land where they could not understand a word of the native languages, went up the river to Asuncion, where they were welcomed by the Dominican Fathers and the whole Spanish colony. These three are thus the pioneer founders of the future Jesuit mission to Paraguay.

The next ten years are filled with the labors of all such pioneer work. Some weeks were spent on a public mission to the garrison of Asuncion, where there was work in plenty to be done. Then began the real work of missionary preaching among the native Indian tribes. The Jesuits were not alone in this task. Dominican Fathers had already made a first beginning in Paraguay, and elsewhere two canonized saints remind us of the enthusiasm which the missionary crusade awoke in all the Orders of the Church. St. Toribio de Magrovejo was at this time Bishop of Peru. A Dominican, he is famous as the director of St. Rose of Lima, but apostolic work among the natives of Peru was the main interest of his life. The apostle of the tribes of the Gran Chaco, St. Francis Solano (1549–1610), was the greatest of the Franciscan missionaries, and a strict contemporary of Father Fihilly. The fame of his preaching, and his repute as being possessed of the gift of tongues, was already a legend in all the Spanish colonies. The Jesuits were thus not first in the field: but in Paraguay little or nothing had been done, and the three first pioneers soon found that the field was indeed white for the harvest. A first journey in 1588–1589 brought them as far north as Guayra, where they reached Villa Rica, a Spanish settlement 500 miles north of Asuncion. Everywhere they were made welcome, and everywhere the work of preaching, catechizing and baptizing went on without interruption. One excursion into the interior ended with the settlement of over three hundred converts in a Christian colony: it was the parent of many such colonies, that were later to become famous in history as the Reductions of Paraguay.

During these first years of the mission Father Saloni acted as Superior, and remained at the headquarters in Asuncion. His two companions, Father Ortega and Father Fihilly, went further afield, and it soon became plain that at least two hundred thousand Indians were within reach of their apostolate, and were for the most part only waiting for the Gospel to be preached to them. These consoling labors were interrupted by a plague which raged across the whole South American continent in 1590. The Jesuits threw themselves into the work of assisting the sick, and a report of the year states that no less than 15,000 confessions had been heard, in addition to the baptism of 1,500 Indians. The plague once over, work in the forests was resumed, and some of the missionary expeditions brought the two priests right across the forests to the neighborhood of the modern Concepcion. We hear of various adventures: rivers that were flooded, encounters with snakes and wild beasts, and the ever-recurring plague. Meanwhile the ranks of the missionaries were being thinned. Father Saloni died in 1599, the two Jesuits from Peru about the same time; and of the recruits sent to their help most went to Cordoba and Tucuman, only one to Asuncion. The result was inevitable. Fathers Ortega and Fihilly were recalled from the northern settlements to Asuncion, much to the grief of the local inhabitants. They left Villa Rica in 1599 after ten years of apostolic labors; eleven years later their place was taken by other Jesuits from Europe, who found that the people of Guayra had kept untouched the sacred books and vessels of their first missionaries.

The ten years that follow Father Saloni's death were years of crisis for the mission. Many of the Jesuit Fathers in Peru held the view that the first ardor of enthusiasm had resulted in missionary work that was scattered over so wide an area as to make all organized direction and regular discipline impossible. Plans were made for the abandonment of the more outlying mission-posts. A conference was held at Salta, midway between Paraguay and Peru, and the Provincial writes home to the General of the Society, Father Aquaviva, that the days which he had spent with these Fathers were the happiest in his life. "I saw them wholly penetrated with the primitive spirit of our Society: humble, poor, mortified, eating little and sleeping less, clothed very poorly, but most contented with their life, in good health, favored by Our Lord in their prayer, most closely united with His Divine Majesty, and with one another in the bond of true charity."

As it happened, Father Fihilly was to play a leading part in the sequel. The conference ended with the decision to abandon the mission of Paraguay, and Father Ortega left Asuncion with his companion, Father Lorenzana. Father Fihilly was left behind, "for reasons of health," according to the report sent home by the Superior of the mission; but we may well suspect that the missionaries had not yet lost hope of saving their work. Letters went to Rome from many of those who knew the local circumstances, and among them one has survived from Father Fihilly (Fildius) to the General, Father Aquaviva. It is a plain, straightforward appeal for the Indians among whom he has worked for so many years. And it ends with a practical suggestion. If the Province of Peru could no longer support the mission, why not make it over to the Province of Brazil, which was more easily accessible, and where the common Guarani language was spoken by the native Indians? So reason the simple; and they are right. But reasons of State too often outweigh the simplest arguments. Brazil was Portuguese territory, Paraguay belonged to the Spanish crown. True, the two crowns were for the time being united; but the political argument proved too strong. Paraguay must go to Spanish Peru, and the order was given for complete evacuation.

But even as he gave the order, Father Aquaviva received fresh appeals from the Superior of all these inland missions, an Italian priest, Father Romero. Were the Jesuit missionaries to do as all the world was doing? Were they to abandon the difficult interior, and concentrate on Peru, the Eldorado of the West? Were souls not worth more than all the gold that had been dreamed of by Spain's *conquistadores*? Father Aquaviva was deeply impressed by this last appeal. His orders had already left Europe, but they were followed by a second letter, countermanding what he had written in his first. Two years and more were needed to clear the situation, for communications between Rome and Peru were slow and uncertain. But in the end Father Romero had won his battle, and Paraguay was saved for the missionaries of the Society of Jesus.

During all these years of confusion and uncertainty one Jesuit had been able to remain and hold the fort—Father Thomas Fihilly, once a young Limerick boy attending the first Jesuit school in the city, and learning his letters from a young Jesuit scholastic for whom martyrdom was waiting. Of his life during these lonely years at Asuncion we have only the following brief narrative. Writing in 1605, when the battle has been won and the mission saved, the two Italian missionaries who had been sent up to assist him give us a glimpse that is precious. "We found in our house, to the great comfort and joy of his soul and of ours, good Father Fildius, who in spite of his infirmities has gone on with his priestly work, and by his religious spirit and dove-like simplicity has edified the whole town very much for the past three years. He is never done thanking God for seeing his brethren again in this far-off land."

One consolation came to Father Fihilly in the midst of all these years of stress and trial. It is usual for a Jesuit to take his final vows, either as a professed father with four solemn vows, or as a spiritual coadjutor with three vows, two or three years after ordination. Father Fihilly had been ordained a priest in 1586, but it was not until sixteen or seventeen years had been spent in the forests of Paraguay that his superiors discovered that he had never been admitted to any but the three simple vows of a scholastic, which he had taken at Coimbra more than twenty-five years before. In the far-off mission of Paraguay he had simply been forgotten, and it would seem that no word came from Father Fihilly during all those years to remind his superiors of their neglect. The discovery was probably made in connection with the conference held at Salta in the year 1602, for later catalogues enter his name with the comment "professed of three vows on March 10, 1603." The technical formula indicates what his superiors thought of Father Fihilly's merits. He had never made the full studies of the Society, which are required for the usual solemn profession. But his superiors evidently felt that some recognition was due to him for his years of devoted labor. The Institute admits of exceptions by way of privilege; and accordingly, twenty-seven years after his first admission into the Society, Father Fihilly was admitted into its highest grade as a professed father of three vows.

With the arrival of reinforcements, new hope came to the missionaries. During the next twenty years young missionary priests were sent from Europe, and the numbers grew so rapidly that a new policy of establishing permanent Reductions for the convert Indians was adopted by the Jesuit Superiors with the full sanction of the Spanish Governors. More than twenty of these Reductions were established within the lifetime of Father Fihilly, who thus lived to see his life's work carried further than ever he or any of his first companions had dared to hope. He himself had grown too old and feeble for such pioneer work in the forests: his part was to remain at home in Asuncion, and there teach to the young Jesuits who were pouring in from Spain and Italy that Guarani language which he himself had learned with such difficulty when he too had been a young missionary in St. Vincent, "very unapt to learn this Brazil's speech." And his pupils did him credit. One of them, a young kinsman of St. Francis Xavier, died of hunger in the forests of Guayra in the year 1614. "At midnight," his companion writes, "he gave his soul to the Lord as peacefully as though he were asleep; the calm beauty of his face showed forth the beauty of his soul."

One last incident remains to be recorded. In the great controversy as to the rights of the South American Indians, the Jesuit Fathers were not slow to stand forth as the champions of a race that was being, so they alleged, most shamefully and cruelly oppressed by their Spanish masters. Slavery was legally unknown in the Spanish colonies, but the lot of the Indian laborers was in fact no better than the lot of the negro slaves in the West Indian islands and at Cartagena. Father de Torres, the Provincial who was responsible for the reorganization of the Paraguay mission, took a leading part in this campaign. He began by publicly setting free those Indians who were at work on the farms belonging to the Jesuit mission, and he then ordered his Fathers to preach a crusade against abuses that were so common. The effect was startling. A Government inquiry was ordered immediately. After a year the Commissioner published his findings, which proved to be a long catalogue of the abuses which had been denounced by the Jesuit preachers. The Spanish landowners were furious, and a boycott was organized against the missionaries. No Spaniard would speak to the Jesuits, no shop would supply them with food. The storm lasted for several months, and for a time the Jesuits had to retire from Paraguay. But once again one Jesuit was able to remain, by reason of his long years of service. Father Fihilly stayed behind in the city to do the necessary work of the church, and two young Jesuit scholastics were allowed to stay with him to teach in the school. The episode ended dramatically. One day a leader of the boycott rode into the town, publicly set free all his slaves, and then rode up to the Jesuit church, entered, and made his confession. It was the end of the boycott, and the Jesuits returned to the town.

Of Father Fihilly's last years we catch no more than a few glimpses. The Jesuit *catalogues* speak of him as "worn out with age and unfit for work" in the year 1623. Two years later the end came, and the valiant missionary died at Asuncion in his seventy-seventh year. The official record of his life and virtues speaks of his virginal purity, his zeal for souls, his love of prayer and religious discipline; and it ends with the enumeration of certain acts of mortification at table to which the dead priest had been faithful all his life. "Such acts," we read, "are peculiarly trying in this hot climate, as good Father Fildio knew by experience in this world, and now has learned from the abundance of his reward in Heaven."[1]

1. Fr. Fihilly's life is more fully treated in a pamphlet by the same author published by the *Irish Messenger*.

MICHAEL O'CLERY (1575–1643)

by VICTOR SHEPPARD, O.F.M.

THERE IS A MYSTERY, AN INDEFINITENESS, ABOUT THE lives of most Franciscan heroes, that seems a sort of heritage from that Divine perversion of things long ago, when men lost the body of St. Francis because they had put it in such safe keeping. Where we think to look down a perspective of ordered events, in reading their splendid story, we often see only grotesque disproportion. There is a blur, where there should be exactness. When, in our human way, we expect to find details plentiful as motes in a sunbeam, there is a cloud of obscurity over the whole. It is true that sometimes the cloud thins and we stumble against a figure, in the way that we stumble with blindness from a sudden light; but even as we turn to gaze, the figure draws back into uncertainty or vanishes with almost elfin irresponsibility. They move in twilight, these heroes, many of them even without a name. It is hardly credible that there are more than fifty Blessed Anonymi in the First Order, and even a Blessed Anonyma, a lady who came to the brethren in man's guise, because she loved virtue and monastic observance.

Brother Michael O'Clery has received a full share of this Franciscan heritage. His past is a book sealed with three seals—oblivion, and neglect, and a seal that has no name, because it seals the truth of things that are forever lost. It is hard to break the first two seals and pry open the book to read therein; and there is much that can never be known now.

One day, in the late Spring or early Summer of 1623, there came to the door of the Irish Franciscan College at Louvain, a man of education who asked to be received into the Order as a lay brother. This was Tadhg O'Clery, of the O'Clerys of Tirconnell, a chronicler by birth and training. His coming to Louvain stands out as a solitary fact, unconnected with any previous event in his life. It is not known when he left Ireland, or what were the circumstances of his leaving. We get our first definite knowledge of him only when he presents himself at the convent door in Louvain.

There was a Don Thadeo Cleri of the Company of Artor O'Neill in the Low Countries, who received a pension of two crowns monthly, on July 23rd, 1621. In a list of Irish troops in the Spanish Netherlands, occurs the name "Clery, Don Thadeo, Soldado, 1622." If Tadhg O'Clery was a soldier before he came to St. Anthony's, one could readily understand the absence of any knowledge about his previous movements. It would explain some of the complete blank that faces us, when we try to link up with his early life in Ireland. To say the least, it is a striking fact that, in all the lists of Irish troops in the Continental armies, down even to the Irish Legion of the First Consul, the name O'Clery occurs only twice, and that both names—this Don Thadeo and a Don Florencio—occur side by side in the same list. For Tadhg O'Clery's presence in Belgium there is another explanation: his elder brother, Maolmuire, had entered at St. Anthony's only seven years before, receiving the habit on August 15th, 1616, with the name of Frater Bernardinus a Sancta Maria.

Tadhg O'Clery was born in the parish of Kilbarron, Co. Donegal, the year 1575 being given, with fair accuracy, as the year of his birth. His family were hereditary ollavs in history (professional historians) to the great O'Donnells, and held large possessions in the Barony of Tirhugh. They had held their office since the days that Cormac

O'Clery, "a proficient in the Civil and Canon Laws," had come with his books into Tirconnell from Tirawley, and won the affection of old Matthew O'Scingin, O'Donnell's ollav in history. O'Scingin loved the lad Cormac for his learning. His own son, his only son, was dead; his name would live no more, but his posterity at least might continue in the tradition. Accordingly, he gave Cormac his only daughter in marriage, and as *tinnscra*—the dower that a husband must pay his bride's father, according to ancient Irish custom—he claimed that the first boy born to them should be trained as an ollav in history. It was thus that the O'Clerys became ollavs to the O'Donnells.

On a steep, jutting cliff, serene above the restless tossing of the waters, stood their castle of Kilbarron, a dear name to chroniclers for the wealth of tradition it enshrined. Here Tadhg was born. For some reason now unknown, he got the nickname of Tadhg-an-tsléibhe, Tadhg-of-the-mountain, a happy name in the light of his trampings over all the mountains of Ireland. Brought up in the tradition of the family, he was sent south to study under Boetius Roe Mac Egan, an acknowledged antiquary and scholar. Mac Egan took the side of Lughaidh O'Clery, cousin of Tadhg, in the great Contention of the Bards in the beginning of the seventeenth century. There is a rather unwarranted assumption that Mac Egan was a Munsterman, living at Ballymacegan in Tipperary. If the assumption be correct, it is remarkable that this Munster poet should stand out against his fellows, who were fighting for the glory of his own province against the bards of Meath, Ulster and Connacht. One wonders what Tadhg O'Clery's presence in Ballymacegan had to do with it.

Thus Tadhg O'Clery was a chronicler by birth and education, and he had come to a College where many of the fathers, scions too of old literary clans, had like him left Ireland's holy hills of beauty "to try another trade" among the brethren at Louvain. In accordance with his request, he was received into the Order as a lay brother, and was given the name of Brother Michael. Then began his year of probation.

St. Anthony's was at this time one of the most important centers of Irish learning on the Continent, and was destined to become greater still. It had been founded in 1606 by Fr. Florence Corny, afterwards Archbishop of Tuam, his purpose being to set up a novitiate and a house of studies for the Irish Franciscans driven in 1601 from Donegal, their last regular house of studies at home. Philip III of Spain became patron of the College, and endowed it. On April 3rd, 1607, the Bull of Foundation was issued, and in May the first friars went into residence. It was ten years, however, before they found permanent quarters. A piece of ground was bought near the south-east corner of the town on May 27th, 1616, and a new College and Chapel were begun by Fr. Hugh McCaughwell, who afterwards became Archbishop of Armagh. By 1611 they had a Gaelic printing press in the College, from which every year they sent books to Ireland "for the greater edification of the Catholics, and the confusion of heretics."

Thither from Paris, in 1623, came a young lecturer in philosophy, aflame with all a young man's ardor for a noble purpose. Fr. Ward had been lecturing in Philosophy in Paris, but even amidst his scholastic arguments and distinctions he had conceived a design that was far more congenial to a scion of the bardic schools. In the year of his coming to Louvain, he had met Fr. Patrick Fleming, for whom he contracted a close friendship, and to him he disclosed his idea of collecting together and publishing all the original *Acta* of the Irish saints and other ancient records. Fleming warmly encouraged him in his project, and promised to cooperate by searching for Irish documents in the libraries of France and Italy that lay on his route to Rome. As has been stated, Louvain at this time numbered in its community several accomplished Irish scholars. Before them Ward laid his plans. To Fleming he evidently sent the news about Brother Michael O'Clery, for in a letter of June 1st, 1624, Fleming tells Ward to inquire *ab ipso laico, germano fratris Mileri Cleri*, if he knows whether there was any king in Ireland named Romanus, and a queen named Plantula, his wife. A letter of August 24th contains good news. Fleming has been appointed to Louvain and will come "laden with documents"; and, in hope of getting Ward to carry through an idea suggested by Ward himself, Fleming adds: "Be sure to carry out your purpose of sending Brother Michael O'Clery to Ireland." So Brother Michael was caught up in the movement, but his return to Ireland was not yet to be.

These two letters of Fleming enable us to fix approximately the date of Brother Michael's entrance into the Order. Fleming left Louvain in April, 1623, but Brother Michael could not have been there at that time, for in his first letter Fleming finds it necessary to describe Brother Michael, not knowing his name. By August, 1624, Brother Michael's year of probation was at least nearing completion, more likely it was at an end, for Fleming writes about sending him to Ireland. Hence he must have come to Louvain some time after Fleming's departure in April and in all likelihood not later than the month of August, 1623.

Fr. Hugh Ward was elected Guardian of St. Anthony's at the Provincial Chapter of August, 1626. It was about this time, too, that Brother Michael was sent back to Ireland. This is easily proved by the Dedications and Addresses prefixed to some of his works. For example, in his Address to the Reader of the *Réim Rioghraidhe*, completed on November 4th, 1630, after telling how it was decided to send him to Ireland, he goes on to say that he had then "spent four full years in the transcription and compilation of every item that pertained to the saints of Ireland."

Even the crossing to Ireland was a perilous venture in those days, holding dangers more fearful than storms and shipwreck. It was only a year before that the Provincial's delegate to the general Chapter, Fr. Thomas Strange, had been captured on the high seas by Algerian corsairs, and carried off to slavery. However, under God's guidance, Brother Michael landed safely in Ireland, and sought his "native convent" of Donegal.

At this time Falkland was Lord Deputy in Ireland, a mild tolerant man, who had no wish to persecute anyone. It was the acceptable time. How acceptable only we can tell, who know of the ruin and desolation wrought by Cromwell but twenty-three years afterwards. Then began through the land the epic journey of that man who was greater than Homer's wandering Ulysses, faithful as Ruth the gleaner in the field of Boaz. Every place in Ireland, wherever he heard there was any book good or bad, he sought and searched, gathering and collecting all that he could discover, transcribing every ancient material concerning the saints of Ireland. By collecting and tabulating the colophons in which he noted the dates and places where he made his transcripts, it would have been possible to form a fairly complete record of his movements, but that is impossible now, for many of his MSS. are lost, or, at least, the place of their keeping is unknown. Still from those that have been saved, we may form some idea of his tireless industry and recognize the effort of these crowded years.

It was at Donegal, on January 24th, 1627, that he made the first transcription recorded in his surviving MSS. This was a very vigorous account of the expulsion of St. Mochuda from Rahen, Mochuda who made the curious half-prophecy, half-precept, that only Kerrymen should succeed him in the abbacy of Lismore. To this, on March 28th, Brother Michael adds three chapters from a book written by Tadhg O'Keenan, thus bringing the whole up to thirteen chapters. He is busy next with Adamnan, who abolished the service of women in war. He copies a brief account of the Law of Adamnan on March 30th. There is an interval of four months, and then, on August 6th, he comes on "an old dark book," from which he copies a description of Adamnan's shrine and relics at Skreen, Co. Sligo. Apparently, it was during this year also that he tramped to Quin, Co. Clare, to examine the *Red Book of Munster*, written by Murrough O'Coinlis. But of this we cannot be sure, for the colophon gives no date. In the manuscript, the next date which occurs is that of the Law of Adamnan mentioned above, but this is separated from the *Book of Munster* extracts by a blank page and a half, and two other transcriptions. It is a pity that we cannot know the year, for Brother Michael made no less than nine extracts on this occasion, and even returned seven years later to the same book—a sign how highly he rated it. Some of the extracts are interesting. There is a *Lorica*, or Breastplate of St. Columbkille, a story of a woman who gave her son to St. Moling, and a report of the first words of Bee Mac De, the prophet, spoken immediately after his birth. The most important is a medley of prose and verse, entitled *The Twelve Apostles of Ireland*, which tells of St. Brendan's meeting with Judas, and how the saint kept Easter on the back of a whale that, raising its shoulders aloft out of the sea, "formed an even, firm, settled, broad, level, beautiful land."

Of Brother Michael's great industry during this year no traces remain but these—just thirty-four—pages. What a vast amount has been lost we can gather from a letter of Dr. Rothe, Bishop of Ossory, written on January 30th, 1628, "To the worthy and much respected friend, Mr. Heagh Ward, Louvain," in which he informs Fr. Ward: "As I was teaching at Cashel upon your patron's festival day,[1] there I met your brother Clery, who made a collection of more than three or four hundred Lives. I gave him the few Lives I had collected, and sent him to Ormond, part of my diocese, to write there for a time…" More than three or four hundred Lives! And so little remains. Dr. Rothe was the author of the famous *Analecta*, an exposure of James' plantation schemes and an appeal for union among Irishmen, which with excellent irony he dedicated to the Prince of Wales—*Serenissimo Walliorum Principi Carolo Brittanicarum Insularum haeredi conspicuo*—in a letter of dedication some 1,150 words in length. He would, therefore, be interested in Brother Michael's literary pursuits; and, indeed, he tells Fr. Ward that he expects Brother Michael soon again: "he shall be welcome truly to me."

When Brother Michael returned to Dr. Rothe, we do not know. In the house of the friars at Cashel he obtained "a vellum book

1. St. Aedh, or Hugh, B. of Kildare: January 4th.

belonging to Eochy O'Heffernan," from which he made rough drafts of two Lives, one of St. Declan, Bishop of Ardmore, and a Life of Ciaran of Saigir, who used to turn stones into glowing coals with a puff of his breath. After this, he trudges northward to "our place of refuge" at Killinure, on Lough Ree, called, through a sort of hopeful fiction, the Convent of Athlone, because the friars of the Athlone Community were living there. From the Book of Eachraid O'Shiel he copies a Life of the saint "who loved malediction," Ruadhan of Lothra, and the so-called Life of Colmán of Lynally, in Offaly—a tiresome piece of reading, "and without a doubt I know that I am writing much of it slowly, tediously, wretchedly" confesses poor Brother Michael. One would almost think that he had broken off in disgust, for it ends with a summary *et reliqua*, did he not tell us "I wrote the little I could find of the Life of Colmán." He dates these lives February 30th, 1628!

During the following March he is in the Franciscan Abbey of Multyfarnham, near Mullingar. Here he copies a long account of the Danish invasion of Ireland, from the time of Airtri, son of Cathal, down to the battle of Clontarf. It recounts the struggles of the Irish against the Gaill—the "azure Gentiles," or Norsemen, and the "fierce, hardhearted Danars or Danes." Chapter LXXX illustrates the security of the reign of Brian, by telling how a lone woman came riding from Torach, in the north of Erin, to Cliodhna, in the south of Erin, and she was neither robbed nor insulted, though on her horse-rod she carried a ring of gold.

Brother Michael is back in Donegal when we hear of him again. He copies the Life of Adamnan from *The Book of the Dun Cow.* In the Vision of Adamnan, the writer gives a striking description of heaven, the rich bright land of the saints, and of hell beneath, with the multitude of its pains and tortures and its punishments.

From Donegal to Dublin; and in Dublin, on July 15th, he copies the Life of the scholar Saint Moling from the Book of Timolling. In this year, too, at Donegal, he writes the first Martyrology or *Félire* of the Saints of Ireland—a small duodecimo volume of 184 pages, with a four-page introduction, dated Donegal, 1628.[2]

The year 1629 is rich in achievement. Brother Michael remains in Donegal until the coming of Summer, copying, ever copying. On January 24th it is the Life of St. Molaise of the Lake, abbot of Devenish, who loved to keep a guesthouse for the men of Erin. Brother Michael completed the Life of St. Naile by January 29th, two days after the saint's own festival. It is not a favorable specimen of Irish hagiology; and, certainly, the story of the cursing match between Naile and St. Ternoc gives little edification. Brother Michael calls it a fragment, and complains that it is obscure; he cannot read it in one or two places.

The month of February slips in, a full month for Brother Michael. On the 6th, he has "a bad old vellum book" belonging to the children of Brian O'Maolconaire, from which he transcribes the Life of Berach, Abbot of Kilbarry, in Roscommon—a life of considerable interest. Then comes Life of St. Grellan, of Creeve, in Roscommon also, on February 12th. On the following day, he transcribes a Life of St. Farannan, whose feast is but two days distant. There is no lull. In quick succession follows a fair copy of the Life of Ciaran of Saiger, which he had written in Cashel the year before, on the 18th a Life of St. Ciaran of Clonmacnoise, St. Declan on the 27th. Finally, rounding off the month, he obtains from "a dark black vellum"—most probably the *Book of Leinster*—another brief account of Adamnan's shrine at Skreen.

March comes. The Life of Ruadhan is written again on the 2nd. On the following day he adds a short tract on the sons of Ua Suanaig, a sort of appendix to his account of Mochuda's expulsion from Rahen. It tells something of what befell the church of Rahen after it passed into the hands of the brothers Ui Suanaig in the eighth century, showing by historical instances the penalties that fell on those who did any outrage to that church. It is only a fragment, and for this Brother

2. The Latin note on page 1 of the MS. (Brussels, 4639) states incorrectly that Brother Michael wrote the Martyrology at Douay. This note was added by a later hand.

Michael expresses his regret: "I cannot find anything more to write in reference to Mochuda and Ui Suanaig in their books… Indeed, I am sorry."

As if for consolation he turns to one of his own transcriptions, a long Life of St. Brendan the Navigator, abounding in marvels. Brother Michael had made his first copy from the book which Seery O'Maolconaire wrote in 1536 for Rose O'Neill, grand-daughter of Aodh Dubh O'Donnell, at Sen-Caislen beside Sliabh Truim in Tyrone. He does not, however, tell us when he made the first copy. His second transcript was made on March 27th, 1629.

He is soon working on a Life of St. Brigid. The MS. is not satisfactory and he takes from it only the first part of the Life. For the second part he goes to the old vellum written by the community of Ciaran of Duleek. The Life was completed on April 1st, 1629.

This was a month of evil change. The Irish Protestants and the people of England had viewed with alarm Falkland's open toleration of Catholicism. They held it to be unpardonable. The question was raised in the House of Commons, and the Lord Deputy was ordered to issue a Proclamation directing that all convents, monasteries and schools should be closed, and that priests should be forbidden to officiate in public. As a result, persecution broke out, spasmodically indeed but of frequent recurrence, so that it was not without risk that Brother Michael began to move southward with the approach of Summer. An added element of danger was the fact that his mission in Ireland was well known. Even a contemporary marvels "that Tadhg O'Clery was not hanged."

In the fair copies of some of his transcripts, made after his return to Donegal, Brother Michael states that he wrote them for the first time in Limerick, but does not give the date of writing. It is practically certain, however, that it was on his southward journey he made these copies, since he returned to Donegal by a route that could not touch Limerick without diverging widely and wastefully. Conaire Og Mac Conaire in Limerick had a book which was full of treasure, copied from "an old dark vellum." Brother Michael makes free use of it. He takes first an account of some miracles said to have been worked by St. Senan after his death, and poems describing St. Senan and others. He copies also the Law of Enda of Aran, a poem of four pages, and adds a few interesting fragments, including a short two-page poem by St. Enda to the ancient saints of Ireland, and three pieces of verse attributed to St. Columbkille.

Then he faces south once more, through Limerick into Cork, across the Blackwater, across the Lee, down to the old Franciscan monastery of Timoleague on Courtmacsherry Bay. Here was kept the *Book of Mac Carthy Reagh*, misnamed nowadays *The Book of Lismore*. From this, Brother Michael transcribes a Life of Mochua, abbot of Ballagh, Co. Mayo, and a fragment of the Life of Baoithin, the cousin and successor of Columba at Iona. It was Baoithin who saw the throne reserved for himself in heaven, a throne of silver "for the brightness and effulgence of his piety." By June 20th, Brother Michael had completed a Life of Finnchua of Brigown, which, it was alleged, the saint had written himself in the *Book of Monasterboice*.

He was in Cork presently, in the Convent of the Order. Less than two years before, a Donal O'Dinneen had copied fifteen Lives from a vellum book in his possession, for Fr. Francis O'Mahony, the Minister Provincial of the time. Brother Michael came for this old vellum. It must have satisfied him for he took more from that book than from any other single source. By June 24th he had finished a Life of Bairre, the flame of wisdom, patron of Cork, and two pages called a Life of the virgin Cranat. He turned next to the Life of Fursa, from whose writings it is said that Dante found inspiration for the *Commedia*. Though Brother Michael does not state it, it is probably from the same old vellum that he copied the Lives of Ailbe who loved hospitality, Carthach also named Mochuda, Abban, Finan of Kinnity, and Molaga who gave his name to Timoleague.

Now came a second evil change. Lord Falkland was finally recalled in August, and the government of Ireland was given over to Lord

Loftus and Richard Boyle, Earl of Cork, as Lords Justices. Agreeing in nothing else, these two agreed cordially in their hatred of Catholicism, and in the zeal with which they strove to have executed all decrees against the Catholics. The storm was near.

Meanwhile, however, Brother Michael had begun his slow return. Going northward, he copies a Life of St. Mochoemog of Liath Mor, near Thurles, a great abbot, whose age, when he died, was "thirteen years above four hundred." Brother Michael grows indignant about a Life of Caimin of Inis Celtra. It is "very disgusting, lying, too short in some places and too long in others, and a great deal of arrant nonsense." Why copy it then? "I make my excuse," he answers, "that it was enjoined on me to follow exactly the track of the old books."

He transcribes another Life of Senan, this time from the book which Maelisa Mac Egan wrote for O'Doran, hereditary Brehon of Leinster. On September 16th, from the book of the priest Roibned Purcell, near Leighlinn, he copies a Life of Kevin of the hard devotion. There follows a Life of Caillin of Fenagh, taken, Brother Michael tells us, from the old Book of Caillin himself. Again, while staying at Castlekevin, near Glendalough, he copies a long metrical life of Kevin. One can sense his gasp of relief as he nears the end. "I am tired," he wrote on the margin of his transcript, "and no wonder." He is not pleased with it either, though it is not worse than many other Lives he has copied.

Having returned to the North, in November, he copies yet another version of the Law of Adamnan, much longer than any previous one, from the old *Book of Raphoe* in Tirconnell. From the *Buile Suibhne*, the tale of Suibhne's madness, he condenses a Life of St. Ronan the Fair, "who cursed Suibhne, because Suibhne had dragged him dishonorably from the place where he was praising God."

Arrived at last at the Convent of Donegal, he sets about making fair copies of his manuscripts for Fr. Ward. On November 17th, he completes a Life of Maedoc of Ferns, long and highly composite. The colophon is interesting. "I wrote this Life of Maedoc from the paper copy which I had previously made myself from the book which Fintan O'Cuirnin wrote...and Fintan says it was taken from old, black, illegible books of the time of the saints and of Sidrac Mor O'Cuirnin and of Gilla O'Cassidy, who wrote and compiled this life from the mouth and words of Maedoc himself...though there are many great and excellent miracles in this life, I do not approve of its diction or order of composition, etc." What does that "etc." hold? Maedoc died in 626; Gilla O'Cassidy died after 1147, yet it was said he had this life from the mouth of Maedoc himself.

Brother Michael completes his fair copy of the Life of Colmán on November 9th. By December 1st, he has rewritten the Miracles of Senan. On December 5th he turns again to Kevin (or Coemgen), transcribing the fragment on that day, and the tedious metrical Life on the day following.

This year, too, he wrote the brief story of the self-sacrifice of Eimine Bán and his monks; also an imperfect Life of St. Brigid, corresponding partly with the Life in the *Book of Mac Carthy Reagh*, and a Life of Cuimin the Tall, of Clonfert, "the vessel of wisdom of his time, and like unto Gregory of the Morals"—but a most repulsive composition.

This account must suffice of what may be called Brother Michael's researches in the field of pure hagiology. Indeed, except for some metrical "Rules" and a few verses dubiously attributed to St. Patrick, St. Cormac, St. Brigid and St. Moling, little else remains. From now on, Brother Michael ceases to be a copyist. With the dawn of 1630, though the storm-clouds had broken over the land, he enters on the second and greater phase of his career.

A glance at the condition of Irish literature in the early seventeenth century will show at once the need of this second phase of Brother Michael's work. The "spoiling of the rhymers," begun in 1537, had effectively ruined the Bardic schools. In parts of the country individual members still clung to their ancient prestige, but as a body their day was no more. Their schools were broken, their pupils scattered, and they themselves were wandering outcasts on the lands that had been their own. Set against the literary background of Europe, this degradation shows up darkly. In France, the seventeenth century was *le grand siècle*, rich in writers of genius, with its ideal of correctness and polish in literature, its prose winged with rhythms that moved and molded themselves upon the thoughts uttered. England had a galaxy of shining names. Shakespeare was at the peak point of his genius. But in Ireland, in Ireland whose sons had taught these nations in the grey of dawn, literature was dying. Verse was still being written. The great Contention had busied many a quill, but those verses had not that indefinable quality which makes poetry. Like a pagan goddess, the Spirit of Poetry seems altogether to have gone over to the conquering enemy. That which stirred the Bards was a brush of wings as she fled away, but they glimpsed not the vision.

Nothing was being produced. On the other hand, in order to break the whole Gaelic tradition, every effort had been made to destroy the sacred and literary relics of the past. Ample evidence of this is given in Dr. Lynch's *Cambrensis Eversus*, published in 1662. "Certain it is," writes Lynch, "that within the memory of our fathers the English burned with savage rage for the destruction of our Irish documents." He tells how, during the Elizabethan wars, the English soldiers rifled the houses of friends and foes indiscriminately, and carried off all Irish manuscripts. When the soldiers were called in to garrison the towns, large leaves of these manuscript volumes were distributed to schoolboys, to make covers for their books, or were cut up in the tailors' shops, to make measures for clothes. In the *Analecta*, Dr. Rothe complained "that if any officers of the government heard of a fragment of manuscript history being in the possession of a private individual, it was at once begged or bought, or, if neither money nor entreaty were strong enough, threats and commands immediately followed." The very efforts used by the Irish to save their manuscripts from this vandalism, threatened the preservation of their contents.

One can, therefore, appreciate Brother Michael's new activity and the value of his efforts to gather and collate the few books that were still left. One can hear the knelling despair in his cry that "should the writing of them be neglected now, they would not be found again to be put on record or commemorated to the end and termination of the world"—a foreboding that was only too drastically realized, since of the many works, whose contents were saved by Brother Michael's industry, but few have escaped the doom that he foretold.

Brother Michael's first work of redaction was a new and enlarged Martyrology of the Saints of Ireland. According to the testimony of Colgan, this was the first occasion on which the Four Masters worked together. The four were Brother Michael, his cousin Peregrine (or Cucogry) O'Clery, chief of the ollavs of Tirconnell, son of Lughaidh of the Contention, Peregrine O'Duigenan of Leitrim, whose sept were ollavs in history to the Mac Dermotts and Mac Donaghs, and Fearfeasa O'Maolconaire of the Clan O'Maolconaire, hereditary bards and historians to the O'Connors, kings of Connacht. It was Colgan, in the preface to his *Acta Sanctorum Hiberniae*, who named them the Four Masters. If Colgan's statement be correct, that the Masters worked with Brother Michael on this occasion, it is strange that Fearfeasa O'Maolconaire makes no mention of it in a manuscript of his preserved at the Royal Irish Academy, though in this manuscript he professes to set forth all the works in which Brother Michael and the Masters collaborated. The omission may be due to the fact that the work was not carried out exclusively by the Masters, as the fathers of the Convent of Donegal cooperated largely, supplying the names of non-Irish saints, about whom foreign historians had written. The colophon attached to the Table of the Martyrology makes no reference to the many collaborators, but states merely where the Martyrology was written and when it was completed: *Finis do'n Martarlaic*, 19 *April*, 1630. *I cconueint Brathar Duin na nGall ro tionnsgnadh acus ro criochnaigheadh.* (End of the Martyrology, 19th of April, 1630. In the Convent of the Friars of Donegal it was begun and ended.)

In general the compilers followed the plan of the *Martyrologium Romanum*. The day of the month is first given, with the Latin form of the date; then follow the names of the saints whose feasts occur on that particular day, their designation, and a note about the saint's life. In the case of Irish saints, their genealogy is added when that is known.

The Calendar of the Martyrology occupied sixty quarto pages. To this the compilers appended a Table of Names, in which they give also curious historical facts not mentioned in the text, and brief notices of ancient wells, relics and reliquaries, that are no longer known. In some instances we find the Latinized forms or equivalents of the Irish names of saints—an invaluable aid to students of Church history in Ireland. The whole work is one of the great authorities of Irish hagiology. It is a compilation of scholars of the greatest eminence, who have condensed into its pages the substance of original records, some of them no longer extant, and all requiring a profound knowledge of Celtic learning for their correct reading and interpretation.

Contemplating the scene of this labor, one envisages a calm retreat, where everything moved forward without haste and without noise, in perfect peace. One certainly does not think that Brother Michael and his associates were in daily peril of their lives. Yet, the storm had burst even while they were planning their task. On St. Stephen's Day of the year before, the Protestant Archbishop Bulkeley, at the head of a troop of soldiers, broke into the Franciscan Church in Dublin, profaned the altar, hewed to pieces the statue of St. Francis, and arrested some of the friars. A Proclamation was issued by the English Privy Council a few weeks later "that the house where so many friars appeared in their habits...be speedily demolished, and be a mark of terror to resisters of authority; and that the rest of the houses erected or employed there or elsewhere in Ireland, to the use of superstitious societies, should be immediately suppressed." The storm spread from the east to the most remote districts of the west and south. The Guardian of Lislaghtin, on the estuary of the Shannon, was arrested. Fr. Owen Field had to flee from Timoleague, where Brother Michael had worked so peacefully a few months before. On April 10th, even as Brother Michael was penning the last pages of the Martyrology, Fr. Field wrote from Cork: "Our house in Dublin has been already utterly destroyed, and the other houses everywhere through the kingdom handed over to strangers, nor is it permitted to any two friars to live together; and this is only the prelude of the persecution that has been determined upon."

Donegal seems to have escaped notice, though, of course, there was no knowing when the marauders might bear down on them. It is likely that Brother Michael remained there for some time; but it would seem also that, in spite of the danger, he tramped about in search of a patron to pay the expenses of a new undertaking he had in mind. At last, a patron was found, and on October 4th his great new work was commenced in the Franciscan Convent of Killinure on Lough Ree. This work was the *Réim Rioghraidhe*, or the Succession of the Kings and the Genealogies of the Saints of Ireland, as they are found in the books of the old writers. It was intended, at first, to treat of the saints only, but, on examination, it was thought better to give also a list of the kings, "because it was impossible to trace the descent of the saints directly to their origins, without first setting down the descent of the kings, for it is from these that the saints sprung."

It "occurred" to Brother Michael that it would not be proper to carry out this work without the authority, confirmation, and examination of other learned historians, men skilled in and conversant with the history of Ireland. Therefore he decided, with the approbation of his superior, to bring together three persons whom he considered best suited and qualified for the task. These were the scholars who had worked with him on the Martyrology; this was the first work that they carried out alone.

It also occurred to Brother Michael that it would not be easy to complete his project without resources. "The Order to which he belonged were so poor by reason of their vow, as well as of their persecution at this time, that he proposed making an appeal to Noblemen who had no vow of poverty." He gives no more than a hint of his wanderings, and of the humiliations of refusal: "Though he made his request to many, he found no one to supply him with the requirements for the completion of his work, except one person... Torlough Mag Cochlain." To this Torlough, Lord of Delvin Eathra, the Four Masters fitly dedicated their book. It took "a whole month of days and nights" to complete; and when it was completed on November 4th, Fr. George Dillon, the Guardian, added his testimony to the industry with which it was completed.

The Masters drew their material from various ancient sources. The pedigrees of the kings are given first, in five great divisions: The Firbolg kings, the kings of the Tuatha de Danaan, the Milesian kings, the kings of Ireland after the Faith, and kings with opposition. The genealogies of the saints begin with that of Patrick, son of Calpurnius. Then follow thirty-eight chapters corresponding to thirty-eight genealogical branches, each chapter consisting of an alphabetical list of saints classified according to their ancestral stock. The whole work, taken with Colgan's identifications and annotations, is of the highest importance in studying the genealogies of the saints of Ireland.

In all these undertakings, one must not lose sight of the fact that Brother Michael's work was part of the Louvain movement; that, great and enduring though his work was in itself, its worth could not be utilized nor its purpose achieved, except in the success of the movement of which it was part. There had been progress at Louvain, too. Fr. Ward had finished his *Life of St. Romold*, the Patron of Mechlin, and was only waiting for some necessary manuscripts from Ireland to hand the work over to the printer. Fr. Fleming's *Collectanea* was actually in the printer's hands. At this juncture, when after eight years of toil success seemed near, the movement received its first setback. Fr. Fleming was removed from St. Anthony's. Early in the month of November he started out for the "triple city" of Prague, where he had been appointed first Guardian of the new Irish Franciscan College. He left his work, however, with the printer, Moretus of Antwerp.

There now ensues a lull in Brother Michael's activity. One cannot imagine him idle, but, whatever his occupation, he must have been greatly hampered by the persecution that was still raging. Soon, he undertook to purge of error, rectify and transcribe "the ancient, honored Chronicle which is called the *Leabhar Gabhála*." It was not possible to undertake this task without the assistance of other chroniclers, at some fixed abode; and, furthermore, it entailed expense, which could be defrayed only by some benefactor of Brother Michael's seeking. Brian Roe Maguire, first Lord Enniskillen, being found willing to pay the expenses, the Four Masters repaired to the Franciscan Convent of Lisgoole in Fermanagh, where with Gillapatrick O'Luinin, Maguire's chief chronicler, they commenced their task on the ancient Chronicle "a fortnight before All-Hallowtide."

Brother Michael clearly indicates the motives that prompted his undertaking. The *Réim Rioghraidhe* was only a skeleton, meagre and wanting without the *Leabhar Gabhála*, for this was "the original fountain of the history of the saints and kings of Ireland"—a motive which the critical historian will acclaim. The lover of Ireland will acclaim a second reason: "I was aware that men learned in Latin and in English had begun to translate this chronicle of Erin from the Irish into these languages that we have spoken of, and that they had not so deep a knowledge of Irish, as that they could put the hard and easy parts of the said book together without disgrace or error; and I felt that the translation which they would make, must become an eternal reproach and disgrace to all Erin, and, in particular, to her chroniclers. It was for this reason that I undertook, with the permission of my superiors, to purify and compile this book, and to collect for it, from other books, all that was wanting to it in history and in other learning, as much as we could in the space of time that we had to write it."

The plan of the compilers was to collate the statements found in old books of history and in the old Books of Invasions that they had gathered together, without discussing or attempting to decide the authenticity of these statements. The compilers of every other

Book of Invasions had commenced with the account of creation in the Book of Genesis, as being, perhaps, the first human invasion. The Four Masters very properly left creation to theologians and students of Sacred Scripture, declaring simply that in their chronology they follow the seventy-two. They keep strictly to native matters, describing the various colorizations of Ireland down to the English invasion, embodying in the work many ancient poems by way of illustration. They completed the task on December 22nd, and the Guardian of the Convent added his testimony on that day, even as Fr. George Dillon had done for the *Réim Rioghraidhe* at Killinure. This was the greatest work in which the Masters had yet collaborated; and it is, perhaps, the most important work preserved to us of the early civil history of Ireland.

The *Leabhar Gabhála* was happily completed. From the Irish viewpoint, the movement initiated at Louvain seemed nearer than ever to success; but even as the Masters were cheerfully working through the early stages of their task, the movement received a second serious setback on the Continent. On November 7th, Fr. Fleming was murdered. The Lutheran peasants of Bohemia, taking heart from the invasion of their country by Gustavus Adolphus and the Elector of Saxony, had formed themselves into armed bands to plunder their Catholic neighbors and to wreck the religious houses. Being warned of danger, Fr. Fleming and three companions resolved to escape from Prague. Fr. Fleming set out with a young deacon, taking a south-easterly direction, but they had not gone more than fourteen or fifteen miles when they were overtaken by a band of peasants, and barbarously murdered. *The Collectanea* was withdrawn from the press.

The Four Masters allowed little time to slip by before they commenced work on their last and greatest compilation—the *Annals of the Kingdom of Ireland*. Their earlier works had paved the way for this. They realized what they might do with the sources at their command, but the work would take years to complete. Who would pay the expenses of these years? It is in many ways a sign of the times that in this, his greatest undertaking, Brother Michael had recourse for help to a Protestant chieftain, Fearghal O'Gara, of Moygara in Sligo, who guaranteed to give the chroniclers the reward of their labor, although he had been "maintained and educated in the English religion and habits, in Trinity College, Dublin."[3]

The Four Masters, accordingly, came to the Convent of Donegal, where Brother Michael's own brother was Guardian, and where he had with difficulty collected "all the best and most copious books of annals that I could find throughout all Ireland." It seems best to state here the exact location of the Convent of Donegal, since this convent is remembered chiefly, and almost exclusively, for its association with the Annals of the Four Masters. It was not to the monastery founded by Finola O'Donnell that the Four Masters came, nor even near its inspiring ruins, but to a residence of sorts—a *locus mansionis*—by the river Drowes, that inconsiderable river flowing north-westward from Lough Melvin into the Bay of Donegal. As in the case of the Convent of Athlone, so here, too, Brother Michael fixes the location himself. *Conueint bhrathar Duin na nGall ag Drobhaois* (the Convent of the friars of Donegal by the Drowes).[4]

On January 22nd, 1632, the Masters began their great foundational task. Maurice O'Maolconaire from Roscommon was there too, but he was to remain only a month; and also Conaire O'Clery, an excellent scribe, a brother of Brother Michael's. Imagination plays about the scene:

> "We can hear them in their musings,
> We can see them as we gaze,
> Four meek men around the cresset,

3. "O'Gara, Farrall (Grandson of Iriell), Moygara, Co. Sligo: Ward. Jan. 12, 1615—1616." Reg. T.C.D.

4. Colophon to *Betha Cholmain Eala*. See other colophons in Plummer's *Bethada Naem nErenn* (Oxford, 1922).

With the scrolls of other days
Four unwearied scribes who treasure
Every word and every line."

As a scene it has the simplicity of greatness.

Maurice O'Maolconaire leaves after a month, and the others settle down to their long, tedious task. Every item is carefully discussed, and comparison is made between the various sources, before the item is written into the Annals. It is the same, day and night. "The sunrise blooms and withers on the hill," the weeks mount up, and years go down into the dust: only here there is no change.

Little occurred to break the even tenor of their labors. On May 15th, the Minister Provincial sends Brother Michael a short letter, bidding him, *ad meritum sanctae obedientiae*, persevere in the work he has undertaken, and subject his collected works to the judgment of those skilled in the Irish language. Only ten days afterwards, on May 25th, poor Peregrine O'Clery was dispossessed, and his lands became forfeited to the king, Peregrine "being a meere Irishman, and not of English or British descent or surname." This incident throws light on Brother Michael's anxiety for a patron who would give the chroniclers the reward of their labors.

In August, with the new Provincial Chapter held in Meelick, there comes a change of Guardian, and Fr. Maurice Donlevy, surnamed "Ultach," is appointed in place of Fr. Bernardine. The work goes on. Brother Michael, in his untiring zeal, engages in other tasks also. On August 18th, he completes a transcript of *The Martyrology of O'Gorman*, and Fearfeasa O'Maolconaire and Peregrine O'Clery write a testimonial that Brother Michael's copy is authentic and entire. At last, in 1634, the first portion of the Annals is completed, bringing the chronicle down to the year 1208 A.D.

It must have been early in summer when this first portion was completed, for in June we find Brother Michael—"that industrious, collecting bee"—in the Franciscan Convent at Ennis, copying a Life of the rather shadowy Mac Creiche, an unfavorable specimen of Irish hagiology embodying several wearisome metrical compositions. From Ennis he turned south-eastward to the Franciscan Convent of Quin, which is also in Clare. Securing the *Red Book of Munster* a second time, he copies again the account of St. Brendan's voyages, called "The Twelve Apostles of Erin." In 1627, as we have seen, he had already made a copy of this narrative. Both copies are in existence, and they prove beyond doubt Brother Michael's fidelity as a copyist.

The two texts agree so minutely, that the same abbreviations and even the same contractions are used. During this visit, he transcribed also the *Amhra*, or Elegy of St. Senan, from a book belonging to the Coarb of Senan, and some brief anecdotes about the saint, differing from those he had copied elsewhere.

The second part of the Annals was begun in 1635, and was exclusively the work of the O'Clerys—Peregrine, Conaire and Brother Michael. But Brother Michael was not satisfied with one occupation, much of which was merely a matter of adapting comparatively recent works. He busied himself with other transcripts also. He has completed a fair copy of the Life of Mac Creiche by May 11th. On June 14th, he rewrites the fragments from the Life of Senan, which he had copied in Quin, Co. Clare.

Meanwhile, however, matters on the Continent had taken a serious turn, the bearing of which on Irish affairs is scarcely appreciated. It might well have meant the undoing of Brother Michael's patient years of copying and travel, the wreckage and lasting loss of the great treasures of Irish history and hagiology collected in St. Anthony's, and the destruction of all the work accomplished for the antiquities of Ireland by Ward and Fleming and Colgan.

The Dutch, having joined the French, decided to attempt the conquest of Belgium. On June 20th, they approached Louvain and proceeded to invest the town. Enraged by a fortnight of disastrous endeavor, they issued an ultimatum to the inhabitants, threatening them, if further resistance was made, with a repetition of the massacres of Tirlemont. Red flags were hoisted as a signal of "No quarter!" The inhabitants were resolute. Irish soldiers rushed out to tear down the flags, but found that the enemy had deserted the fort on which the red flags floated. The siege had been raised. The following Sunday the victorious defenders marched in solemn procession to celebrate their delivery. The Franciscans walked in two lines, the one Belgian, the other Irish. One gladly shares their act of thanksgiving, remembering the might-have-been, had the enemy been successful.

All unconscious of these dangers, Brother Michael and his associates worked on without dismay, with a great joy. The Provincial Chapter of August 14th brought the reinstatement of their old Guardian, Fr. Bernardine. Peregrine and Conaire toiled on at the Annals. In November Brother Michael rewrote the *Wars of the Gael and the Gaill* from the copy which he had made at Multyfarnham in March, 1628. He was making all these fair copies for Fr. Ward, but Fr. Ward died on November 8th, even as he was penning the first pages of his manuscript. We do not know when Brother Michael received the sad news. He never ceases from his labors. He copies the ancient *Martyrology of Tallaght*. This work is defective from November 1st to December 16th. "I did not find the other part of the Martyrology in the old Book," he writes. He copies the Martyrology of Oengusso Céli Dé, and two metrical genealogies of Irish saints—copies, he tells us, that are without alteration of arrangement, or exchange (that is, paraphrase) of the writing. Brother Michael makes good use of his opportunities: he copies one of the metrical genealogies from the vellum book of the Clan O'Maolconaire, which they used in the compilation of the Annals. Fr. Bernardine and Fr. Maurice Donlevy add a testimony on April 25th, that Brother Michael's copies were made *de verbo ad verbum, sine styli ordinis aut substantiae rerum inversione aut corruptione*—a testimony that might be applied to all of Brother Michael's transcripts.

Finally, on August 10th, the last entry is made in the Annals, the last lines are written, and the work of tedious years is brought to an end. A preface is added, setting forth the names of those who wrote the various parts of the Annals, and the old books they used. This preface is signed in turn by Brother Michael, by Maurice O'Maolconaire, who had returned to Donegal, by Fearfeasa O'Maolconaire, Conaire O'Clery, their assistant, and by Fr. Bernardine and Fr. Maurice Donlevy. A long dedication to Fearghal O'Gara was written later, and signed by the Four Masters; Fr. Bernardine and Fr. Maurice Donlevy adding a testimonial which took the place of the earlier preface. Thus was completed the last and greatest of our Irish Annals.

The contents of the Annals deal mainly with the affairs of the native Irish. At first there are only brief references to names and deeds, and derivations of names. Deaths, battles, the clearing of primeval forests, the building of forts, lake-eruptions, reigns, successions, genealogies, political changes, raids, famines, plagues, the foundation and occasionally the overthrow of churches and monasteries, the making of roads, strange occurrences—"the condensed pith and substance of the old vellum books of Ireland then in existence"—all are given under their respective dates, as accurately as the Masters can give them. Occasionally, from 106 A.D., ancient verses are quoted in corroboration. Towards the end the Annals take on the proportions of a literary history, and are largely devoted to the affairs of the O'Neills and O'Donnells.

The language of the Annals is archaic even for that time, and hard to understand. The work was not intended for the people, but rather for scholars. Compiling this chronicle of their country in their own learned diction was a last gesture of the bardic schools in the face of the English civilization that had doomed them. Reaching from far antiquity to the very century in which they were composed, the Annals were a memorial of a dying civilization, fittingly couched, therefore, in the language of the schools which that civilization brought forth.

One need not dilate on their value. That is perhaps, best summed up by Dr. Hyde, when he declares that there is no event in the whole of Irish history, from the time of Christ down to the beginning of the seventeenth century, concerning which the first inquiry of the student must not be: "What do the Four Masters say of this?"

After the completion of the Annals, there is a touch of finality about Brother Michael's movements. As the Provincial had directed him, he sets out to get the approval of men learned in the language and antiquities of Ireland, but he takes with him not merely the Annals, but also the two martyrologies, the *Réim Rioghraidhe*, and the *Leabhar Gabhála.* His first destination was Ballymacegan in Tipperary. On his way he stops at Killinure, where he transcribes an Irish version of the Rule of St. Clare and the approbation of the Rule by Innocent IV., which Fr. Aodh O'Reilly and Fr. Séamas O'Shiel had made from the English—*as berla an Riaghail si*—for the Poor Clares of the nearby Convent of Bethlehem on the lake shore. These transcriptions are dated October 19th and 21st, 1636.

In Ballymacegan, Brother Michael submits his works to a last representative of the hereditary ollavs, Flann Mac Egan, the old scholar about whom Rory O'Moore was to grow so enthusiastic in the first successes of the Confederation, that he wanted to have an Irish school opened before Mac Egan died, and heartily wished "that those learned and religious fathers in Lovayne did come over in haste with their monuments and with an Irish and Latin print." Flann Mac Egan gave his approbations on November 1st and 2nd. He pays a glowing tribute to the Annals, declaring that in all his experience he had never found, as a book of history and Annals, one of better order, more universal, more copious, or more to be approved of, than this book. Unwisely for himself, he added: "I think that no intelligent person whatever, of the laity or clergy, or of the professions, who shall read it, can possibly find fault with it."

From Ballymacegan in Tipperary to Kilkee on the coast of Clare. Here Brother Michael submitted his works to Conner Mac Brody, son of Maoilin Og. He and his associates had used the Book of Maoilin Og in compiling the second part of the Annals. Conner Mac Brody, who, rather curiously, signs his name in English first, and then in Irish, entirely endorses the opinion of Flann Mac Egan. Likewise he adds: "It is difficult to find fault with, censure or criticize it. To attest what I have said, I now put my hand upon it at Kilkee, 11th November, 1636."

A little attention to dates will show that Conner Mac Brody could not know much about the works he recommended. Ballymacegan was situated in the extreme north of Tipperary. Brother Michael did not leave it earlier than November 2nd. He was now an old man, though one hardly adverts to that fact, and in travelling could make only the slow progress of age. Yet, Conner Mac Brody's approbations appear on *all* of Brother Michael's works on November 11th, nine days after Flann Mac Egan's. These approbations, both of Conner Mac Brody and of Flann Mac Egan, have been quoted widely in proof of Brother Michael's scholarship, but the truth is that they are worthless, and have no more significance than an empty courtesy. How empty we shall soon see.

It may have been during this visit to Clare that Brother Michael received the fragment of the supposed *Psalter of St. Caimin* from Flann and Bernard, the sons of Mac Brody. Clearly, this Mac Brody is not the same who gave his testimony to Brother Michael's works, though this has been taken for granted. On folio two of the manuscript Brother Michael wrote a colophon in which, among other interesting details, he states that he saw Flann and Bernard Mac Brody living in Termonn Caimin after their father's death. According to the *Book of Forfeitures and Distributions*, Conor, son of Maoelin Mac Brody, was living in 1641, holding property in the townlands of "Kilkie and Lisheenrahanick."

Brother Michael turns northward. Through Co. Clare into Connacht, around the inner reaches of Galway Bay he plods, to the city of Galway. Here on November 17th and 18th, he obtains the *imprimatur* of Malachy O'Queely, Archbishop of Tuam, for all his works. This he also secures on November 27th, at the Convent of the Order in Rosserilly, near Headford, Co. Galway, from Boetius Mac Egan, the Franciscan Bishop of Elphin.

We have no further tidings of Brother Michael until the New Year, when his works were approved by Ross Mac Geoghegan, O.P.,

Bishop of Kildare, whose name in religion was Fr. Rochus a Cruce. From this approbation we learn that Flann Mac Egan and Conner Mac Brody were appointed by the Franciscan Provincial to examine Brother Michael's works. The approbation is given *in loco nostrae mansionis die 8° Januarii, anno Domini 1637*, but we are not told where this place of refuge was. Ross Mac Geoghegan is described as an alumnus of the Dominican foundation at Mullingar, and as being forced by the stress of persecution frequently to change his abode.

From this Dominican place of refuge Brother Michael turns to Dublin. There on February 15th, all his works are approved—a special approbation being given to the Annals on the 18th—by Thomas Fleming, O.F.M., Archbishop of Dublin. Then northwards to the Franciscan convent at Carrickfergus, on Belfast Lough, goes Brother Michael; and here his long tramping end. The *nihil obstat* of the Franciscan censors is given on July 2nd.

Brother Michael's last days in Ireland were saddened through attacks on his work by a fellow Franciscan, Tuileagna O'Maolconaire. This critic, author of an Irish Grammar and Prosody, gravely charges Brother Michael with putting in his works five statements that have no justification in the old books. To this charge Brother Michael made "a learned and well-informed reply," but without avail. Through the influence of Tuileagna, Flann Mac Egan wrote withdrawing his approbation from Brother Michael's works, until the points in question should be settled, an action which shows the slight importance that Flann Mac Egan attached to his own solemn attestation. Tuileagna continued his attacks on the five points until after 1646, when Fearfeasa O'Maolconaire, one of the Masters, decided to silence him in the traditional manner, by writing a poem against him.

However, we can thank Tuileagna for one thing—he enables us to know approximately when Brother Michael returned to Louvain. In a letter to the Minister Provincial he states, in reference to his five points, that he had made preparations "to have the matter discussed in the general chapter held in Thomond in the year 1638, when the Brother had gone away." Though Tuileagna uses the expression *caibidil ghenerálta,* he means the ordinary triennial chapter of the Province. This Chapter of Thomond was held in Quin, Co. Clare, on August 15th, 1638. Hence, Brother Michael left Ireland sometime between July 2nd, 1637, and August 15th, 1638. Tuileagna mentions other interesting matters in the same letter to the Provincial, as, for instance, that Mac Brody came to the Chapter of Thomond and publicly withdrew his signature from Brother Michael's works, and that, before Brother Michael left Ireland, Flann Mac Egan had written to him, withdrawing his approbation.

In Louvain, Brother Michael's influence is very evident in the work of Colgan, who had taken up the task laid down at death by Fr. Ward. Colgan shows an astonishing knowledge of Irish topographical data. He can indicate the position of rivulets, lakes, mountains, ancient abbeys, churches, chapels, small and obscure localities, with surprising exactness. Naturally, he would have had the assistance of the Irish living in Louvain, but that minute and pertinent detail he could have had only from Brother Michael, who, making his transcriptions on the spot, would have a special care for all such points.

Brother Michael was not, however, satisfied with being a mere helper. In his readings and transcriptions he had come upon many obsolete words, whose meaning could be understood only by those trained in the schools. The schools were no more; so he decided to compile a dictionary of ancient and obsolete Irish words, lest the knowledge of them should be lost. This dictionary was issued from the college press in 1643. It is dedicated "To my very honorable Lord and Friend, Boetius Mac Egan, Bishop of Elphin." The dedication bears the date October 28th, 1643, but the work was finished some months earlier, for the approbation of the Royal Censor of books is dated August 7th, 1643.

The first word in the dictionary is *A .i. árd nó cnoc* (a hill), the last is *Usarb .i. bás* (death), and these two words image Brother Michael's whole life, for Tadhg-of-the-mountain climbed not only the hills of

Ireland but the mountains of great toil, at last to find death gloriously upon their summit.

Brother Michael died soon after the completion of his dictionary. Strange to say, his death is not recorded in the Necrology kept at St. Anthony's, though the Necrology begins with the year 1614, and includes the names of his colleagues, Colgan and Ward. Colgan, who on November 24th, 1643, gave formal permission to De Witte to print the *Ada Sanctorum Hiberniae*, wrote, in the preface to that work, an account of Brother Michael, whom he describes as *ante paucos menses mortuus*. A manuscript chronicle in St. Isidore's, Rome, states definitely that Brother Michael died in 1643. The writer gives a brief account of him, referring to Colgan as his authority, and concludes with a reference to the dictionary *impressum in Collegio año 1643 quo Lovanii obiit.*

Had Brother Michael been as vain as Horace was, he might with more truth have written upon his works *aere perennius.* His works are his memorial. No monument makes his tomb a glory. His grave is unknown. It was in death as in life. He was aloof, not inscrutable but little known, reserved, silent. This silence is of his very character, only intensified for us by the revealing flashes that all too rarely play upon him, showing him always a man great of mind, great of will, greater in obedience, the scholar exclaiming at absurdity and slovenliness, yet working faithfully, copying without change, because such method had been enjoined upon him. Add to this his courage, his almost superhuman activity, his greatness of accomplishment, and we may glimpse the man. We may follow, we may watch him at work, but we never see his face. We think of him as a figure keeping ever on its unhurrying way, now ascending the climbing paths of a mountainside, now a silhouette against the brilliance of the summit, now making its slow pace down into the cloistered valley. We see only a figure; we do not see the face, the serious deep eyes. He is the most impersonal hero in all history.

BLESSED OLIVER PLUNKET (1629–1681)

by PHILIP HUGHES

THE SEVENTEENTH IS, OF ALL THE CENTURIES OF IRELAND's history, surely the most tragic! It is the century when the old Gaelic Ireland that had escaped Rome and survived the Middle Ages, and which, baptised into the Church, had successively assimilated the different conquerors and adventurers who from England had set forth for its undoing, rose for the last time against the power that was its mortal enemy. It is the century which, opening to the despair of the flight of the Earls, sees the great plantation scheme of James I, the iron rule of the Earl of Strafford, the new hope of the ill-starred Confederation of Kilkenny, the splendid apparition of Owen Roe O'Neill, and then Cromwell and death. And if for a moment hopes rise high once more when, thirty years later, there comes the last Catholic king, it is, appropriately, with the Boyne and the broken treaty of Limerick that this tragic century ends. As in 1607 the broken and defeated lords of Tyrone and Tyrconnell had fled to Spain and Rome, and as in the years that followed Cromwell's bloody triumph the nation's soldiers had gone to swell the armies of the Catholic kings, so was it now once again. From the desolated country there went forth the flower of its manhood, and its last human hopes. There remained only its faith, its Catholicism, its poor and its priests. The priests survived. Theirs it was to assist at every stage of the national tragedy. They blessed the hopes and aspirations, they encouraged with prayer and sacraments the captains and their men, they shared in the brief glories of the Catholic revival, and in the hour of defeat they remained to console the remnant that must pay the price—themselves more than all to pay it most heavily.

Blessed Oliver Plunket was of the generation whose childhood lay in one of the less miserable periods of the time. He grew up to manhood while the land was most given over to the forces of destruction, and his maturity left him only this role of consoling the remnant in the stillness that succeeded to the tramp of the last defeated soldiers going abroad, of consoling them and of suffering in their company. With the tragedy in its every phase he was then in most intimate relation, for his kinsfolk were among the leading actors of its early stages, and in the latter he was himself its chief figure. This century of national heroism, rich in great figures, knows none greater than this Archbishop of Armagh. The great O'Neills, Hugh and Owen Roe, the scholars Colgan, O'Clery, Geoffrey Keating, the mighty Wadding himself, yield each of them something to his primacy. The noble, the scholar, the administrator, the reformer, the suffering exile and the faithful fugitive missioner, he was all of these, the martyrdom the fitting crown to his life of hidden prayer and accepted destitution.

Blessed Oliver Plunket was born in the year 1629, at Loughcrew in the County Meath. He belonged to a clan already famous. Plunkets—Anglo-Irish by origin—there were everywhere in contemporary history. There were for example the four Plunket peers, the Earl of Fingall, Lord Louth, Lord Dunsany and Lord Rathmore, Catholics as true as those ancestors of whom the Jesuit Nuncio, David Wolf, wrote fifty years earlier: "[They] are of the same house, and all in time of war gather under the banner of Lord Plunket of Killeen (the later Earl of Fingall), not that he is stronger than the others but because his ancestors are more ancient…and the Lord of Rathmore told me that these Lords of the Plunket family can put into the field 500 knights well armed besides as many foot soldiers." Of the same generation was that Sir Oliver Plunket listed with the Earl of Desmond and some score of others in a document of 1567, as one of the "Irish Lords in Prison." Another, more illustrious, namesake was the young Oliver Plunket butchered at Smerwick by the Lord Deputy's orders in 1580 for his valiant profession of faith. Of a later generation were the two brothers Patrick, Bishop of Ardagh, and Sir Nicholas, Envoy of the Irish Catholics to Pope Innocent X, "the best lawyer in the kingdom and the only defender that poor ecclesiastics had in such circumstances" said Blessed Oliver years later—solicitous for the defence of the Archbishop of Tuam then in gaol for *premunire*, and recommending Sir Nicholas as counsel. A Bartholomew Plunkett was President of the Irish College at Brussels, Luke Plunkett ruled successively the Sees of Raphoe and Derry as Vicar-General in the long years when they lacked a bishop. There is mention of a Robert Plunkett suggested as bishop for Kilmore, and the Michael Plunket who was to do his share in creating history as Roman agent of the Irish bishops and later as a bishop himself, was the nephew to whom was addressed one of the martyr's last letters.

Nor was Oliver Plunket of family less illustrious on his mother's side, for thence he was kin to the Dillons, Earls of Roscommon, and to the Talbots, one of whom was to rule in Dublin while he held Armagh, and to lie with him a fellow prisoner in Dublin Castle.

Of Oliver Plunket's boyhood nothing seemingly is preserved in record except the all-important fact that it was in the household of his kinsman, the Bishop of Ardagh, that he was bred until, at the age of sixteen, he passed to the old Irish College at Rome under the care of a returning papal envoy. Handsome the boy was surely from the later man's portraits, grave perhaps, more certainly studious and devoted, with just as certainly a sense of humor for later it forces its way through his most serious letters and turns the edge of his life of privation.

It was in the Ireland ruled by the Earl of Strafford that these early years were spent. Strafford was not a persecutor of Catholics as such, though what penal laws were a source of gain to the crown were systematically and rigorously administered. His mission was to unite the country and organize its resources as a basis upon which he might build a government less at the mercy of parliamentary schemers and fanatics than the system he had seen growing up at Westminster. Whence to the viceroy the interest of the crown was all decisive. Five years before his coming Charles I had consented, in return for a lavish grant of money, to concede substantial "graces" to the Irish Catholics, notably permission to substitute a simple Oath of Allegiance for the heretical Oath of Supremacy that was the formula *sine qua non*, admitting to all public appointments and validating the most important transactions of private life. For the first time for a generation, Catholics could now take up an inheritance without forswearing their faith, practice the law and medicine, graduate in a University. The concessions were judged a weakness, and in 1634, on Strafford's advice, Charles revoked them.

Two years after this betrayal the able governor planned a second. In the face of royal pledges to hold as good all titles to land that had weathered the upset of the last sixty troubled years, he proposed to resume, for the King, practically the whole of the province of Connaught, relying on an alleged grant of a thirteenth-century king to a nobleman whom Charles I could number among his hundreds of more remote ancestors. By personal assistance at the jury sessions where the decision lay, by much browbeating, imprisonment and fining of reluctant jurymen the Earl forced his will on half a dozen counties, until he met, in Galway, so formidable a resistance from the Earl of Clanricarde, that the affair halted. It never advanced any further, but the scheme, the bad heart it revealed, and the lack of all scruple in the pursuit of injustice, were not without their effect on the Catholic nobility and gentry. Where on this occasion six counties had fallen and only Clanricarde had been strong enough to resist, who could be sure, Antrim, Fingall, Roscommon, that tomorrow he might not be faced with the like iniquity and, under the menace of like threats, fall in his turn. Strafford, it has been recorded and truly, was not unpopular with the mass of the people he ruled, but he left Ireland hated as bitterly by the Catholic lords whose beggary he had planned as by the corrupt Castle oligarchy whose swindling he had exposed, and, where possible, punished.

The Earl of Strafford, his Irish achievement barely laid in foundation, returned to England to help his king against perils more difficult by far than what threatened from Ireland. The eleven years of personal government without personality strong enough to carry responsibility and direct, were bringing in now the inevitable harvest of crisis, and while the agitation in England was hardly come to seething, the Scots rose, and their armies invading England compelled the King to reverse his policy and, summoning a Parliament once more, give disaffection a means to organize and an instrument to destroy himself. The disaffected of a hundred sects, political, religious, economic, were now to have their day, and, achieving power, establish themselves—an oligarchy that grew ever more restricted in number as it grew more fanatic in word and in deed.

One of the first signs of coming change was a cry loud, fierce, and persistent for Catholic blood. It gave to the Church martyrs in England, and in Ireland it was as a last fatal dose to explode the mixture and blow sky high the crazily built construction of the last sixty years. The Parliament was to rule, and extirpation of Papists and Papistry was, avowedly, a leading aim. So Papists in Ireland, with Presbyterian Scots for patterns, were, for once, realist in policy and there broke out that movement of a thousand complications, where at first sight each rebel seems almost a separate rebellion, the Irish rebellion of 1641. It was at one time as valuable a piece in the anti-Catholic armory as the revelations of Maria Monk and the horrors of the Inquisition. Milton, notably, was one of the foremost of those whose industrious lying established the legend. In fact it was a political movement, as well as a religious movement. Anti-English, pro-Catholic, it was also anti-planter, an agrarian movement, the dispossessed of yesterday turning on their despoilers. Violence there was in plenty, looting and murder, outrages of every sort, of course, but for the modern historian the six figure totals of Protestants massacred for Protestantism, scale down to 4,000 unhappy victims of a peasant *jacquerie* with perhaps twice as many who died from cold and exposure. It was only a matter of weeks before this anarchy was in hand, and the rising, a disciplined ordered thing, in the control of national leaders. By the summer of 1642 they had in their hands the whole of the country save Dublin, some few other towns and parts of the eastern coast line.

The rebellion, so far, was a rising of the old Irish stock, but in December 1642, at a meeting on the Hill of Crofty in Meath, the great Anglo-Irish lords joined the Irish by a treaty that pledged common action until the free practice of the Catholic faith was secured and the King's enemies—since August in the field against him—defeated. In that company that rode out to Crofty at Lord Gormanstown's summons, were two at least of the Plunket peers, Lord Fingall and Lord Louth who was Oliver Plunket's godfather. The century had opened with the Catholics oppressed, indeed, but still well able to battle against their oppressors because still possessed of the greater part of the country's wealth. Now at last, with Crofty, the old fatal division between Irish and Anglo-Irish seemed to have healed before the threat of extinction from the Puritan-inspired Parliament at Westminster. At Kilkenny in the May of 1643 a provisional government was set up by the confederates, allegiance sworn to the King, whose handsome head adorned their coinage, and throughout the country the Catholics entered once more into possession of lands and buildings long since ravished from them. The ancient cathedrals were restored and with unbelievable swiftness the effects of a hundred years were rolled away.

It was not to be. The King's representative in Ireland, the Marquis of Ormonde, following the example of his master, played fast and loose with these Catholic defenders of the monarchy and he ultimately sold them to the monarchy's bitterest foes. The old trouble between Irish and Anglo-Irish broke out once more, the Confederate Constitution was ill-devised for a time of war, and slowly through the next five years the cause drifted to the rocks. Assistance had been sought from the Pope, and Urban VIII sent, in 1643, the Oratorian, Scarampo, as envoy to observe and report. Two years later that Pope's successor, Innocent X, sent a more imposing mission headed by the Archbishop of Fermo as Nuncio, the famous Rinuccini. Before he arrived his predecessor had returned, and, from this troubled Ireland where five different factions and their armies contended, took back with him, to make his studies for the priesthood, Oliver Plunket, sixteen years of age.

So from the fringe of the world Oliver Plunket passed, as adolescence dawned, to its very center, from the distant province where all was menace, to the capital resplendent with triumph.

There was a new Pope, Giovanni Battista Pamfili now styled Innocent X; and, as ever in the first hours of a new regime, the morning was all promise. Innocent X was typical of the new race of Popes bred by the Council of Trent, trained theologians, practiced jurists and diplomatists, who from the great schools of the Catholic capital had mounted step by step in a long career of service, nuncios and legates to the Catholic princes abroad, administrators of the Papal States at home. Able, prudent, wary, men of the world under their cassocks of scarlet, they were of all men the least likely to mistake the personal piety of Catholic rulers for a willingness to serve uniquely, in public action, the cause of Our Lord and His Church. A hard task they had, these great clerical statesmen of this last renaissance of the Catholic Commonwealth. The ravages and raids bequeathed by the last century had been fought back now to the last ditch. Italy, Spain and France were safe, most of Germany had been recovered. Poland had been strengthened for the future. But at price of what arrangement between rival Catholic States! Spain, France, the Empire, Venice, and a score of petty princelings besides, ready to call in against one another the heretic and even the Turk! In the war still raging in

Germany while the armies on the Spanish side were led by one Cardinal of the Holy Roman Church, had not another, France's Prime Minister, planned and devised for the heretic enemy, planned indeed so successfully that the Catholic victory was thereby made impossible?

Such colleagues had the Popes of Oliver Plunket's Rome in their cardinalitial days, such a novitiate through thirty and forty years of service, before it fell to their lot as Supreme Pontiffs, themselves to ache under the impossible burden.

Innocent X (1644–1655) was followed by Alexander VII (1655–1667) who as the Nuncio Fabio Chigi had such a share in the diplomacy that ended the Thirty Years' War, that, when archives reveal it, he will rank high indeed among the Popes. Then came Clement IX (1667–1669) last of Papal crusaders.

It was the baroque Rome where Bernini ruled supreme, building for Innocent X the Church of St. Agnes where he lies entombed, and for Alexander VII the splendid porticoes that make the approach to St. Peter's. It was that artistic capital of the world, that happy center of elegant and cultured *flanerie*, of lovely formal gardens, cypress and ilex and diversifying sculpture, where the ecclesiastical world was courtly as never before; Horace and Vergil and Lucretius in the hourly service of that wonderful life where, in the leisured charm of easy scholarship, diplomacy allusively decided fates of churches and of empires. Particularly, of such a Rome, was Alexander VII Chief Priest and King, perhaps a little too much its King, not discerning in the splendor of the sunny sky the presaging tints of afternoon. Later Oliver Plunket, too, was to have his place in this world; but at sixteen he passed it by to enter as a student the tiny Irish College founded a few years earlier by the young Cardinal Ludovisi. Here he lived, and for his studies went to the most famous of all modern theological schools, the Roman College of the Society of Jesus. He made here the usual studies of Philosophy and Theology, and passing thence to the University called the Sapienza graduated in Law, Civil and Canon. He was fortunate in his generation as in his colleges, for it was, in studies as in all else, an age of revival, of great teachers and a new intellectual alertness. In France the glories of the Benedictines of St. Maur were slowly rising, and in the Spanish Netherlands the first generation of Bollandists were laying the foundations of critical historical scholarship. Here in Rome were De Lugo and Pallavicino, the last named ever a treasured friend. Jansenism had hardly travelled as yet beyond the little summer-house where the *Augustinus* was composed. The day was not yet come when the influence of the controversies aroused by it and by the pest of Quietism which was its contemporary, would overshadow the happy optimism that characterized the age's spirituality, and through contagious fear make all men rigorist.

Oliver Plunket loved his College all his life. As Scarampo paid his pension in those days of poverty when he was entered, so in later years he in turn maintained a student out of his tiny professor's salary. He gave to it a vineyard—how acquired or begged we know not—and books too, when, twenty-four years later, he left Rome for ever. In his last hours of life, he willed it the pictures that had decorated his room, and still remained there—to his regret still unframed.

In such surroundings, in that life of monastic seclusion set in the heart of the world's most splendid pageantry which, such is its happy, unique prerogative, detracts nothing thereby from the reality of the seclusion, like thousands of other fortunate alumni of his College and University, receiving in the best years of life the best that life can offer, and Rome, he came to his ordination in the summer of 1654.

He should now, in the normal course of things, have returned to Ireland. Instead, urging to the General of the Jesuits in whose hands dispensation lay "the impossibility, as your Paternity well knows, of now returning to Ireland in accordance with the oath which I have taken," he sought and obtained permission to delay his departure. Rooms were assigned him—no doubt through Scarampo's good offices—in the little house for ever associated with the most Roman of saints, St. Philip Neri, at San Girolamo della Carita, and there for the next few years he lived. Only a few yards away, across the same street, is the venerable College of the English, and as seventy years earlier St. Philip used to hail the future martyrs issuing thence, so now there must often have met the students this destined last of the English Martyrs, the young Irish priest of San Girolamo, lecturer in Theology now at the Missionary College of the Congregation for the Propagation of the Faith.

The years went steadily by. Scarampo in 1655 died one of those holy deaths which so often crown the hidden heroic lives that fill a hundred unsuspected corners of the Roman Pageant; and Oliver Plunket, at Propaganda, began to show himself as a Reformer. "You know well in what condition the studies were when I entered on my duties," he was to write many years after this to the Secretary of Propaganda "and in what condition I left them." He was named as one of the official theological experts who advise the different Congregations, and his gifts—the appointments providing the occasion—brought him acquaintances and friends in all that varied official world. It was now he first made friends with Cerri who was to be his patron and superior when Secretary to Propaganda, with Marcantonio Odescalchi and his more famous kinsman who as the Venerable Innocent XI was to be the great glory of the modern papacy.

With all this brilliance of a learned career, through all the fabric of the splendid life, there ran, of course, threads of a most decided asceticism, for such, again, is the Roman formation. Prayer, regular, fervent and unostentatious, pilgrimages to the shrines, the seven churches, and—to modern notions severest of all self-inflicted penances—the methodical service of the poor patients in the great hospital of S. Spirito: here above all was his spirit formed and the lesson learnt, so that to endure patiently, without hope of release, the well-nigh unendurable could be in years to come his everyday affair, his very life.

Ireland he did not lose sight of during these twenty-five years of Roman life. Thence the news filtered through slowly but continuously, and continuously bad. From the Nuncio at Paris and the Internuncio at Brussels, from the exiled bishops and a hundred individual sources, the ceaseless tale came into the Catholic capital. Closely related to one of the few bishops who contrived to remain in Ireland unmolested, for some time his agent in Curia, related to so many of the Catholic leaders and himself already within the circle of those who mattered in Rome, it was not possible for Oliver Plunket to be other than well-informed of the later phases of the Irish tragedy.

The year in which he had left Ireland was the year of King Charles' last fatal defeat at Naseby. Thenceforward the royal cause slowly sank below the surface in England and in Ireland too. There the Catholic Confederation, betrayed by the King and its dissensions given new life and permanence by the betrayal, saw, after the promise of Benburb, its last armies defeated. In 1649 the Nuncio, despairing, sailed away to France, the one man of military genius died, Owen Roe, and on a black day Oliver Cromwell landed at Ringsend.

The tale of the next few years is horrible still, after all the repetition, but to Oliver Plunket the horror came fresh and actual, the blacker since rapine and massacre seemed destined to permanence as a system. It was a tale of sieges, of surrenders and betrayals, of covenants broken as regularly as made, and breach of covenant followed by simple straightforward massacre of whatever confiding townsfolk came within reach. The country was laid waste, houses, crops, cattle, until Government commissioners could report three-fourths of the cattle as destroyed and four-fifths the arable land a wilderness, and a Cromwellian commander noted a thirty-mile march through what had been the richest of Irish pasturelands with now not a sign of life, no trace of either man or beast. The revenue sank until it was less than half the annual cost of maintaining the English army in occupation. The very garrisons of the conqueror came themselves near to starving. By 1652 of the million and a half inhabitants some six hundred thousand had perished, while thousands more had been sold into slavery in the West Indies and America.

With the conquest went persecution, for a hatred of the Mass and the priests who offered it was, admittedly, the English commander's most powerful inspiration. Hence from whatever pardons were granted the priest was excepted, and for the next terrible years the search was so thorough, its results so sure, that only in the remotest hills and most dangerous bogs were any clergy to be found. Those captured, and they were numbered by the hundred, were shipped aboard the first vessel that lay in harbor bound for foreign parts, and the country where so lately a hierarchy of twenty-six bishops had presided over a Catholic restoration saw those reduced now to a poor half dozen, too old and infirm either to go into exile or to be able to carry out their functions at home.

Cromwell died in Oliver Plunket's first year at Propaganda, and on his death there followed the inevitable anarchy when all the hundred factions of the "saints" fought, squabbled and intrigued to fill the place he left, until in less than two years the Stuarts were once more on the throne. But to the wretched Irish Catholics the Restoration meant little beyond the cessation of the Puritan Inquisition. The economic question, the ownership of the vast lands confiscated from the Catholics since 1642, was solved by giving the first claim to the Cromwellians and Adventurers. The monarchy's Catholic supporters appeared in the arrangement as "Papist rebels." A court was, it is true, appointed to adjudge their claim, but so busy did it promise to be, that a special Act of Parliament decided it should hear no more, and the class which in 1640 still held more than a half of Irish land, now saw its share reduced to a mere one-eighth. Scarce three gentlemen in his diocese, Oliver Plunket wrote to Propaganda, in 1671, had re-acquired their lands after Cromwell's confiscation. And so it was universally.

The desolation in things spiritual was as great, and may be judged from the state of the religious orders where corporate continuity has best preserved the record in detail. The Friars Minor, by 1656, had lost every one of their sixty-four convents and the ten houses of their nuns, while some thirty of their number had glorified the Faith on the scaffold. The Dominicans similarly had lost all their houses—forty-three in all. Thirty friars had been martyred, others were dead of exposure, or exiled beyond the seas. Of the total six hundred a mere hundred and fifty survived. The Jesuits had lost their six colleges and sixty-three of their eighty members. So few priests were left—over a thousand were forcibly exiled—that, in Munster especially, many Catholics were as long as six years without the chance of receiving the Sacraments. Three of the bishops had been put to death, and of the remainder so many had been driven into exile that for a moment it seemed that there lay in wait for the Church in Ireland the fate that afflicted the sister Church in England where the persecuted faithful were mysteriously left a century and a quarter without a bishop at all!

To preserve the hierarchy—reduced now to one bishop in residence, Dr. Patrick Plunket of Ardagh—was the great problem of the day. It was a problem that concerned very nearly Dr. Plunket's agent at Rome. "If our Church at the present day," Cardinal Moran has written, "does not present the sad desolation of England and Scotland, we are indebted under Heaven to these indefatigable men who labored in season and out of season to preserve unbroken…the succession of our chief pastors." Notable among such indefatigables at this most critical of times was Blessed Oliver, and on January 21, 1669, four vacant sees were filled, an old schoolfellow and close friend William Burgatt being appointed to Cashel, and a cousin, Dr. Peter Talbot—for many years during the exile, a confidant of the now restored Stuarts—Archbishop of Dublin. The four new bishops straightway named the Bishop of Ardagh's agent to be their agent too, and his future seemed fixed in a Roman life fuller even than before, when two months later the exiled Archbishop of Armagh died at Paris, and Clement IX cut short the long discussion as to the better man for the vacant see by pointing personally to the best possible, "the certain thing before our eyes…in the city of Rome itself, Oliver Plunket."

The twenty-five years of exile then were ended, and at forty he returned to rule in its hour of desolation, the land he had last seen as a boy of sixteen. He left Rome in the late August, not yet consecrated, despite his most urgent petition, lest a Roman consecration should be an additional embarrassment in the difficult life ahead. Before he went he paid a last visit to his hospital of Santo Spirito, and its Polish superior, taking leave of the Irishman, prophesied the glory to come.

He made his way slowly north to the Internuncio at Brussels—still the official channel for the Holy See's Irish business—to confer with him and to arrange the details of his consecration. This finally took place, in the greatest privacy, at Ghent on Advent Sunday, the bishop of that city officiating with the exiled Bishop of Ferns as one of the assistants. Six weeks later the new Archbishop was in London, lodged in the royal palace (so curious the time in its juxtapositions) in the apartments of the Catholic Queen's chaplain Fr. Philip Howard, the Cardinal of Norfolk to be.

The Queen received him most favorably. He saw the sights in Fr. Howard's hospitable carriage—perhaps secretly met the half Catholic Charles II whom his colleague of Dublin was reputed already to have received into the Church. Then in the first weeks of the new year, passing, as he turned north for the Holyhead road, the gallows whose last hallower he was eleven years later to be, he came at last, late, through the usual vexations of that terrible road and crossing, to his kingdom and his See (March, 1670).

He plunged without an hour's delay into the work awaiting him, the work which was to occupy him unceasingly until the day of his arrest, nine and a half years of the continuous labor that only genius and sanctity can accomplish. His predecessor had long been an exile. The diocese was a prey to dissension, the Archbishop of Dublin had warned the Holy See in recommending candidates. In the province there was but one suffragan, the old Bishop of Ardagh now translated to Meath. (He had found it best to live in the Capital, and thence ruling his diocese, had contrived in his hiding place to ordain some two hundred and fifty priests). Derry, another suffragan See, had not known a bishop for a century, and even in the "good" days before 1641 Raphoe, it was reported, had only sixteen priests and in all its wild territory no more than seven hundred discoverable Catholics.

Confirmation was the first necessity and within six weeks he had administered the Sacrament to ten thousand eager candidates. There remained—so he estimated—another fifty thousand in his province to whom it must be given, and in 1673 he was able to inform Propaganda he had, in four years, confirmed 48,655. They marveled in Ireland at the gently-bred bishop's endurance. "We have no fixed churches or oratories, and celebrate Mass and the Sacraments often in the fields, now at one place now at another" a report of 1669 had informed the Sacred Congregation, and it was in fields and woods and caves, with the wind and the rain often enough for setting, that the rite was given—"nor often enough" wrote the admiring Vicar-General of Raphoe "is there other food for him beyond a little oatcake and salt butter, nor had he drink other than milk." For during the whole of his episcopate Oliver Plunket suffered acutely from lack of money, was never, in fact, very far removed from destitution. His revenue, nominally, was £62 a year, a pound from each priest of his diocese, but he never in any one year received more than £55. Sometimes it sank to a single figure sum; and when for his trial he was taken to London, he had to sell chalice and pectoral cross to pay the expense of his journey.

The greatest tax on his poor purse was his correspondence with Rome. Never was there a more faithful Roman than Oliver Plunket and never did any bishop do more to keep the Holy See informed of the fortunes of the church committed to him. "He renewed or rather established anew at great expense," say the Prelates of the Provincial Synod of 1678, "correspondence with the Holy See which for many years before he arrived had been interrupted, or rather become extinct." Scarcely one letter a year had passed before his time. "I do not hesitate to say that I wrote more letters during the last four years than the Irish Bishops during the preceding thirty years," he wrote to the Internuncio in 1673, and he appeals to the Archives of the Congregation in proof. It is one of the most frequent themes of his astonishingly regular correspondence—the necessity of the Holy See being well informed, the expense of the inevitable letters and the fear that this will soon prove too much for his pocket. The cost amounted in fact to practically the half of his tiny income, and his petitions, despite the humor that would laugh the strain away, are often near indeed to tears. "I have done and written and labored more these ten years than all the other prelates of this kingdom together, and I now find myself without a house, and all my money amounts to fifty-three crowns." As for the assistance so continually promised him by the Congregation, "Through Mgr. Airoldi I received 100 crowns; Mgr. Falconieri sent me fifty more. This is all I received for myself during the ten years." And after another such exposition:

> I hope Their Eminences will compensate my expenses and labors and faithfulness in serving them. I hope they will not reply: "When you shall have done all these things say, *We are unprofitable servants*."

The contrast could not have been greater than between the ordered secure dignity of the Roman life, ascetic though it might be, and the daily round of this archbishop, hunted from the woods to the hills and thence once more down to the woods and bogs to find his refuge in the very ditches. For hunted he was often, living for months together in the open, and liable to the hue and cry at any moment. "All enjoy liberty and ease," the Holy See had been informed in 1670 "thanks to the benign influence of the King of England. Ecclesiastics may be publicly known, and are permitted to exercise their functions without any impediment." Nevertheless at this very time the Archbishop went about as Captain Brown, complete with sword and pistols, and the years that followed the anti-Catholic reaction in 1673 were years when he scarcely ever was at ease. In 1674–1675 for fifteen months on end he lived in the wilds, as he did again in the anxious year that preceded his arrest: and this although personally he was on good terms with the Viceroy, Lord Berkeley of Stratton, the two powers more than once working together for the pacification of the distracted country. With Berkeley's predecessor too, the Presbyterian Robartes, he stood in good repute and the Earl of Essex, who ruled from 1677, was also to bear witness—too late, to the King's indignation, to save him from death—that in all things he had worked loyally for the cause of peace.

He was never in any sense a politician, and never strove, as did perhaps his colleague of Dublin, to use what influence he had in high places to promote the affairs of the Church. And in a day when episcopal appointments went, almost universally, by court favor, he was bold enough to discourage the practice at Propaganda. "I believe," he wrote, "it is not desirable to advance those who seek for promotion through the English Court, for such persons will always adopt the doctrines of the Sorbonne, and should any question arise they will adhere to the King and not to the Apostolic See." From the politico-religious activity which in these years following the Treaty of Dover was making a last bid to regain England for the Faith through the Stuart Kings, he kept himself carefully aloof. There was more urgent work to hand, occupation for a lifetime in caring for the spiritualities of the seven bishopless dioceses of his province, in restoring ecclesiastical discipline, establishing schools, confirming and ordaining; working off the arrears of a whole generation where all had been left to decay.

In Drogheda, the chief town of his diocese, he set up a college and brought the Jesuits to teach. They had been his masters of old, and now for a time he lived with them once more. "They assist me," he wrote, "in resolving difficult cases, and in writing letters to different parts of the kingdom when necessary." This college, where also some of his clerics read their Theology, was perhaps the work nearest his heart, and the Jesuits, for their labors in it, especially dear to him. Of the College's hundred and fifty boys some were destined for the priesthood, and many of the onetime professor's long letters recur to this pressing problem of how best to train the future priests for this difficult mission. Rome he considered the best school of all. Men educated there "enter more fully into the views of the Holy See." And he had in mind not the schools which had trained him, but the College of Propaganda where he had taught with such distinction. "For missionary priests there is no college in the world better suited" he declared, and urgently protested against less adequate solutions by which "our priests will be *infra mediocritatem.*"

To review and set in order the whole machinery of ecclesiastical government he held more than one synod—two indeed within three months of his arrival in 1670, one of the Bishops at Dublin, and, in the October of the same year a Provincial Council at Clones. Systematically he visited the other dioceses of his province, courageously facing the unusual problems they presented, and where drastic action alone could cure, never shrinking from the unpleasantness to himself involved therein.

One such controversy must have been a sorrow to him, that with the Archbishop of Dublin, his cousin, as to the precedence of the two Sees, in which Oliver Plunket temperately, but no less forcibly than his heady opponent, defended the traditional claims of Armagh. The dispute did not strain the personal relation, and when Blessed Oliver was taken to Dublin Castle after his arrest he found himself in a cell adjacent to Peter of Dublin who had preceded him by a good twelve months, and who twelve months later died there, Confessor for the Faith. More important in their results to himself were the troubles that arose from his zeal to correct clerical abuses—among his own secular clergy and among the Franciscans too. Of the Franciscans he would no doubt have agreed with what his friend the Archbishop of Cashel wrote to Rome in 1684. "The Franciscan Friars of strict observance do more good in this kingdom than any other religious order." But in 1670 they still suffered unduly from the effects of the ecclesiastical anarchy that had prevailed for twenty years, and where Blessed Oliver thought the remedy lay in new methods and stricter administration he conscientiously pointed it out. There were he considered too many small convents (seventy in all Ireland), too many novitiates by far (twelve or thirteen in his province, thirty in Ireland altogether), and a province that included all Ireland was more than one provincial could be expected to govern. Of these tiny novitiates, he wrote to Rome that they were not real convents but they "live in a sort of huts, without choir and without real education."

Again he speaks of the novices "bred amongst the serving men and maids, guests and other chance strangers," and complains of the candidates that "they bring in the halt and the blind and compel them to come in, and whilst gourds are sown it cannot be expected that melons should be gathered." Moreover Ireland was a convenient dumping ground for the awkward subjects of superiors abroad, and it is not surprising that the Archbishop was able to complain of extravagance in dress and living. "Almost every friar has a horse and servant…would not the money be better spent on books…especially as many of you say your order is in great need of money?"

In a kindly letter he brought these points to the notice of the Provincial Chapter, and little by little they were no doubt corrected, though Blessed Oliver did not live to see the novitiate system he complained of abolished, and the novices sent abroad, as he had suggested, for training under more settled conditions.

"Franciscan dissensions have for many years disturbed the spiritual tranquility of the kingdom and they still disturb it," he wrote bluntly in 1672 and a contemporary letter of the Earl of Essex, then Viceroy, throws such light on the character of some of the dissensions, and on the power of a few to create nationwide trouble that it is worth recalling. The letter is addressed to the Duke of Ormonde:

> "…beleeving it to be one of the most important things I could do both for His Majesties Service and the security of his Protestant subjects here, either to keep these men divided or, if they were united to breeke them again, I made use of some of their ffriers, who alwaies have their little wrangle with the Secular Clergy, to set up faction against their Bishop, and by encouraging these little annemostys among themselves at length brought them to that pass

> that they openly accused one another of exercising Ecclesiasticall jurisdiction contrary to the Laws of the Land. Severall examinations were taken and the Bishop brought to swear one against another. Which has renewed their division to that degree as I beleeve they are now irreconsilable. By the addresse of the house of Commons all the regulars are to be banished, and should I put this exactly in execution, I must send all these poor Friars abroad who have done us this service and expose them to great severity there… They are but very few, I am sure not above six or eight who have been principally instrumental in this affaire"—and though no public provision can be made no doubt some gentleman in the country will look after them!

Like every reformer Oliver Plunket made enemies, bitter enemies, and incorrigible religious whom he was the means of exposing and some of his own secular clergy who were at least as bad—ex-priests turned banditti who had long been familiar figures in Irish jails—were to be the instruments of his betrayal and death, their opportunity the Popish Plot.

Beneath the apparent gaiety and folly of the reign of Charles II there seethed a menacing life of plot and counterplot, where the rival conspirators were on the one side the King, and on the other his more crazy subjects. The return of the Stuarts in 1660 was the end of an all too short golden age for a whole world of fanatics of the Fifth Monarchy type, their minds filled with the prospect of joy to come in massacring the enemies of the Lord who abounded outside the confines of their little assemblies. They had found patronage and support in the days of Cromwell, and for one dangerous moment they showed their willingness to put theory into practice in the first days of Charles II. They were sternly put down, but their activities ran on continuously below the surface, providing a useful reserve of enthusiastic, Bible-inspired hate for any politician vile enough to enlist and direct it. From this underworld were to come the actors and the legends of the Popish Plot, and the pious zeal which hoped, through the "revelations," to destroy, along with Papistry, the monarchy which, to the faction's disgust, had survived 1649.

The other plot was much more subtle, for its leading spirit, the shrewdest and ablest man of his time, had in continual play half a dozen conflicting worlds to none of which could he trust himself, and on all of which he must yet depend to defeat the latent republicans, keep his throne and life itself. Charles II was a bad man with good instincts matched against men worse even than himself with whom, in their hatred of all that savored of Catholicism, any wickedness that was useful passed for virtue. The support of Presbyterians fearful of the anarchy of the wild Independents had alone made the Restoration possible, and it was on a coalition of Presbyterians and Cavaliers that his throne rested. He was to be the instrument of their policies, and to secure his docility they systematically kept him short of even the moneys they voted him. To Charles, meaning in his own phrase "to be a King and not a doge," a short cut to monarchy independent of the ever recurring factions seemed to offer itself through an arrangement with France, hard cash as the price of the foreign policy which he kept in his own control. Whence the Treaty of Dover. Whence also growing dissatisfaction on the part of all sections in his Parliament, and, after the first ten years of the reign a fairly universal distrust of the King, and a growing fear of what he intended—a fear none the less powerful because it was vague.

One thing all parties had in common, a hatred and a fear of Catholicism which the propaganda attributing the Great Fire of 1666 to Catholics fanned as nothing before had fanned it save the Gunpowder Plot in the time of the King's grandfather. That grandfather, James I, and the King's own father were almost the only wholehearted Protestants of the family Englishmen had known. Whether Charles II was Catholic or not, his mother was a Catholic and his wife, his only surviving brother and sister too, and more than one lady of his *seraglio*. Catholics came to court, and were admitted to the King's intimacy and his council, while for the services of the Queen, there was in the palace itself the Catholic chapel-royal, elaborately served by a score of foreign friars.

Material for trouble of the very worst kind where Catholics were concerned lay then to hand in plenty all through the years of Oliver Plunket's episcopacy, and it needed only the ingenuity of some highly placed opponent of the King to rouse an all powerful anti-Catholic storm and commit the King to the suspicion of being on the Catholic side, and there would be achieved the aim of all the underground political activity of the last seventeen years. Charles II would go down and the monarchy, as the monarchy had gone down before a like cleverly organized piece of work in 1641. This criminal achievement is the chief title to fame of the first Lord Shaftesbury, whose villainy, unfortunately, Dryden's genius has so wonderfully etched that the degree of his wickedness is forgotten in admiration of the artist's skill in picturing it. Oates, Bedloe and the rest of the vile crew are, beside their chief, poor pale satans indeed.

They came forward and told their tales, the nation believed, the panic grew, and Catholic blood began to flow once more. One man in the country knew the truth and all the truth, knew the Catholics innocent, but saw no hope of surviving the storm and defeating the power that had raised it, save by allowing it for the moment to wreak its worst where it would. So he signed the death warrants for the many martyrs. "More he could not do: had he insisted on exercising his right of pardon, with the mob up and the city armed, revolution must almost certainly have followed… 'Let the blood lie on them that condemn them,' he said, 'for God knows I sign with tears in my eyes.'"

A time then when in a State Trial a Catholic had but to be shown to a London jury for his condemnation to follow.

The storm had been raging for a good eighteen months before it struck the Archbishop of Armagh. The last illness and death of the old Bishop of Meath had brought him to Dublin in the last days of

November, 1679, and on December 6 he was arrested and taken to Dublin Castle.

An apostate religious, MacMoyer, had earlier in the previous year denounced him as conspiring to murder the King, but the Grand Jury, knowing MacMoyer's manner of life, had thrown out the bill. Once more in gaol himself MacMoyer found there another ex-priest, Edmond Murphy, a secular of the Archbishop's own diocese, a one-time dignitary degraded for his double life of parish priest and leader of the local banditti. These two enemies aching for revenge found their opportunity in a third gaol-bird, an Englishman in Lord Shaftesbury's service as tutor and trainer to the perjured witnesses who in the London courts swore to the different details of the plot, one William Hetherington. The Protestant Bishop of Meath—ex-officer of the Cromwellian armies—lent his influence and with that and Shaftesbury's too the plan of campaign was settled, and instructions for the arrest sent to Dublin.

The next seven months were spent in hunting up likely perjurers, the Viceroy, Ormonde, well disposed, delaying the trial until, once more, instructions from London forced his hand, and on July 23, 1680, the Archbishop appeared in the dock at Dundalk before a jury on which, by special command from England, no Catholic sat. To repel the charges against him of conspiracy to bring in the French and to murder the King he had thirty-two witnesses, but the case was never heard. For two whole days the court waited for the crown witnesses to put in an appearance and when, on the third day, MacMoyer arrived, half-drunk, it was to ask that the trial be put back as Murphy had not yet been found. After this fiasco there should have remained for the Archbishop nothing beyond the formality of presenting himself at three successive assizes and he would regain his liberty. But the ex-Cromwellian Bishop was insistent and between him and Shaftesbury, apparently, the thing was arranged, and in October Oliver Plunket was cited outside the kingdom to stand his trial in London. Thither he sailed on October 21, 1680, ten months after his arrest.

A like procedure had been followed more than a century earlier with Oliver Plunket's predecessor, Dr. Richard Creagh. The Lord Deputy had advised Elizabeth that she stood a better chance of killing her man through a London jury. No Dublin jury would convict him. So it fell out. At the Dublin trial he was acquitted. The jury were imprisoned and fined for their verdict and Archbishop Creagh thereupon taken over to London, where, however, he was never tried again but left to rot in the Tower till his death twenty years later.

Blessed Oliver reached London and was straightway confined in Newgate, in the cell lately occupied by the martyred provincial of the Jesuits. He was kept very strictly and for six months allowed to see no one, not even his servant. The case came on at the Winter Assizes, but so gross and evident were the contradictions of the crown witnesses that the Grand Jury would not find a bill. He lay, therefore, in Newgate yet another six months until May 5, 1681, the day fixed for the trial. One accused of treason in those days was not allowed counsel for his defence, his witnesses were not sworn, nor was he allowed to know precisely the nature of the charges against him before the indictment was read as the trial opened. Hence the Archbishop's immediate plea on May 5 for a respite until such time as he could gather from Ireland witnesses and the necessary documents. Five weeks were granted him—a delay all too short at a time when the single journey might take a fortnight and more. Contrary winds detained the few witnesses who could be found courageous enough to testify, and the Irish judges, for a legal quibble, refused the authentic copies of the record of the previous trial. Hence when the Archbishop reappeared in court on June 8, 1681, he had no defence but his denial of the charges.

The trial proceeded in the usual fashion, judges and crown lawyers combining to protect the crown witnesses from effective cross-examination, and to harass and browbeat the prisoner. Nine witnesses were brought against him, four of them, alas, ex-priests. The worst of these, Edmond Murphy, repented when too late. He went into hiding and was only discovered after much search—praying in the chapel of the Spanish Embassy. When he came into court, he so hedged and faltered—to delay the case, it has been suggested, until Blessed Oliver's witnesses could arrive—that night found him too in Newgate for wasting the time of the court. The Archbishop made skillful use of what opportunities were allowed him to cross-examine these wretched perjurers and break down their credit, but lacking witnesses and the corroboration of documents it availed nothing at that bar where he was already condemned. He made a dignified protest against the unjust novelty of the whole affair. "I am come here where no jury knows me nor the quality of my adversaries. If I had been in Ireland I would have put myself upon my trial tomorrow, without any witnesses, before any Protestant jury that knew both them and me." From the London of that day Ireland was as remote as Egypt is today, its inhabitants a people as strange and unfamiliar. "Your Lordship sees how I am dealt with," he protested in conclusion. "I have not time to bring my witnesses or my records...I am brought out of my native land where these men and I lived, and where my witnesses and records are." The end was of course inevitable. Jeffreys addressed the jury for the Crown, the Lord Chief Justice summed up against him, and the jury duly found him guilty. To which he answered simply: *Deo Gratias.*

A week later he was brought up for judgment. It was the longed-for opportunity to bring out a public declaration of what inspired his prosecution and the whole bloody business, the Faith he and his fellow-sufferers professed. In a skillfully prepared speech he exposed the worthlessness of the testimony on which he was condemned, protested his innocence and cited the witness of one viceroy after another to prove his continuous loyalty. The criticism was unanswerable, and unable to defend the indefensible, unwilling to face the ridiculous task of proving this evidently harmless innocent man the leading traitor in a scheme of foreign invasion, the Lord Chief Justice took the easier road, and went to the heart of the matter, that his Faith and his labors for it were the greatest treason of all. "Yours is treason of the highest nature, it is treason in truth against God and your King and the country where you lived. You have done as much as you could to dishonor God in this case, for the bottom of your treason was your setting up your false religion, than which there is not anything more displeasing to God, or more pernicious to mankind in the world—a religion that is ten times worse than all heathenish superstitions, the most dishonorable and derogatory to God and His glory of all religions or pretended religions whatever... So that certainly a greater crime there cannot be committed against God than for a man to endeavor the propagation of that religion." He then invited him to apostatize and passed on him the degrading sentence that in England was the traitor's lot.

There remained to him seventeen days of life. They were what all the days had been since his first coming to prison, days of prayer and recollection and penance. Once more he was back in his little room at San Girolamo, not a care in the world now to worry him save his soul's salvation. The weary business of the trial, the duty of making a good fight, the anxiety lest the real reason for his death should be so covered that his death would add to religion's difficulties, all these now were ended. There were left himself and God. An English Benedictine, Dom Maurus Corker, lying in the same gaol, assisted him, and like some young inexperienced novice the Archbishop placed himself in his direction. The long solitude that had been the regime of his first nine months in Newgate was at last relaxed. He received visitors, he wrote his last letters. They are full of that affection for family, friends, and old associations that was his characteristic, and they preserve to us in golden letters the names of his benefactors. The death that lay before him, the detail of its horrors, he prayed over and accepted so often in spirit that by God's grace he could write "compared to the death of the Cross, that of Tyburn, as I hear the description of it, is but a flea biting." Easily, as only a man can whose natural courage is supernaturally informed, he writes in the same tone to his nephew Michael Plunket at the Irish College: "I expect daily to be brought to the place of execution, where my bowels are to be cut out and burned before my face and then my head to be cut off, etc., which death I embrace willingly. I desire to be dissolved, *cupio dissolvi*, etc." And again: "I did expect yesterday to be brought to execution, but finding I am not to be brought to it until Friday or Saturday, I thought fit to write you these few lines." "In truth his holy life merited for him this glorious death," said his friend the Archbishop of Cashel, and we may well think that in these weeks when the prison cloistered him, holiness matured to sanctity, and the martyrdom came to a bishop already confessor.

On the appointed day, July 1st, 1681, he was drawn at the horse's tail from Newgate through London, the long two miles or more by which so many had already gone to their victory and crown. Of all that glorious band he was to be the last, and of them all he was the only bishop, for the one other bishop martyred in England had suffered on Tower Hill. At Tyburn, before an immense crowd, he preached his last sermon, prayed his last prayer, calling on Our Lady and the Saints to aid him. Then the Law had its way.

To the Catholics of the country where he died he left his body, and in unforgettable words an acknowledgment of their thought for him. "The English Catholics were here most charitable to me. They spared neither money nor gold to relieve me, and in my trial did all that even my brother would do. They are rare Catholics and most constant sufferers." Irish bishops in the past had pleaded at Rome the cause of England's desolated church, and now in the person of their Primate had given to it the last of its martyrs. His passion had been for the London Catholics an opportunity gratefully accepted. Is it too much to see in this brotherly charity when an Irishman came to glorify by his death the English capital, an augury of the happier relations between the two churches that mark the present hour? And of such a happier age who more suitable as protector and patron than Blessed Oliver Plunket?

THADDEUS MORIARTY, O.P. (c. 1605–1653)

by ALICE CURTAYNE

THADDEUS MORIARTY WAS BORN EARLY IN THE SEVENTEENTH century in Castledrum, a district which extends along the coast, five miles west of the village of Castlemaine, in the County Kerry. All nature might have combined to make that coastland secluded: immediately to the north, a towering great shoulder of land, Slieve Mish, rises up to thrust its arm far out into the Dingle peninsula, overshadowing Castledrum in the heights of Cahirconree and Baurtregaum. If the boy went down to the shore, the very waters on which he gazed are almost land-locked, shut off from the Atlantic ocean by Inch strand, a tongue of land stretching across Castlemaine Harbor, inside which the waves ripple softly in a quietude apart.

Moriarty's father was the chieftain of a powerful Kerry clan. The name is still ubiquitous there. King, in his history of the county, estimated four hundred and thirty-seven families of the name. Thaddeus Moriarty was born in the family mansion of Castledrum while his people were still in the noontide of their strength. But he lived to see that home in ruins, and his eldest brother, who had inherited the chieftaincy, driven out and dispossessed in the rising of 1641.

Yet in that remote spot, doubly enclosed from the world by mountain and harbor barrier, communication with the Continent was close and constant. The culture that persisted in the mountain homes of the chieftains was astonishing in its vigor and modernity. Catholic education being then banned in Ireland, every Irish family of standing sent its sons abroad to be educated. In this way, and particularly when a vocation to the priesthood declared itself both in Thaddeus and in his brother, Dominic, they were sent as a matter of course to Spain, where they had the choice of six or seven Irish ecclesiastical colleges. No record exists of the whole course followed by Thaddeus, but he chose the Dominican Order. In the year 1627, he was certainly in St. Peter Martyr's, Toledo, at that time the foremost theological college in Spain, for his name occurs in a list sent to Propaganda of the Irish Dominican students of that year. Thaddeus further appears to have been one of the novices of Dominic O'Daly, called "Dominic of the Rosary," sometime while the latter was prefect of the Lisbon convent between the years 1634 and 1640. It is O'Daly who tells us, in his *History of the Geraldines*, that Thaddeus completed his studies in Lisbon.

His intellect was keen and it developed rapidly in that cultural and artistic world so far removed from the rugged scenery of his birthplace. He followed his academic studies up to the highest point permissible in his Order and received the degree of Master of Theology. In college it was said of him that he was fully as much a man of prayer as of study. About the year 1634, the Bishop of Ardfert, Moriarty's native diocese, established a seminary in Tralee. The next time we hear of Thaddeus, he has returned from Spain and is teaching in this seminary as one of the Professors.

He seems to have come immediately to the fore in the ecclesiastical world of his day. His character was as outstanding as his intellectual acquirements. In the year 1643 he was appointed Prior of Holycross Abbey in Tralee. The same year his name appears as Definitor at a Provincial Chapter held in Kilkenny. This city was the most interesting place in Ireland that particular year. During the previous Autumn, the Confederation of Kilkenny had gathered there. Its meetings continued all during 1643. It is possible, even likely, that

Thaddeus Moriarty was present at some of them.

In the year 1645, the Archbishop of Fermo, Baptist Rinuccini, sailed into Kenmare Bay with supplies of money and arms for the Confederates. Yet they met with no success. After four years of a losing fight, when peace was broached, the Confederation was not in a position to dictate. The Papal Nuncio returned to Rome, considering his mission a failure. Peace was concluded in 1649, mainly on the understanding that the penal laws were to be repealed. But they were not repealed. One fortnight after the signing of that treaty, the English beheaded their king, and later Cromwell sailed for Ireland, where many were still upholding the royalist cause.

During those two years Prior Thaddeus Moriarty had been quietly fulfilling his duties in Holycross Abbey, Tralee. Without entering largely into the historical happenings of the period, the reader should recall the kind of news that was being brought to Kerry in the months after Cromwell's landing in Dublin in the August of 1649. Every fresh tidings tolled the dirge of the Irish Catholic cause. Cromwell had commenced with Drogheda, which showed a spirited resistance. Now whenever this happened, whenever a town offered resistance, he retaliated by a massacre of the garrison and inhabitants as soon as he had effected an entrance. This he did in order to deter other towns from resisting and in general the lessons he gave were effective. His method made his task easier and quicker. After Drogheda was taken, Trim, Dundalk, Carlingford and Newry surrendered in quick succession. Wexford held out for a while, so a garrison of three thousand with two thousand civilians were put to death in the marketplace when the walls were stormed. Then New Ross, Cork, Youghal, Kinsale, Dungarvan, even Kilkenny and Clonmel were taken. Cromwell's campaign had been impressive; he felt so sure of the situation that he was able to leave Ireland within less than a year, the country firmly gripped again and his son-in-law, Ireton, in command.

The thunders of the conquering army—terror flying before them—plague, famine and death in their wake, came steadily nearer.

In October, 1651, Limerick was taken, but Ireton died of plague shortly afterwards and was replaced in command by Edmund Ludlow. The story of this town's surrender had a personal interest for Thaddeus Moriarty. The siege had lasted five months, and in that interval five thousand had died of famine or plague within the city. When at last the Cromwellians forced an entrance they came upon Terence Albert O'Brien, Bishop of Emly, and Provincial of the Irish Dominicans, administering the Last Sacraments to the dying in the pest-house. They seized him, hanged him on All Saints' Eve, then battered the dead body with clubs until it lost human semblance and left it hanging a considerable time as a warning, finally setting the head on a pole over one of the city gates. O'Brien's mother was alive and a witness to these things; she was given her son's pectoral cross. Now Terence Albert O'Brien and Thaddeus Moriarty had been class-fellows at St. Peter Martyr's in Toledo. The two Irish students had together shared exile and experience of foreign lands. Moriarty conserved all a student's memories of O'Brien: memories of gaiety, of restiveness, of long silent hours of study, of raillery, of unspoken pride in each other's achievements. The story of the fall of Limerick should have been Moriarty's cue to take to his heels. He went on with his work in Tralee.

After Limerick, Galway surrendered to Ludlow in May 1652. Then the army came south, taking various small castles on the way. Their work became increasingly easy. Things had gone fearfully hard with the civilian population, who, decimated by plague and famine, were now almost wiped out. Horrible pictures are painted of the plight of the people. Ludlow, in his march, saw along the roads of Ireland what Moryson had witnessed fifty years previously: crowds of skeleton corpses, their mouths stained green from eating nettles and docks. The English were in Kerry by the Autumn. Ross Castle in Killarney surrendered. Ludlow then opened negotiations with the last of the Irish Catholic leaders to lay down arms, Piaras Ferriter, Chieftain of West Kerry, who was bard as well as soldier.

This brings the Confederate War very close to the subject of our study, for Piaras Ferriter's wife was Margaret Moriarty, sister to Thaddeus. Ferriter's name lives on today as one of the four great poets of Kerry. His praise of his wife's beauty gives us the only clue we possess to the appearance of Thaddeus. Margaret is described as "tall, slender, blue-eyed and beauteous." It may be that Thaddeus had some share in the family good looks.

While the negotiations were proceeding between Ludlow, entrenched in Ross Castle, and Ferriter, who held a stronghold in Dingle, the latter was seized by treachery and imprisoned. The Cromwellian victory was complete. The manner in which that victory was ratified filled the people with sickened dismay. All except the very poor (who were needed as serfs on the land) were ordered to leave their homes in the three provinces of Ulster, Leinster and Munster and transplant themselves by a given date to the waste lands of Connaught, where they were permitted to hold small allotments. "Any Catholics of those ordered away—young or old—men or women—found in any of the three provinces after that date, might be killed by whoever met them. Moreover, they were not permitted to live within four miles of the sea or of any town, or within two miles of the Shannon." The remnant of the Confederate army, thirty-four thousand men, fled from the country to enlist in foreign service under the flags of France, Spain, and Austria. Widows and orphans met a fearful fate: they were rooted out of their hiding-places and sent overseas in slave gangs to the West Indies; even children of twelve and fourteen were thus sold into slavery. All the transported population succumbed to the foreign climate within a few years.

This exodus of a people was in its full tide when the threat for which Thaddeus Moriarty was waiting came to him. During the happenings described, he had labored on among the stricken people. Now the penal laws against Catholics, especially against priests, began to be enforced with increasing severity. In January 1653, all priests were warned to leave the country within sixty days under pain of death. When the time limit had expired, Moriarty was still in his place as Prior of Holycross Abbey. Particular concern was shown for his welfare. I know not how to account for this except that, Tralee being what is called a "planted" town, and its taking having cost Ludlow nothing, he was disposed to temporize in this case. It is probable that Father Moriarty was very popular even among aliens to his race and faith. At any rate, he was not arrested even when he was known to be ignoring the edict. Instead, a friendly caution was privately conveyed to him and he was offered a safe-conduct out of the country. He refused to go.

It had indeed become the practice among the native Irish to ignore rulings on the part of the foreign power when these were both preposterous in their nature and impossible in their enforcement, as they frequently were. Often a sort of grim humor characterized the situations. The fixed resolve of the defeated people to preserve their religion had become a huge perplexity to their prosperous aggressors, who imagined at times that if they could make them conform exactly with their conquerors in externals, a change of religious heart would follow in due course. Thus statutes were passed defining the manner of riding a horse, of clipping the beard, of speaking, the number of yards of material for a woman's dress, even its color, and the type of hat to be worn!—all with the object of forcing the Irish to look and behave exactly like the English. But such statutes as these were never enforced; they remained dead letters, because no nation could provide the machinery for enforcing such legislation. It is unlikely however that Thaddeus Moriarty was acting on the precedent of successful defiance of law. He knew that the edict against him would be enforced. He remembered Terence O'Brien.

Sometime during the Autumn of 1653, in his Abbey of Holycross, he was handed the warrant for his arrest. On the facade of the Abbey were sculptured the arms of the Desmonds who had founded it: an arm and hand wielding a sword. Some of the carved stones of the ancient facade are preserved in the present Dominican church in

Tralee, which was built in 1862 when the foundation was restored. Thaddeus Moriarty was the last Prior to pass out through the portals of the old Abbey, where twelve of the Geraldines were buried. If his eyes rested for a moment on the sculptured hand and sword, he must have seen the symbol with a great sadness. That sword, although not native, had fought well for the Catholic cause. But the sword of the Geraldines had been broken long since. No hand was raised that day in defence of Father Moriarty.

The military escort whom Ludlow's Commander in Kerry, one Brigadier Nelson, had sent with the warrant, informed the Prior that he was to accompany them to Ross Castle, where the trial was to take place. Father Moriarty set out with them immediately, for they were to walk and the distance is long, eighteen miles, assuming that they took the direct route—that old road to Killarney, which runs straight as an arrow from Tralee past the base of the Slieve Mish mountains. It was and is a rough road and even soldiers trained to route-marching would take the best part of six hours to traverse it.

The priest had thus plenty of leisure to reflect on his choice. His road to Calvary was a long one. Under the heavy military guard, he passed out of Tralee by what is now the Ballymullen road. At Farmers' Bridge, where no bridge then stood, the pace was relaxed while they forded the Lee. Here the roughest part of the road begins in the ascent over Garraun, where the oddly notched peak of Knockawaddra shifts away to the right. Father Moriarty stumbled and fell, but immediately resumed his march. On cresting this road at its highest point, at what is now called Quill's Cross, the MacGillycuddy Reeks that rise beyond Killarney swing suddenly into view with a quality of sheer surprise. The prisoner lifted his eyes to those mountains whence he knew no help of man would come to him. Death was dancing before him all the way.

Yet in that long road some sorrowful and comprehending eyes must have rested on the escort. Father Moriarty is said to have been a man of markedly mild disposition, slow to anger, to whom violence was foreign. There was no cause cited against him save the religious one. If it be asked why no hands were raised to rescue this man of peace and learning from armed soldiery, the answer is in his country's defeat. No better symbol of it could be found than Thaddeus Moriarty disappearing over the brow of the hill under such a guard. The whole nation was keeping step with him on a martyr's way. The Confederate army was by this time no more. The civilian population who were not dying of hunger or plague were mostly hiding, fearing death or transportation. One remembers the story of Ludlow in his march discovering a band of these in a cave and, since weapons could not reach them, trying to smoke them out; when all the fugitives had been killed, the soldiers noted that a priest must have been among them, because a chalice and vestments were found in the cave.

The road traversed by Father Moriarty is beautiful, particularly in Autumn, when those uplands are full of the music of streams and the copses are touched with gold. He marked at intervals along his way where the flame of some late rowan-berry still lingered. But the blue splendor of the Reeks beyond Killarney is the glory of that journey. These, as the road falls and curves, seem momentarily to dip and swerve out of sight, only to tower again majestically, as though crowding around the pilgrim in solemn surmise, or in benediction. The Gap of Dunloe, with a patch of sky shining through, is visible all the way; and there are perfect glimpses of the reaping hook that is Caran Tual, inverted to the heavens.

The soldiers with their steady jog-trot constantly outpaced the priest. Not that he was out of training, for he was accustomed to scouring the glens with the miserable remnant of his people, but he was hardly in military training. He was noticed to stumble a second time. There was little converse between prisoner and guard; no sound for mile after mile but the even tramp of feet, the rattle of the soldiers' muskets and the friar's labored breathing. Nevertheless those hard-bitten ironsides were aware of something that emanated from their prisoner, something which filled them with, I do not say compunction, but a sort of subdued gravity. If these men were among the thirteen thousand who had come over with Cromwell and had gone through the whole campaign, they were incapable of compunction. They reeked of blood. Yet in this instance they showed an unwonted humanity. Unable to relax their pace, for they were under stringent orders and their arrival timed, the third occasion Father Moriarty fell, one of them cut a stout stave from a wayside tree and gave it to the priest to help him along.

A second river had to be forded, the Maine, not negligible as rivers go, sufficiently broad here and beginning in Autumn to show white caps on its surface. This river was full of memories for the priest; it joins the sea near his old home at Castledrum. At this date it was twelve years since the Moriarty family mansion there had been destroyed.

Beyond Longfield Cross, the ancient road to Killarney wound to the right over Buille Hill, skirting what used to be a thick wood, and ran by Aglish to Lough Leane. The third river to be forded was encountered on this part of the old road. Killarney's approaching nearness is signaled when that whimsical little flat hump of a mountain, so appropriately named Stoompa, comes clearly into view, as though blocking the end of the road. There follows the long, silver line of Lough Leane and finally the dark battlements of Ross Castle.

Pending his trial, Father Moriarty was imprisoned in a dungeon in Ross, within sound of the lapping waters of the lake. Those into whose power he had fallen were curiously anxious not to condemn him, but this anxiety only prolonged his martyrdom. It is said that he was whipped to force from him an undertaking to leave the country. He refused to give it. Before the trial, the wife of the Judge, Nelson, intervened with a warning to her husband to have nothing to do with Moriarty, lest he (the Judge) should expose himself to greater perils. But the issue of the trial was clear. The priest was guilty of having disobeyed the laws of the land. Asked why he had done so, he answered that when such laws conflicted with the law of God, he was bound to obey the law of God. He was condemned to death by hanging. There are dark stories of other tortures inflicted upon him in his dungeon in order to force from him information he was known to possess. This much is certain: that when he was next seen many who had previously known him well hardly recognized him. His face had become so emaciated, darkened and discolored that his appearance was totally altered.

When sentence of death was pronounced upon him, Father Moriarty asked to see a priest, but his request was refused. There were still fugitive priests in the district. One of these, having heard of the new prisoners in the castle, went cautiously reconnoitering there at dusk and ventured in. He came upon Father Moriarty, was given the news in hurried whispers, and administered the last rites. This priest walked out of the castle again, miraculously unperceived by the guards.

Next morning Father Moriarty was led out to execution. He found himself in the company of his sister's husband, Piaras Ferriter, who was executed with him. The gallows had been erected on the Fair Hill, Killarney, a distance of two miles from the castle. The two prisoners' hands were tied to a hurdle and they were rushed to the site. A group of witnesses had gathered and when the long-suppressed grief of these poor people broke out around him, Thaddeus Moriarty, the noose about his neck, encouraged them not to despair. You can still see the very spot on which the gibbet stood. It is in the triangle of waste ground made by the railing and the railway wall, opposite the Franciscan church. This place of holy memories was marked with a circle of chamomile plants until the Famine days. There is nothing to mark it today. The date was the 15th of October, 1653, when Prior Thaddeus Moriarty was hanged by the neck as a warning to many, his body left twisting in mid-air until he was dead. After death, the discolorment of his face, so deplored by those who knew him, cleared away marvelously and he seemed transfigured.

The parallel with a divine model was continued in the manner of his burial. His grave must have been somewhere within military enclosure and the people were strictly prevented from having access to it. Some attempts to venerate it must have been made, because the grave was closely guarded for an incredible length of time. Dominic O'Daly, who wrote his *History of the Geraldines* two years after the occurrence, stated that Father Moriarty's grave was still being guarded by soldiers. Today that grave is unknown.

CATHERINE MCAULEY (1787–1841)

by FERGAL MCGRATH, S.J.

DUBLIN, DURING THE LATTER HALF OF THE EIGHTEENTH century, presented a strangely diverse picture of splendor and misery. A native Parliament inspired by the glamour of Grattan's oratory, a viceregal court setting the example of profuse and magnificent hospitality, a wealthy resident aristocracy ready and able to follow that example, all combined to justify the common phrase which styled Dublin the second gayest city in Europe. On every side the graceful lines of magnificent buildings like the Four Courts and the Custom House rose into the sky. Splendid mansions sprang up along the wide thoroughfares or in the pleasant suburbs. Sober John Wesley in 1775 pronounced one of the salons of Lord Moira's residence on Usher's Quay, with its great window paneled with mother-of-pearl, to be "a far more elegant room than any I have seen in England." And these splendid mansions housed a brilliant and accomplished aristocracy. Round Delville at Glasnevin there clung the memory of the beautiful Mrs. Delaney, grandniece of the first Earl of Bath, wife of an amazing clergyman and writer of perilously witty memoirs. At Leinster House, the residence of his father, the Duke of Leinster, lived Lord Edward Fitzgerald and his Pamela; he, the darling of the crowds, who cheered him as he drove through their midst wearing a feloniously green neckerchief; she, the mysterious beauty who had won his love at first sight in a Paris theatre, who was idolized by the poet Southey, whose lovely portrait hangs in the Louvre. Out at Castleknock the Honorable Luke Gardiner, later Viscount Mountjoy, who was to fall in the fight at New Ross in '98, gathered a brilliant circle of friends around his private theatre, where he and his beautiful wife were to be seen playing Macbeth and Lady Macbeth before the Lord Lieutenant and his court.

During the term of office of the Duke of Rutland as Viceroy, from 1784 to 1787, the social gaiety of Dublin was at its highest. Every Sunday afternoon long lines of coaches and six and coaches and four, led by the Duke and his consort in their magnificent equipage, were to be seen rolling up and down the North Circular Road. Castle balls alternated with crowded assemblies in the newly-built Rotunda, to which the ladies, on the authority of John O'Keefe, the actor, went in sedan chairs, for the reason that their mountainous hairdressing was incompatible with the dimensions of a coach.

Round the theatres, too, wit and fashion thronged. The year 1742 witnessed the famous first performance of *The Messiah* in Fishamble Street Theatre, to which the gentlemen were requested to come without their swords and the ladies without their hoops "in order to make more room for the public." A couple of years later the Smock Alley Theatre began its career of success under the management of Thomas Sheridan, the father of Richard Brinsley Sheridan. Among the brilliant assembly that filled it were the Bucks, all too successful imitators of the earlier London Mohawks. Sheridan had the courage to prosecute at the risk of his life one of these elegant nuisances, who had first pelted the company with oranges and then led a party of his friends, sword in hand, on to the stage to punish the manager. To the amazement of all Dublin, the roisterer was fined and imprisoned, and a new era of personal safety for actors ensued. Not all the Bucks treated Melpomene so rudely. Buck Jones, who prided himself on his resemblance to George the Fourth, was himself one of the managers of the Fishamble Street Theatre. But the Bucks in the main were kinsmen of the orange thrower. The most famous of them all, Buck Whaley, once for a bet threw himself from his drawing room window in Stephen's Green into a passing barouche, and kissed the fair occupant.

The Bucks formed a link between the brilliant aristocracy and the brilliant commoners. And of these latter there was no lack. Grattan was at the height of his fame during this period. Robert Emmet was a student at Trinity College until he was expelled for his rebellious sentiments in 1798, whilst out at Rathfarnham his Sarah, daughter of John Philpot Curran, the orator, was growing from girlhood into womanhood. Emmet had a lock of her golden hair sewed into his neckerchief on the morning he went to execution; and the story of their love inspired one of the loveliest of Moore's ballads. Moore was born in Aungier Street in 1779, and went to school at Mr. Samuel Whyte's Academy in Johnston's Court, off Grafton Street, where also were educated Richard Brinsley Sheridan and the Duke of Wellington. A few years before the gates of Trinity College opened to Robert Emmet, they closed upon a clever, lazy young man named Wolfe Tone, the son of a Dublin coachmaker.

But all this brilliance was confined to a small and privileged section of the population of Dublin. Over the vast majority rested the shadow of poverty and misery. Never, said an English parliamentary reporter writing from the capital in 1785, was so splendid a metropolis in so poor a country. The whole century was one of agricultural and industrial decay and of chronic famine which came periodically to a crisis. The poverty of the country was reflected in its capital. The number of the destitute was commonly estimated at 5,000. Dr. Whitley Stokes at the close of the century paints a vivid picture of the tenements that even then disgraced the capital, nine or ten persons living in a room ten feet square, ninety persons lodging in some houses, lodgers who paid 6½ d. a week for room to lie down on straw, dunghills at the rear, ash heaps on the stairs. Another writer adds further squalid details; insanitary churchyards and slaughterhouses in the midst of dwelling places, offal allowed to accumulate in the front or rear of every narrow lane. Warburton, writing at the beginning of the nineteenth century, states that there were then 45,000 poor patients yearly in the hospitals out of a population of 182,000. This figure is hardly credible; but disease certainly claimed a heavy toll in these wretched surroundings. The typhus, when it came, attacked as many as a hundred persons in a day. Public effort for the relief of poverty was confined to the establishment of state institutions. One of them, the Foundling Hospital, had a record grim enough in itself to cast a shadow over all the splendid picture we have just sketched. In 1797, a Sub-Committee of the Irish House of Commons reported that during five years five thousand infants were sent to the Infirmary, of whom a solitary one recovered. In the March quarter of one year 540 children were admitted, of whom 440 died. In the evidence a good deal was heard of a certain "Bottle" after taking which the infants "were quiet." A set of reforming Governors were appointed, but thirty years later forty thousand out of fifty thousand infants had died. It was then gravely considered that the Foundling Hospital had had a fair trial, and it was closed.

This picture of old Dublin has been drawn at some length, for it helps us to enter into the mind and appreciate the work of Catherine McAuley, whose destiny it was to form a link between the gay life of the great mansions and pleasant parks of her native city and the squalor that lurked in its alleys and laneways. She was born, indeed, not into the aristocracy—the Penal Laws had ousted almost all Catholics from its ranks—but into the wealthy upper middle class; and her mature life belonged not to the century that preceded the Union, but to that which followed it. But as a young girl she saw and mingled with that brilliant eighteenth-century society. It is the triumph of her achievement that its dazzle did not blind her to the darker side of Dublin life, and that side by side with that other great Irishwoman of her time, Mary Aikenhead, she brought to the making of the new era a new and ennobling element, practical compassion for the miseries of the poor, transfigured into an even nobler thing by the love of God.

At Drumcondra, in the northern suburbs of Dublin, still stands solid Georgian Stormanstown House where Catherine McAuley was born on September 29th, 1787. Her father was a well-to-do gentleman of private means, an earnest Catholic and a benefactor to the poor. Her mother was a handsome attractive woman, fond of society, and somewhat impatient of the ragged petitioners that flocked to her husband's gates in the all too frequent times of trouble. On his death, Mrs. McAuley, bent on social ascent, let her children abandon their religion. Catherine grew up without other creed than a benevolence inherited from her father; her brother and sister became Protestants. Her mother died when she was eleven, leaving the three children to the care of a worthy but rigid Protestant surgeon. All communication with priests was sternly prohibited, but delving in the theologically-flavored library of her guardian, the serious-eyed little girl read herself back into the Catholic faith before she was sixteen. At that age she was adopted by a Mr. and Mrs. Callahan, a wealthy couple returned from India. When one reads that on a visit to the surgeon they were instantaneously fascinated by Kitty's golden hair and blue eyes, one scents a biographical convention. But both hair and eyes are authentic. I cannot do better here, since we are to have the figure of Catherine McAuley constantly before us, than quote from a hitherto unpublished memoir written by Mother Mary Clare, one of her contemporaries. It describes Mother McAuley as she appeared at their first meeting in 1829.

> She was then upwards of 40, but looked at least 10 years younger. She was very fair, with a brilliant color on her cheeks, still not too red. Her face was a short oval, but the contour was perfect. Her lips were thin and her mouth rather wide, yet there was so much play and expression about it that I remarked it as the most agreeable feature in her face. Her eyes were light blue and remarkably round with the brows and lashes colorless; but they spoke. In repose they

> had a melancholy beseeching look; then it would light up expressive of really hearty fun or if she disapproved of anything they could tell that too. Sometimes they had that strange expression of reading your thoughts which made you feel that even your mind was in her power and that you could not hide anything from her. Her nose was straight but thick. She wore bands made from her own back hair which were so well managed as to be quite free from the disagreeable look bands of the kind usually give. The color was pale golden, not in the least sandy, very fine and silky. She was dressed in black British merino which, according to the fashion of the time, fitted tight to her shape. She was remarkably well made, round but not in the least heavy. She had a good carriage. Her hands were remarkably white but very clumsy, very large with broad square tips to the fingers and short square nails.

A miniature executed shortly after her death, and preserved in the convent at Baggot Street confirms this description. It adds one detail missed by Mother Clare, a most inspiring expression of calm strength, which instantly suggests constant and vivid reliance on a help that could not fail.

Installed with her new guardians out at Coolock House, some miles to the north of the city, Catherine's first care was to be reconciled formally to the faith of her father and mother. A shopping expedition gave the opportunity. She deserted her carriage—fit omen of her coming contempt of the world—outside a milliner's in Sackville Street, and hurrying breathlessly to a Catholic chapel in a dark by-street, was received by Dr. Murray, the future Archbishop. It was thirty years before Catholic Emancipation and her kindly foster-parents were puzzled, and somewhat troubled when they heard of her step. Even on her deathbed, a few days before she herself received the grace of conversion, Mrs. Callahan gently chided Catherine for having joined "a vulgar sect."

But though their Catherine had become a Papist, her foster-parents retained all their affection for her. The years slipped peacefully by at Coolock. Miss McAuley worked among the poor not only of the adjoining village, but of the narrow lanes and alleys of Dublin to which Dr. Murray introduced her. Mrs. Callahan died, becoming a Catholic a few days before her death. Her husband, heart-broken at her loss, became seriously ill. Catherine pleaded with him to enter the Church. He smiled indulgently at such folly, but a day or two later sent for a priest and spent the last year of his life as a fervent Catholic. When he died, he left to Catherine his entire fortune, thirty thousand pounds in the Bank of Ireland, six hundred a year in perpetuity, and Coolock House with its furniture, jewelry and plate. The thought of it is enough to make the mouth of any struggling philanthropist water. Catherine did not waste her chance. She decided to transfer her charitable activities to the city and to give them more corporate shape.

Early in July, 1824, she purchased from the Right Honorable Sidney Herbert a site in Lower Baggot Street and proceeded to erect a large house suitable for a school and a home for poor girls. The choice of one of the most fashionable suburbs was characteristically courageous. Only six years before, the first Catholic church bell since the Reformation had been rung in the Church of Saints Michael and John. A local alderman instituted proceedings to silence it, but luckily O'Connell himself was at hand to silence the alderman. In Baggot Street House Catherine gathered a few friends of her way of thinking. The last thing in the world she thought of was the founding of a convent. She and her ladies dressed in ordinary style, and at this period there was still a dashing Major who sighed hopefully in Catherine's direction. But Catherine had eyes only for the poor, and after some months of persevering wooing, the Major abandoned his suit.

But, as so often happens, Providence began to shape Baggot Street House into a convent. The ladies began to call one another "Sister," at first in jest and then in earnest. The Archbishop allowed them to assume a distinctive black dress and asked Catherine to choose a name for the community. She had always been attracted by the ancient Order of Our Lady of Mercy founded by Saint Peter Nolasco for the redemption of slaves, and on the spot chose the now familiar title of Sisters of Mercy.

She had a great love for the word Mercy, noting in it somewhat fancifully five letters corresponding to the wounds of Christ, and the same initial and final letters as the name of His Mother. And beyond a doubt the most shining of all her virtues was an overmastering pity for the pain of others. One of the earliest events that set her upon her path of succor was the tragedy of a pretty little servant maid of only seventeen, who was employed in a mansion near Coolock House. She was ruined by her master's blackguardly son. Catherine made desperate but unavailing efforts to save her, and the incident filled her with that noble anger that the sight of the strong destroying the weak always does produce in good men and women. And in Catherine it was a sternly practical emotion. The *saeva indignatio* that just a century before, in the deanery of St. Patrick's, had set her great fellow-citizen stabbing with gall-dipped pen the pages of his undying satires, sent her hot-foot to landlord, attorney and architect, and stands today embodied in her House of Mercy in Baggot Street and in a hundred other such homes throughout the world. And it was the same with the mere bodily pains of the poor and sick. They really wrung her heart, and wrung it to immediate sacrifice. There is the ring of utter truth in the words found in one of her letters: "God knows that I would rather be cold and hungry than that His poor should suffer."

The inevitable opposition that attends the birth of every good work at once manifested itself. A spate of piously unpleasant letters flowed into Baggot Street. One clerical correspondent, forgetting the shining and recent examples of Nano Nagle and Mary Aikenhead, and wishing to intimate that the founding of a congregation was not within the sphere of woman's work, addressed his letter to C. McAuley, Esq. He dropped dead in the street a few days later, a salutary warning to amateurs of heavy sarcasm. Even Dr. Murray wavered for a while, but finally decided that the hand of God was in the work, and urged the Sisters to become a Congregation of Religious.

Nano Nagle's foundation was thought to be the best cradle for the new Sisters of Mercy, and accordingly Catherine and two companions retired to the Presentation Convent at George's Hill to make their novitiate. Two incidents of that time of probation are worthy of note. They display great virtue in very different ways. On one occasion as a penance for a slight omission through mere forgetfulness, Sister Mary Catherine, as she was now called, was told by the novice-mistress to kneel at the foot of the novitiate table with her arms extended in the form of a cross. The novice mistress was called suddenly away and, returning more than an hour later, found her forgotten child still kneeling with arms outstretched, trembling and half-fainting. The other incident was at Catherine's reception. Her companions wore the orthodox white, but she had only a rich lavender brocade left of all her wardrobe. The Reverend Mother, as an especial favor, begged to be let arrange her dress, and zealously coaxed it into her most recent recollection of fashion, which happened to be of the year 1798. Another good Mother, mature, but somewhat junior, hastened to mend matters by a few pulls and pinning which brought the general effect up to about 1808. A young postulant coming on the scene made a few despairing last-minute efforts, but the combined effect was devastating. As the nuns filed into the Chapter-room decorum broke down hopelessly, and the Reverend Mother hastily whisked Sister Mary Catherine off for a radical remodeling of her costume. Catherine smiled through it all.

On the 12th of December, 1831, the three Sisters were professed and led back to Baggot Street by the Archbishop, who canonically installed Sister Mary Catherine as Superior. Thus was born the Congregation of the Sisters of Mercy.

Its growth can be depicted here only in merest outline. It was largely a matter of the simple multiplication of the original good works of Baggot Street House, the teaching of poor children, the sheltering of homeless girls and the care of the sick poor in their homes or in hospitals. It was a multiplication that was literally to fill the world.

The year after the foundation was the awful year of the cholera. No sooner had it appeared in Dublin than Dr. Murray came to the convent and appealed for help. Almost the entire community followed him to the Cholera Hospital where the deaths at first averaged six hundred a day. It was a time of heroic deeds on all sides. One only of Catherine McAuley's need be set down here, in a passage from a letter of Sister M. Moore.

> Once a poor woman died of cholera just after confinement, and Rev. Mother had such compassion on the infant that she brought it home under her shawl and put it to sleep in a little bed in her own cell, but as you may guess, the little thing cried all night and had to be given to someone to take care of.

This, be it remembered, at a time when the terror was so great that the appearance in a street of one of the chairs in which the victims were carried to hospital was enough to cause a stampede. But Catherine had a conquering courage. The cholera passed, but left hundreds of widows and orphans in its trail. At her wits' end for money Catherine took refuge in that unfailing form of religious piracy, a bazaar. To the usual pessimists on the committee she announced a bold stroke. They gasped, but Catherine was as resolute as in the face of the cholera. She sat down and wrote off to the Duchess of Kent, guardian of the fourteen-year-old Princess Victoria, calmly suggesting that she and her royal charge should send contributions. Catherine's sublime audacity was rewarded with a large assortment of fancy work, an embroidered muff and some drawings wrought by the royal fingers and autographed. Compassion for the poor became all the rage in fashionable Dublin and the bazaar was an overwhelming success.

The rules were drawn up and approved in 1835. Novices flocked in, many of them of good family. Dr. Murray laughingly declared Mother Catherine to be "the greatest enemy the fashionable world has." Then came expansion. The first new mission was to a strange race of heathens living within a few miles of Dublin. Years before, a richly-freighted vessel had been wrecked in sight of Dunleary harbor and its cargo looted by the inhabitants of the little village that then stood there. The clergy ordered restitution, and according to one account excommunication was declared against those who refused. At all events their children grew up in total ignorance of religion and in great moral degradation. The Sisters of Mercy opened a school for them in 1834. It was an immediate success, but was destined later to cause Mother McAuley much anxiety. All over Ireland convent after convent was opened, and the history of the remaining sixteen years of Mother Catherine's life reads like a series of passages from Saint Teresa's *Book of the Foundations.* Especially is this so in the account of the foundation at Charleville in County Cork. The journey was by canal boat, in a cold and wet October. Arriving on the vigil of All Saints the Sisters found the house so damp that when they entered it, their very clothing became rapidly saturated. A stream flowed right under the walls. After a day or two, Mother Catherine was on the point of abandoning the project, but while visiting the sick she heard a poor woman exclaim "O it was the Almighty God, glory to Him, that drove you among us!" The combined poetry and piety of this were too much for her, and the Sisters stayed in Charleville.

In 1839, at the invitation of Dr. Griffiths, the Vicar Apostolic of the London district, the first English foundation was made at Bermondsey. The convent was designed by Pugin, and the severely practical eye of the Reverend Mother detected in it the elements of artistic discomfort. "Mr. Pugin," she wrote, "was determined we should not look out of the windows, they are up to the ceiling. We could not touch the glass without standing on a chair." Later on in Birmingham she was to become more reconciled to the great mediaevalist. "Mr. Pugin would not allow cloth of any kind in the parlors. We have rush chairs and oak tables, and all is so admirable and religious that no want can be felt." Despite the last generous protestation one feels that the Reverend Mother was afraid that it was all going to be somewhat chilly.

The shrewd humor of Mother McAuley's verdict on Pugin's convent is found in many places elsewhere in her letters and recorded sayings. Of Pusey, who was present at the first profession at Birmingham, she writes: "His appearance is that of a negligent author." One of her favorite sayings was: "If everyone would mind their own business, the convent would be a heaven upon earth." It was a constant practice of hers to send instructions or to describe events in her letters in humorous verse, in which, be it confessed, good spirits preponderate over literary merit. There is very deep wisdom in four lines of one of these rhymed epistles addressed "To a Newly Appointed Superior."

> Avoid all solemn declarations,
> All serious close investigations;
> Turn what you can into a jest,
> And with few words dismiss the rest.

Other foundations both Irish and English followed fast. There were soon fourteen convents and over four hundred nuns. The incessant round of work and the journeyings, often under primitive conditions, began to tell. In 1840, the year the Sisters of Mercy settled in Birmingham, we hear the first mention of what Mother McAuley gaily called her "real old man's cough." In 1841 she journeyed to Birmingham, and the stay in the freshly built Gothic building did not improve her. The journey home was made in damp weather, Reverend Mother's clothing was poor, her shoes old and worn, and on her arrival the Sisters noted with alarm the racking cough and flushed cheeks. She rallied for a while, and began to plan settlements in Newfoundland and Nova Scotia, but towards the end of October it became clear that she was a dying woman.

I have remarked that in the most authentic portrait of Mother McAuley there is an inspiring expression of calm strength. This characteristic is most marked in the accounts of her death. A month before it, she began to put her papers in order, destroyed any correspondence that might cause pain to others, arranged and indexed wills, deeds and legacies. When she took to her bed she showed not the slightest sign of fear, but a wonderful joy. Her old friend Dean Gaffney of Maynooth, who wrote an account of her life for the *Dublin Review* of March, 1847, records that one of her last sayings was: "Oh, if this be death, it is very easy indeed."

A couple of days before her death an incident occurred that told significantly of her combined austerity and humility. It is related somewhat baldly and unconvincingly in the early biographies, but I have been able to verify it by the testimony of one who read an account of it, now unfortunately destroyed, written down by an old nun who had it from the lips of the Sister concerned. This Sister was acting as infirmarian during the night and heard a rustling noise as of some objects being wrapped up in paper. The dying woman then called her and asked her whether she would be afraid to go down to the kitchen and burn a parcel unopened. The young nun heroically conquered both her curiosity and her fear of the cockroaches that were known to lurk below in the dark, and burned the parcel unopened. Reverend Mother, however, had said nothing about not feeling it, and the Sister averred that it contained among other things her discipline. Whether there is any more evidence than this for the early biographer's epithet "bloodstained" I do not know. Certainly after her death her discipline was missing, as were also her broken and uncomfortable shoes.

Right up to the end there was that air of ordered calm about Mother McAuley's leave-taking that had characterized her life. The day after her death Mother Elizabeth Moore, who said the prayers for the dying at her bedside, wrote down a detailed account of her last hours. We do not find in it any very startling revelations, any strikingly original religious reflections. Such things are rarely found in the dying words of the saints. Rather as they get nearer to God they seem to become more like little children and to be content with the very simplest expressions of love. In one of the most moving of all death-scenes, that of St. Catherine of Siena described by Ser Barduccio di Piero Canigiani, we find only such commonplace expressions as "Thou, O Lord, callest me, and I come to Thee, not through my merit, but through Thy mercy alone." Yet Ser Barduccio avers that "at hearing her, not only our hearts, but the very stones might have been broken." So it was with Catherine McAuley. It was the ordinary prayers for the dying that she said, but the Sisters were weeping all around her as they listened.

The day of her death came, November 11th, 1841. Twice at least on that day she showed the exquisite feeling for others which had been the inspiration of her whole life. To little Sister Camillus, her god-child, she said, using the lovely old Irish term of endearment: "Kiss me, my heart, and then go away." "Thus," adds Mother Elizabeth, "she sought to prevent her from weeping." The evening wore on; she had the blessed candle in her hands; she was but a few hours from eternity. Around her the Sisters had been praying for hours; some of them had come from a distance. They were surely tired. Their Mother thought of them to the last. She beckoned one of her own community over and whispered "Be sure you have a cup of tea for them when I am gone." I cannot help thinking that the startlingly matter-of-fact view of death that these words reveal had been learned by Mother McAuley from the Dublin poor amongst whom she had worked so long. It would be no strange thing to find a poor woman dying in a Dublin slum so unappalled at the thought of going before the throne of God as to busy her mind about the humble hospitality that should be shown her neighbors when she was beyond caring for them. Death for the Dublin poor, as all know who know them, is as familiar a matter as turning in at the church door for Mass on a Sunday.

It was now close on eight o'clock. To the last the Mother did not wish to trouble her children. The end is best narrated in the words of Mother Elizabeth Moore.

> We then commenced the last prayers. I repeated one or two she herself had taught me, and she said, with energy, "may God bless you." When we thought her senses were failing, and that it might be well to rouse her attention by praying a little louder, she said, "No occasion to speak so loud, my darling; I hear distinctly." At a few minutes to eight she calmly breathed her last. I did not think it was possible for human nature to have such self-possession at the awful moment of death.

Her grave is in the little cemetery of the convent at Baggot Street, where also are to be seen the simple room in which she died, and the wooden crucifix she held at the last. From the day of her death the growth of the congregation she founded has been most striking. In December, 1931, the Sisters of Mercy celebrated the centenary of their foundation. In that year the American Sisters published an official list of all the Mercy Convents in the world. Though it is a bare enumeration of names and figures, it runs to over a hundred pages. According to it, there were in that year 1,464 convents with 19,980 Sisters. Of these convents 200 were in Ireland, 102 in England, 255 in Australia and 813 in the United States. In all their institutions, higher and elementary schools, hospitals and homes, the Sisters had about a million souls under their care.

Of the outward achievement of Catherine McAuley we have an ample chronicle. On the contrary, of her inner life, her love of God and her communion with Him, we have strikingly little direct knowledge. There are several reasons for this lack. She wrote a great many spiritual instructions, but on one occasion, looking for some document, she dropped a taper amongst her papers and they were nearly all destroyed. She kept no record of her own spiritual progress, or if she did, burned it, as she did contentious letters, before her death. She constantly gave spiritual exhortations; but the early Sisters were too busy with their incessant round of work to take notes of them. On the whole her letters, too, contain little self-revelation. Here I speak with some reserve. It is over seventy years since the first biographies were published, and those that have appeared since have been mere sketches. The older Lives are accurate and frank enough in the recording of events, but in the estimating of Mother McAuley's virtues they abound in generalities, most of them probably quite true, but unsupported by evidence. No really critical Life has ever been attempted, and it is possible that the letters and other documents treasured in various Mercy convents might reveal more of the Foundress's soul. In preparing this sketch I have had access to the letters preserved in Dublin, but they do not reveal much. They are warmly pious and affectionate, but simple and business-like. One of them indeed praises highly a "sweet holy reserve" in all religious matters which may perhaps have been what prevented Mother McAuley from speaking more in them of herself.

But about the intense holiness of Catherine McAuley there can be no manner of doubt. Already as a young girl her foster-parents noticed how, when she thought she was alone, her lips were constantly moving in prayer; and as a nun she was apt to become so absorbed in prayer that on ceremony days she took care to have another Sister near her to remind her of her duties. From her childhood to her death she never tasted food or drink of any kind from Holy Thursday till Easter Saturday. When travelling on feast days, she thought nothing of fasting until after one o'clock and walking several miles to have the joy of communicating. When new Sisters arrived at the convent, if, as often happened in the early days, there was no cell for them, she would give up hers and sleep in an old armchair of Mr. Callahan's. A host of other evidences of this kind leave no doubt that union with God and self-abnegation were hers in a very great degree. One of her confessors, Dr. Blake, could say boldly of her: "The Foundress was holy, and eminently holy. Her heart overflowed with the charity of Jesus," and Archdeacon O'Brien of Limerick, who was in close touch with her for thirty years, could speak of "her heroism of every description," and "her sinless life."

And indeed even in this short sketch we have seen enough to justify these testimonies. As we recall the whole striking story, the young heiress scattering her fortune upon the poor, the band of young women, many of them rich, talented, and beautiful, who gathered round her, the convents springing up all over Ireland and across the seas, the enthusiastic support of the ablest men of the time, the countless souls palpably saved in hospital, prison, slum, school and refuge, we feel how superfluous it is to seek for further proof of the great holiness of this brave, able, affectionate, witty Irishwoman whom God inspired to embody in herself and in her followers the noble virtue of pity for the suffering and the afflicted.

MARY AIKENHEAD (1787–1858)

by C. P. CURRAN

MARY AIKENHEAD WAS BORN IN CORK IN 1787. HER grandfather was a Scotch military officer who had married and settled in Ireland and her father was a physician practicing in Cork. To count a soldier and a doctor amongst her immediate forebears is precisely the ancestry one would have presumed from her work, and the dash of Scotch goes well with her plain and powerful common sense. It is more surprising to find that she was first baptised Protestant for, though her mother was a Stacpole of a well-known Catholic stock, it had been a condition of her marriage that the children, of whom Mary was fourth, should belong to the Established Church. The other curious circumstance of her childhood was that for the first six years she should have been wholly given over to foster-parents to be reared in a little thatched cottage in the suburbs of the city. It was a fortunate circumstance because it gave her the franchise of two worlds. In the Roches' cottage she was the ally of Shaun the coal-porter, and shared Jeanie Keating's supper of sprats.

Mary Roche brought her, as Irish nurses do, to her parish church where she was baptised a Catholic. She fell in with the Catholic practices of the household, went to Mass, joined in the Rosary, and grew up enveloped in the wholehearted simplicity of faith and submission to the Divine Will which fills every cranny of such an Irish cottage.

Having once breathed this atmosphere the nominal social division of classes into upper and lower remained permanently in her mind as a very irrelevant valuation.

In 1793 she returned to the world of her class, bringing the Roches back with her into the service of her father's household. He was then in full practice, a wealthy, generous and public-spirited man and like many of his profession and race of a strong, democratic bent, sharing the new ideas of his time. He is stated to have belonged to the United Irishmen, some of whose most distinguished leaders like Addis Emmet and the brothers Sheares were his coreligionists and fellow-citizens. Lord Edward Fitzgerald was a secret visitor at his house. Through her mother's family and other visitors she had glimpses of an older, disappearing Europe. The Stacpoles had fought at Aughrim and being dispossessed of their lands became, in the way of such families, soldiers and merchants. They trafficked with the Continent in swords and wine. One of her collaterals, holding the commission of Maria Theresa, had held Frederick the Great prisoner for a moment at Künersdorff until a pistol shot disabled him. One of the family circle was a Hennessy, connected on one side with Edmund Burke and on another with relatives who had been busy at Dettingen, Fontenoy and Cognac. Another habitue of the house was Roche, the banker, educated as usual in France and intimate with Count MacCarthy at Toulouse and with the Girondists at Bordeaux. These families, with associations both aristocratic and popular, formed a genial, hospitable and cultured society which molded and fed the intelligence of the growing girl. They shared the general prosperity of the Cork merchants which was so considerable in the middle of the eighteenth century that it is said that though they lost £70,000 in the Lisbon earthquake, not one of them broke. Their wealth was maintained in supplying both services in the Napoleonic wars and though change was imminent there was still in the hands of these Catholic families the means to equip the new foundations of Christian enterprise and charity to which the new spirit of Catholic liberty and the new feeling of social responsibility were giving birth. They represented the unregimented, resurgent Catholic body which was opposing itself at the beginning of the century to the entrenched ascendancy with its institutional wealth derived from tithes, glebes and public endowments of ecclesiastical commissions. These families worshipped in chapels and Mass-houses hidden from the public view like Fr. Mathew's Friary "between salt-house and stables." But in Mary Aikenhead's youth in Cork, no doubt, as in Dublin they went to the mid-day Mass in state with their best horses and carriages, their equipages cluttering up the narrow lanes about the parochial and conventual chapels.

In 1801 Dr. Aikenhead died. He had become a Catholic shortly before his death and his daughter was received into the Church in the following year. A sermon on Dives and Lazarus is characteristically associated with her final determination. She was already well known to the Cork poor for devotion to them, and soon after her reception it became plain that she proposed to dedicate herself wholly to their service. At this time there were only two convents in Cork, one of the Ursulines who were beginning their admirable work in education but not specifically the education of the poor, the second of the Presentation Order who maintained schools for the poor but as an enclosed order. Mary Aikenhead, familiar with the homes of the poor and the daughter of soldier and doctor, would engage with poverty in its own territory and with a freedom and mobility denied to an enclosed community. While debating alternatives and before she saw her way to a third solution, she went to Dublin to visit the convent of the Poor Clares which her dearest friend was about to enter. The visit was critical inasmuch as it brought her into close contact with two individuals who had a decisive influence on her future, her hostess, Mrs. John O'Brien, and Dr. Murray. Mrs. O'Brien was a conspicuous member of Dublin society who had the heart of a Sister of Charity under the guise of a woman of fashion. She had a clever woman's knowledge of the world and, tireless in works of charity, was a zealous co-operator with Dr. Murray in some of his manifold charities. Dr. Murray, who from a curate had been made Archbishop and coadjutor of the See, was then at the beginning of a career which changed the Catholic face of Dublin. He had come to Dublin in 1798 as a refugee priest from Arklow where his parish priest had been murdered in his bed. He came to a Dublin where even years later a German traveler would observe as little of Catholicism as of Protestantism in Prague. "Concealed in I know not what by-lanes of the city" the chapels occupied a place in the city guides and directories after the meetinghouses of Kelly's and Walker's Society. On his death in 1852 ninety-seven churches and numerous schools had been built in his diocese and some twenty-nine communities established in the service of education and the poor. This achievement was the work of a man whose suavity and modest demeanor hid a real strength which showed itself conspicuously in the veto controversy. His quiet continuity of purpose, patience and foresight are nowhere better shown than in his correspondence with Mary Aikenhead whose character he had quickly divined. He had resolved to set up in Dublin some congregation of Sisters of Charity. A conversation between himself and Dr. Moylan of Cork, at which Mary Aikenhead was present, showed him that his instrument was at hand. A complete and permanent understanding was established between bishop and apprentice-superior; his firm and kindly letters sustained and guided her early steps and the project rapidly matured. In June, 1812, he accompanied her and Alicia Walsh to York to the Convent of the Institute of the Blessed Virgin Mary at Micklegate Bar where, having taken the name of Sister Mary Augustine, it was arranged that she should pass her two years' novitiate and ground herself in the principles and practice of religious life. The Institute founded by the Ven. Mary Ward was chosen as incorporating most fully the spirit with which she wished to inspire her own foundation. The uncloistered nun was unknown in Ireland. To seek out the destitute and afflicted and to minister to them in their own homes or in hospitals or asylums was the outer life to which she looked forward and her first and most searching problem was to frame a Rule which would harmonize the interior life of the religious with this external purpose. All her practical sagacity and sound judgment went into this task while still in the novitiate. She turned down a *projet d'accord* with the French Sisters of Charity of St. Vincent de Paul and with Dr. Murray's assistance studied alternative Rules and Constitutions. In August, 1815, she returned with her companion to Dublin to the house in North William Street provided by the Archbishop and was professed there on September 1st. Awaiting a constitution they made their vows for one year only. Sister Mary Augustine Aikenhead was nominated Superior-General and Sister Mary Catherine Walsh, Mistress of Novices. Two days later their first postulant, Miss Catherine Lynch, was received to be followed immediately by three others. On September 10th the visitation of the sick poor in their homes began and the dress of the new community became a familiar sight in the Dublin streets. In January, 1816, the Rescript of Pius VII dated November, 1815, was received for the canonical creation of the Congregation of Irish Sisters of Charity and the perpetual vows were taken, though it was not until August, 1833, that the Constitutions were confirmed by Brief of Gregory XVI.

The community under the spiritual direction of the celebrated Fr. Peter Kenney, S.J., lived at first under the Rules of the York Convent in so far as these were compatible with the characteristic fourth vow of devotion to the service of the poor. When Tullabeg College was opened Fr. Kenney resigned his charge to Fr. Robert St. Leger who placed at the disposal of the young Foundress, in Dr. Murray's words, "his deep research and profound judgment in all spiritual matters." He came into association with her when the Mother-General was also acting as Novice Mistress in the Novitiate, now separately established in the Stanhope Street House in 1818, and when the Constitutions were still under consideration. His first efforts, in the words of the Annals of the Congregation, "were directed to forming the Superior herself," instructing her in the "whole arcanum of spiritual life"; his second to the task of framing Constitutions. The Rules and Constitutions of the York Institute were originally based on the Rules of the Society of Jesus. Time and custom had altered them and Fr. St. Leger set himself so successfully to remodel them to the archetype that the new Constitutions remain impregnated with the Ignatian spirit. The Institute, Mary Aikenhead wrote, is formed on that of St. Ignatius. The conventual observance followed the Rules and Customs of the Society. "It is the system of St. Ignatius" an observer wrote to a postulant. "You will find it to be high perfection and difficult, but at the same time totally practical. The soul formed on it will be truly interior and will have learned that death to self by which alone it can begin to live to God."

Her letters and homilies inculcate the mortified will, the perfect surrender of liberty as the first condition of the service of charity. The interior life should be the source of action. Novices must learn "the (with us) indivisible duties of Mary and Martha." Not compassion nor natural charity but the pure love of God must be their motive: "of little avail will be all our exertions if each act does not flow from the interior spirit of genuine charity."

Fr. St. Leger sets out in one memorandum on the training of novices his conception of the leading virtues of the Institute: the perfect indifference to occupation, the entire resignation of themselves into the hands of the Superior, the spirit of labor, recollection of heart and union with God, humility under correction, minute compliance with discipline, renunciation of will, judgment and self-ease. This is the language of the Jesuit novitiate. It recurs in her letters but she stresses "not so much those rules that regulate the minor practices of religious life as those which inculcate the fundamental principles of asceticism." Austerity is tempered by insistence on the Sister of Charity's privilege of serving Christ personally and directly by laboring in the service of the poor. Her housewifely common sense chimes with Jesuit practicality. No one should be aggregated who has not a real spirit of labor. Their job is not walking about distributing alms. If they cannot keep accounts and manage the household concerns they must spend themselves in helping those who are so capable. "We want women who have sense and who know how to use it."

In this spirit she worked for ten years in the Motherhouse and novitiate and ensured the future of the Congregation in conducting a school of spiritual leadership. A group of remarkable women were trained in her likeness, women of indomitable courage and unflagging energy and perseverance as Dr. Walsh described one of them. Her lineaments were generally reproduced. A future sister, at that time not much in love with nuns, thought she would like to have a look at one of them and knocked at the door of the Gardiner St. Convent. "The Sister who received me struck me as totally different from what I expected. She seemed a frank, reliable sort of person who had a clear intelligence and could use it." She meets a priest and tells him she has seen a Sister of Charity with a man's strength of character and intellectual power. "Ah," said he, "this comes from the grand old Mother—she puts her stamp on them."

After this period of training the Congregation rapidly expanded in all the directions which have characterized its activity. Houses were established in Cork, where they had almost immediately to combat a violent typhus epidemic, and in Waterford, Galway and Clonmel. In Dublin in 1831, free schools were organized in Gardiner Street with the assistance of Edmond Ignatius Rice and Mr. Duggan, of the newly established Congregation of Irish Christian Brothers. The schools became a model of their kind and an anchorage of the faith in a district engirdled with proselytizing institutions. In 1833, St. Mary Magdalen's Asylum was founded in Donnybrook for rescue work. In 1835, St. Vincent's Hospital was opened. In 1845, the Mother House was moved to Harold's Cross where the admirable Hospice for the Dying is now housed, and meanwhile colonies had swarmed off to England and Australia. The most notable of these enterprises and the one dearest to her heart was the foundation of St. Vincent's Hospital. Inured to Hospital work the sisters were called on by Dr. Murray in 1832 to face it in its most terrible aspect when the Asiatic cholera, which was then sweeping over Europe, reached Dublin and Cork. During two years the nuns did heroic work among the terror-stricken population. The cholera had hardly abated when she bought the Earl of Meath's fine Georgian town house on St. Stephen's Green, and with the devoted aid of Dr. O'Ferrall equipped and conducted there the first Catholic hospital in Dublin. Its success called for the highest qualities of prudent administration and the institution stands as a notable monument to the judgment and courageous initiative of the foundress.

Much of this work was conducted from a sick room. A woman of indomitable energy, she had been in the early William Street days missioner, mistress of novices, portress and cook. Regarding the last avocation it is true that at times the only dinner was of stirabout. There is a well-known story from this period of a bishop who called to see the Superior and was admitted to the parlor by the portress who had been scrubbing the stairs. Removing her apron, the portress returned to His Lordship who failed to recognize in the dignified Superior the businesslike person who had opened the door. Someone describes her later appearance:

> Mrs. Aikenhead came to the parlor. She was an elegant looking woman, tall and slight with dark, grey eyes almost black, and an aquiline nose. Her bearing was majestic, but there was great benignity in her countenance and her smile was very sweet. Her manners were simple and playful.

In 1831 her health completely broke down. For two years she was a helpless invalid with spinal trouble, and for five or six years she lived perforce in a recumbent position suffering intense pain with fortitude. Appointed Superior-General for life by Gregory XVI in 1843, she labored inexorably till her death in 1858 in the closest touch with her business, interviewing and writing. Here is a fellow-worker's account of her:

> I was particularly struck by her greatness of soul and her perfect freedom of action, irrespective of worldly opinion; the ease with which she referred everything to God; and her open, genial, good-natured manner of acting with everyone who came in contact with her. Her nobility of character was shown by her universal benevolence. She never did a little or a small thing; her smallest actions bore the stamp of greatness of soul.

Her conversation is reported as full of good sense, earnestness, cordiality and variety; at one moment the breadth and power of a strong, masculine understanding, at another full of humor and quaint expressions. Much the same qualities mark her enormous correspondence with the daughter houses, which in their published form occupy a stout volume of some six hundred pages. One does not look for humor in such letters, but there is in them the pithy shrewdness which is its foundation. They are practical home-spun letters, straightforward in expression and without verbal decoration. She looked for "truth without quibbles," and gave it. Her criticism and admonitions are outspoken but kindly, and point directly to a remedy. They are written in an intense spirit of faith and are saturated with trust in Providence. She worked in the spirit of St. Paul. "I can do all things in Him Who strengthens me." "Labor," she writes, "as if all depended on our poor endeavors, all the while convinced that God is all-sufficient"; and again repeating what she calls "the cuckoo-song of an old woman"—"Labor as if all depended on our own exertions, but with peaceful mind." She was not a woman of many books, but incessantly refers to two or three writers, to St. Ignatius, à Kempis and St. Augustine, upon whom she made her soul. The same integrity and sense of justice which shine in her letters impressed the men of business she met in the lay world. She saw things in a big way, would not huxter and commanded the respect and willing service of both worlds. A Dominican who had watched most of her life wrote of her as an Irish St. Teresa or St. Catherine of Siena: "She was a woman to be revered and loved; gifted with high spiritual knowledge and proficiency; sometimes brusque perhaps in manner, but making you understand that honesty was the great point with her. Looking like what she was, the Foundress of a great Institute."

THEOBALD MATHEW (1790–1856)†

by JAMES O'MAHONEY, O.M. CAP.

TWO MEN TOWERED ABOVE THEIR CONTEMPORARIES OF the nineteenth century in Ireland: they were Daniel O'Connell and Theobald Mathew. They shared between them a power over the Irish people that is almost unique in history. At their call drooping hearts looked up; beneath the spell of their personality spirits almost broken caught new strength and fire; the people marched out into the light of day, they ran together, when O'Connell spoke or Theobald Mathew preached.

Opinion may be divided as to the ultimate success of the work of both. In his own day O'Connell was superseded; by 1844 he was leader only in name. Theobald Mathew also lived to look upon a land that was almost ruined by famine and to see the broken remnants of crowds that once were entirely his.

† The best-known biography of Theobald Mathew is that of John Francis Maguire, *Father Mathew: A Biography* (London, 1863). There is another by Frank Mathew (Cassells). A very interesting account of him is given by J. McGlashan in the *Dublin University Magazine*, Vol. 1 (1849), Our Portrait Gallery, No. 54, pp. 694–706. There is reason to believe that McGlashan had access to the invaluable sourcebook, the MS. *History of the Temperance Movement*, written by Father Mathew's Secretary, James McKenna (died in 1846), at present in the Archives of the Capuchin Friary, Church Street, Dublin.

The human and historical issues, however, remain untouched by such eventualities. The movement that emanated from Theobald Mathew was its own success. It is of a past that is unchangeable. It brought before the world a man whose fame will live as long as the Irish Race survives.

On the 10th of April, 1838, Theobald Mathew took the decisive step. It was then, with dramatic gesture, that he uttered the memorable words, "Here goes, in the name of God," as he launched the movement that was to bring him before the eyes of the world.

A Quaker, William Martin, with whom he sat on the Board of the House of Industry in Cork, would constantly say to him: "Oh, Theobald Mathew, if thee would only give thy aid to the cause, what good thee would do for these poor creatures!" Reading his biographer one has the impression that a Total Abstinence society existed and that nothing had to be done except to throw in his lot with the members of that society.

The matter really was not quite so simple. As first initiated, the temperance movement was only a form of "moderation society" which excluded the use of whiskey. It was soon realized that this was not enough, and moderation was succeeded by total abstinence as an ideal. The moving spirit of the new association was William Martin. Some eight years later a deputation awaited on Theobald Mathew. The only reason alleged for this choice of Father Mathew was that "he was a young priest, well-liked, and very popular amongst the working classes." Nothing came of the deputation. For two years things went on much as before until a little incident threatened the very existence of the association. It was a rule of the society that no religious or political topics should be broached. On one occasion the rule was broken by one Mr. Lombard, a Protestant clergyman. The Catholics present, discerning the thin end of the wedge of proselytism, strongly objected and left the society as a protest.

It was then that Father Mathew was prevailed upon to take up the temperance campaign. He was approached by one of the Catholics who had protested. A preliminary meeting was arranged at which William Martin was again present. The date was fixed for April the 10th, and it was then that things began really to move. It was Father Mathew made the temperance movement.[1]

Within three months the number of his followers amounted to 25,000; in five months it was 131,000; and in less than nine months the numbers ran up to 200,000 people. These growing numbers summon up an image of a constant stream of pilgrims to the little house in Cork City where Father Mathew lodged. Day after day the people came. They were to be seen on the roads that led to Cork, poor, tired, foot-sore after long journeyings. They crowded in upon him. His little house was over-run. The people sensed instinctively the warmth and tenderness of the man by whom they were attracted.

This enthusiastic response fanned the flames that burned within the breast of Theobald Mathew. Before his eyes he saw the people whom he loved grow in beauty and self-respect. Out from Cork he would go. He would carry the crusade for temperance into every corner of the land. First came Limerick. Word went out from town to town that he was coming. The day before his arrival the roads were black with people waiting for him. For four days the streets of Limerick were packed with people. When he spoke crowds surged in upon him in a moving mass; the horses on which Scotch Greys were striving to keep order were literally lifted off their feet; people knelt before him to receive his blessing and to make an act of renunciation that for many was heroic.

After Limerick he went on to Waterford. He was back in Cork for Christmas, and later he journeyed to Dublin and Maynooth. Within two years he had travelled the length and breadth of Ireland. The

1. The foregoing facts are not to be found in Maguire. They are furnished by two independent witnesses, and are borne out by Father Mathew's own account. See interesting article, "Father Mathew and Temperance," in *Capuchin Annual* (1930), pp. 162–168. This article is signed F. S. (V. Rev. Fr. Stanislaus, O.M.Cap.), who probably knows more about Theobald Mathew than any other living historian.

rapidity of his movements became proverbial: in the North yesterday, in the South today. By then the number of names on the Roll of total abstainers was 5,457,030.

O'Connell, who must have been watching this rapid progress of Father Mathew, expressed his idea of him by saying that Theobald Mathew was a "miracle." In 1840 he himself launched the movement for Repeal. He saw the vast possibilities of the new enthusiastic organization of the people. On one occasion the two great leaders met. On Easter Monday, 1840, they walked together at the head of 10,000 people in the City of Cork. When the Liberator knelt to receive the priest's blessing an onlooker might have thought that the supreme moment of his career had been reached by Theobald Mathew.

But it was not so. The temperance leader was uneasy. His aim, as he conceived it, was broader. "I utterly disclaim any political object; my ardent desire is to promote the glory of God by drying up the fruitful source of crime, and the happiness of His creatures by persuading them to the observance of temperance." So wrote Father Mathew, after the meeting, to a friend.

From 1838 onwards, it might be said, Father Mathew lived for the temperance movement. No words could convey the gigantic toil of these years. When almost every parish in Ireland was organized he crossed to England.

A graphic picture of him as he then appeared to his contemporaries has been left by one who had an eye for heroes, Thomas Carlyle, who caught a glimpse of him by chance as he conducted one of his meetings in Liverpool. This is how Carlyle expressed himself: "Passing near some Catholic chapel, and noticing a crowd in a yard there with flags, white sticks, and brass bands, we stopped our hackney coachman, stepped forth into the throng, and found it to be Father Mathew distributing the temperance pledge to the lost sheep of the place, thousands strong of both sexes; a very ragged and lost-looking squadron indeed. Father Mathew is a broad, solid-looking man, with grey hair, mild, intelligent eyes, massive, rather aquiline nose and countenance. The very face of him attracts you. We saw him go through a whole act of the business, do, as Darwin would say, a whole batch of teetotalers. I almost cried to listen to him, and could not but lift my broadbrimmed hat at the end when he called for God's blessing on the vow these poor wretches had taken. I have seen nothing so religious since I set out on my travels as this squalid scene—nay, nothing properly religious at all."

All this outward success was not without its inner core of suffering for Theobald Mathew. Some were found to suggest that he preached an abstinence that he did not practice: on one occasion he heard, without betraying his identity, this very charge rather crudely made by a fellow traveler in a coach. Others were not beyond believing that the crusade was a money-making affair, and at the time the man was thousands of pounds in debt. All his life, in fact, he was struggling with debt. It could not have been otherwise. He was one who received with one hand and gave away with two. In his temperance movement he had nothing to gain, but all to lose. Money was the least of the things he lost.

He spent himself entirely in the Cause. Theobald Mathew was of that highly-strung temperament for which success itself brings dark moments of reaction. There is plenty of light and shade in his human life. By 1845 the Famine appeared and began to eat its way through the land into the hearts of the people. During one of his journeys from Dublin to Cork the Apostle of Temperance saw the people sitting on the fences bewailing bitterly the destruction of everything around them. Temperance was then almost forgotten for the moment by its advocate. Back in Cork, we find him feeding the hungry, hammering at the British Treasury with suggestions and appeals for help, and trying to save his people by the establishment of soup-shops from the merciless profiteering of flour and corn merchants. The trip to America in 1849, though it aroused enthusiasm everywhere, was succeeded by a sad return to a changed inglorious Ireland.

For a short time he went to live with his brother, Charles, at

Lehenagh House in Cork, and he retired to Cobh for the winter. There he was to end his days. There are few scenes more touching or more pathetic than these last days of the great leader of the people. We are reminded forcibly that "Man born of woman living for a short time is filled with many miseries. Who cometh forth as a flower, and is destroyed, and fleeth as a shadow, and never continueth in the same state." The man who had led thousands was now old and feeble, the fire of his personality was almost dead, he tottered through the streets of Cobh. After a life so full, great must have been the dread reaction of these last days. To complete the picture of the suffering Father Mathew we have but to listen to the voice of self-reproach that welled up within him and frequently escaped his lips: "If only I had taken up the work of temperance sooner. If only my motives were always pure in the sight of God—no man can be pure in the sight of God."

There is more insight into the real Father Mathew in these few words than any scene witnessed by a Carlyle could convey. These heart-searchings reveal beneath the powerful exterior of the great Apostle the spiritual man, the man of God. They warn us that no full understanding of his personality is possible until we have situated his work for temperance in the broader context of his life as a whole.

The immense popularity he enjoyed because of his crusade for temperance may even falsify the perspective of his life. The man who worked for temperance is so well known that the rest of his life has been obscured. I am quite confident that my readers will be surprised to know that Theobald Mathew had spent twenty-four years of his life working for the spiritual and corporal welfare of his co-citizens in Cork before the temperance movement lifted him from his surroundings and made of him a public figure. I am also of opinion that not a few will be surprised to hear that Theobald Mathew was a Capuchin and a follower of St. Francis of Assisi. The statue of him that honors the principal street of Cork, seeming to extend a welcome to every casual visitor to the City, tells nothing of this latter fact. Neither do the many pictures of him with which we are familiar. The Franciscan cowl and habit are missing; in his day it was not permissible to wear them. Yet, we must see Theobald Mathew in the Franciscan habit, not merely to do honor to Franciscans, but simply to understand the great Apostle: never was man more naturally endowed with the Franciscan temperament than was Theobald Mathew.

Of the family of Mathews, who could boast kinship with the Earls of Llandaff, Theobald Mathew was born at Thomastown not far from Cashel in County Tipperary. The date of his birth was October 10th, 1790. He was the fourth son of the marriage of James Mathew with Anne Whyte of Cappa-white, and Thomastown House, where he was born, was celebrated for its hospitality.

As a youth there was nothing outstanding about him in the intellectual line: he was a boy of warm character and good nature. Of an affectionate disposition, he was more ready to bestow than to receive. In a special way he loved his mother, and while the other members of the family sought their pleasures out of doors, Toby, as he was called, was satisfied to remain at home.

The unselfishness of his character saved him from any little jealousies that might have arisen from his mother's partiality. It was his brothers who benefited, for he was the acknowledged mediator of the family. He was popular. He shared his gifts with others, and he was not averse to surrounding his giving with a certain amount of ceremony. To give a feast was his greatest joy. Down through life the same propensity remained with him. A day or two before his death his doctor surprised him in the act of feasting with little children.

Nor was this generosity a respecter of persons. Himself of gentle birth, he experienced no difficulty in gathering around him the servants of his home. In the last days at Lehenagh House he would leave the table of his friends and go to meet some poor beggar who was seen to approach the house. He was ever the friend of the poor and the downtrodden. The Clerk of his Chapel in Cork depicted rather well this generosity of Father Mathew: "Look, sir, here is my notion on the subject: if the streets of Cork were paved with gold, and if Father Mathew had entire control over them, and could do what he liked with them, there would not be a paving-stone left in all Cork by the end of the year."

Who can forbear from thinking of Francis of Assisi, refined and generous, the giver of feasts, ever generous to the poor, ready even to take his father's bales so as to supply the needs of those in want? When we are told that Toby Mathew actually abhorred any sport that entailed the death of animals, is there not another little trait that reminds us of him who loved the birds and called the wolf his brother?

Theobald Mathew, however, was not all tenderness: there was power and force beneath the gentleness of his character. He was in fact impetuous by nature, and in presence of the crowd the innate force of his personality went out and swayed his audience according to his desires. His prevailing gentleness in disturbing moments was certainly not the pure result of nature. By birth he was a gentleman and he was ever mindful of the fact. By grace he submerged himself in the very poor, but grace did not destroy his human character. "It is almost the definition of a gentleman," says Newman, "that he is one who never inflicts pain. He carefully avoids whatever may cause ajar or jolt in the minds of those with whom he is cast. He guards against unseasonable allusions to topics that may irritate; he never takes unfair advantages, never mistakes personalities or sharp sayings for arguments; he never insinuates evil which he dare not say out."

Father Mathew verifies the definition of Newman. We see him moving amidst all creeds and classes. All were attracted by him. He was all things to all men. Contemporaries such as Carlyle and the Duke of Devonshire speak of a countenance that was marvelously winning and divine. The Russian traveler, Kohl, said that Theobald Mathew was of such distinguished appearance that he found it no longer difficult to understand the influence he exerted over people. His manner was persuasive to a degree, simple, easy, humble. And Thackeray who had little good to say of things Catholic wrote: "On the day we arrived at Cork, and as the passengers descended from the 'drag,' a stout, handsome, honest-looking man, of some two-and-forty years, was passing by, and received a number of bows from the crowd around. It was Theobald Mathew with whose face a thousand little print shop windows had already rendered me familiar. He shook hands with the master of the carriage very cordially, and just as cordially with the master's coachman. The world likes to know how a great man appears even to a *valet de chambre*, and I suppose it is one's vanity that is flattered in such rare company to find the great man quite as unassuming as the very smallest personage present... There is nothing remarkable in Mr. Mathew's manner, except that it is extremely simple, hearty, and manly.... He is almost the only man, too, that I have met in Ireland, who, in speaking of public matters, did not talk as a partisan. With the state of the country, of landlord, tenant, peasantry, he seemed to be most curiously and intimately acquainted; speaking of their wants, differences, and of the means of bettering them, with the minutest practical knowledge."[2]

Endowed with such a natural character, influenced also by his upbringing, Theobald Mathew was prone to be broadminded and extremely tolerant. When he first walked the streets of Cork, arm in arm with a Protestant parson, he was the talk of the city. The fact that the Quaker, William Martin, turned naturally to him for help with the total abstinence movement shows the friendly relations that obtained between them. This broad outlook also pervaded his work for temperance. He administered the pledge to all who looked for it.

It would be false, however, to infer from this that Father Mathew's work for temperance was merely humanitarian and had no religious motives at the back of it. It may well be that Father Mathew erred in the desire of making temperance a movement that would unite all creeds. At his meeting in Waterford, however, he had the comfort of hearing the Bishop of that diocese, Dr. Foran, declare: "Why should I

2. *The Irish Sketch Book* (London, 1843), pp. 78, 79.

not encourage this movement, and sanction and support it by every means in my power? If I did not do so, I would not be an Irishman; if I did not do so, I would not be a Christian; and if I did not do so I would not be a Bishop."[3] We must remember that Father Mathew was living at a period when Catholicism in Ireland was struggling out of the dark gulf of persecution. It is significant that his predecessor, the Capuchin, Fr. A. O'Leary, had made his name on his written pleas for toleration.[4] In the social uplifting of the people Father Mathew had to accept the co-operation of those who were not Catholics.

There can be little doubt as to the motives that guided Father Mathew personally. It was only after long and arduous prayer that he acceded to the request of William Martin. Legend tells of one mysterious night spent alone in his little Chapel which was supposed to have had a decisive influence upon him. His biographer recalls that Father Mathew was on one occasion sorely tempted to alleviate depression by having recourse to some cognac that was in his room. Nor was the priest himself beyond the confession that it was for fear of consequences to himself that he became a total abstainer. "If only one poor soul," said he on that first occasion when he signed the Roll-book, "could be rescued from destruction by what we are now attempting, it would be giving glory to God and well worth the trouble."

His contemporaries were well aware that Theobald Mathew was a Catholic priest. On one occasion he told them rather forcibly. It was during his mission to America where in some place he was welcomed "*not* as a Roman priest, but as a preacher of temperance." All his gentleness suddenly fell from him, and in a passionate outburst he said to those gathered before him: "I am proud, justly proud, of being a humble servant in that holy Church which has done so much for the glory of God and the civilization of mankind, which has stood bravely in the van unchanged from age to age, which has outlived, and shall

3. Maguire, *Father Mathew*, p. 134.

4. See O'Leary, Rev. A., O.M.Cap., *Miscellaneous Tracts* (Dublin, 1781).

outlive, both calumny and oppression." Here was a profession of faith worthy of the man. For himself Father Mathew was first and last the priest, and if he could do good to others outside the fold by social reformation he was not averse to allowing them to share in a work that had for object the glory of God and the salvation of souls.

From the days of his infancy the eyes of Theobald Mathew were turned towards the priesthood. There is scarcely an Irish mother who has not the secret ambition of one day seeing a son of hers a priest. Toby's mother was no exception. A pathetic little incident reveals the fact. Her son, George, had shown some signs of a vocation. A friend had actually presented him with a chalice and vestments against his Ordination-day. But nothing came of George's leanings towards the priesthood. The mother felt the disappointment keenly. One day her feelings found expression. As her children sat around her she remarked: "I have nine sons, and not one of them to be a priest." In an instant Toby was on his feet: "I will be a priest," he declared.

At the age of twelve he was sent to a school at Kilkenny. Possibly there he came in contact with the Capuchins or heard of them. When he was seventeen he entered Maynooth. But there his feast-giving propensities proved his undoing. He gave a feast to some companions in his room, and this was a thing forbidden by the Statutes. While his case was under consideration he left Maynooth. He joined the Capuchins in 1810, and was ordained a priest in Dublin on Easter Saturday, April 17th, 1813. In 1822, he was chosen Provincial of the Capuchins in Ireland and held that office for twenty-nine years.

His first mission was to Kilkenny. He did not spend a very long period there as we find him stationed in Cork in 1814. He succeeded here in Cork to the title of his illustrious predecessor, "a poor friar buried between salt houses and stables." The church wherein he ministered, his biographer tells us, "exactly measured 43 feet in length and about the same in breadth; and from the rails of the altar to the interior of the porch the space did not exceed 28 or 30 feet."[5] It had been built by Father Arthur O'Leary. "It was not much bigger than a respectable barn, and but for the galleries might have passed for one. Yet, it served its purpose; it had its day, and was not unknown to fame. For half a century it was celebrated far and near as 'Father O'Leary's Chapel'; and for a subsequent generation it enjoyed if not a better merited, at least a more widespread notoriety, as the church to which the world-renowned 'Apostle of Temperance' was attached."[6]

This little Church in Blackamoor lane was situated in the very poorest part of the City of Cork. Father Mathew had full occasion to submerge himself in the poor, which he did without hesitation. St. Francis himself could not have looked for greater poverty. The tradition there was good. "I saw that little church," says an eyewitness. "It was the real expression of seraphic poverty and religious piety. I was witness of the austere life of the Capuchins, their contempt of the world, their humility, modesty, simplicity and love of solitude. I saw their vigils, fasts and mortifications, their devotion to mental prayer, their prompt obedience and the spotless purity of their lives."[7]

That Father Mathew had the Franciscan sensitiveness about poverty may be inferred from the fact that as Provincial he applied to his superiors in Rome for permission for the use of money; his journeyings outside of Ireland were also sanctioned by obedience from his higher Superiors.[8] That he had the real Christian traditional outlook on poverty may be seen from his sermons to the people. At this

5. The present Church administered by the Capuchins in Cork is that of the Most Holy Trinity situated on the other side of the river from that of the older Capuchins in Blackamoor lane. The foundation stone was laid on the birthday of Father Mathew, October 10th, 1832. He was responsible for it, and it was known as "Father Mathew's Chapel." It was only completed in 1890 to celebrate the Centenary of Father Mathew's birth. Cf. F.S.K., "A Notable Cork Centenary," *Capuchin Annual* (1932), pp. 158–165.

6. M. B. Buckley, *Life of Rev. A. O'Leary, O.M.Cap.*, p. 20.

7. *Historia Missionis Hibernia Capuccinorum*, f. 457.

8. Cf. *Bullarium*, vol. 10, p. 219. Decree from S. Congregation of Regulars, dated February 12, 1894, Rome.

time there is a phrase constantly on his lips that is significant. "Every time," he says, "I see a barefooted child in the street I seem to see Jesus Christ Himself." Have we not here simply an echo of Christ's own identification of Himself with the poor? This serves to show what, in the mind of Father Mathew, lay at the basis of all social reform, if the example of his own choice of poverty and of an Order which in his time in Ireland was unknown and obscure does not convince us.

His life in Cork for twenty-four years before the temperance movement uprooted him from the soil of his choice was one long effort to improve both socially and spiritually his fellow-Catholics. His principal concern was undoubtedly the spiritual interests of his people, but that did not prevent him from seeing that health and well-being of soul and spirit were intimately dependent on the good of body and on suitable environment. The three evils of his day, ignorance and idleness and intoxicants taken to excess, were the enemies he fought in turn.

His first endeavor was to supply education. He set himself to build schools for children. He succeeded, and had ladies to teach them. By 1824 there were 500 pupils, boys and girls, in the humble schools opened by Father Mathew. Soon he had gathered young men and boys around him and had formed a society for visiting the sick and for giving religious instruction.

When cholera broke out in the City in 1832 the people of Cork began to learn something of the priest they had in their midst. He was everywhere. "I have at this moment," writes a contemporary, "the most vivid and grateful recollection of the generous and heroic zeal displayed by my revered and beloved friend, Father Mathew, when, with the unselfish devotedness of a martyr and an apostle, he threw himself into the midst of the peril, when the terrible *reality of* Asiatic cholera smote my parish first of any locality in Ireland, April, 1832.... Two or three days after the first terrific outburst of the pest, and as soon as the awful tidings reached Father Mathew's ears, he hastened to my house, and, with open heart and arms, embraced me; and, while offering his sympathy and consolation, tendered me his valuable services and the offices of his sacred ministry, for the comfort and spiritual aid of my poor afflicted parishioners, at every hour by night or day that I should refer to him. This offer, unexpected and unsolicited on my part, was, of course, promptly and gratefully accepted; and nothing could equal the noble untiring efficiency of the support he then gave me until the benefit and blessing of his ministrations to the sick were required away from my central district, in the southern quarter of the city, which, in less than a fortnight after, was doomed to undergo its own share in the prevailing scourge."[9] Back in his own parish, Father Mathew was even more untiring in his charity. When night duty was to be undertaken in a hospital near Cove Street the hours from midnight until morning were selected by Father Mathew. Meanwhile he was engaged in schemes for the whole City, and the Botanic Gardens which he had leased in 1830 were handed over to be a burial-ground for the poor. When he came to die himself it was here he chose to be buried with his own. To this day it is frequently called the Father Mathew Cemetery, and not a few pious pilgrims are seen to kneel at the grave that contains his mortal remains.

Already in 1820 his fame as a preacher had begun to be noised abroad. By 1824 he was looked upon as one of the most popular preachers of his day. Fr. M. B. O'Shea, afterwards Pastor of St. Patrick's, gives a touching account of his preaching: "We have ourselves more than once gone to hear this preacher, with the express intent of duly and fairly estimating his powers as a speaker, and have summoned to our aid as much of our critical bitterness as we conceived sufficient to preserve our judgment uninfluenced by the previous charm of his character. We were not listening to his affectionate, earnest, and pathetic exhortation more than ten minutes, when our criticism—our bitterness—our self-importance, left us; all within us of unkind and harsh was softened down—our heartbeat only to kindlier

9. Maguire, *Father Mathew*, p. 67.

emotions—we sympathized with our fellow-Christians around us. We defy the sternness and severity of criticism to stand unmoved, though it may remain unawakened, while Mr. Mathew is preaching; and this surely is no mean criterion of the excellence of his character, and the efficiency of his ministry in the pulpit."[10]

Father Mathew's life, we infer, was his greatest sermon. Dean Collins, another contemporary, summed up his opinion in that way. "I have been listening to a sermon from Father Mathew," said a lady to the Dean one day, "and I have been greatly edified." "My dear," said the Dean, "his life is a sermon."

In 1847 the name Theobald Mathew, O.C., was sent to Rome as *dignissimus* for the vacant Bishopric of the diocese of Cork. Fifteen years had elapsed since the cholera episode: time could have dulled the memory of the Christian heroism he then displayed. For almost ten years a publicity was thrust upon him that might have been perilous for the reputation of a lesser man. That fellow-priests, who knew him intimately, selected Theobald Mathew to be their future Bishop is a fact significant. Rome did not confirm their choice. His name will not be found in the list of Cork's past Bishops. But nothing can efface it from the unbroken scroll of Ireland's gloriously Catholic past: it is written in vivid characters across the period marked by the nineteenth century in Ireland's history.

10. Ibid., pp. 78, 79.

JOHN HAND (1807–1846)

by THOMAS O'DONNELL, C.M.

Father Hand was not a bishop or a prelate of any degree, he never had charge of a parish, nor was he a member of any religious institute; in fact he was nothing more than a simple priest, exercising his ministry in the Archdiocese of Dublin. That ministry did not exceed a single decade. The first five years, 1836–1842, were spent with a group of ardent young clerics who, under the leadership of Dean Dooley, had dedicated themselves to the teaching of the young and to the giving of missions in country parishes, and who subsequently became the first Irish Vincentians.

He rose at four o'clock, taught every day for many hours, visited the poor, heard confessions, and preached on Sundays. His many natural gifts helped him to be a persuasive preacher—sweetness of voice, clarity of ideas, a frank and pleasing countenance, an extensive knowledge of the Sacred Scriptures, and a fund of nervous English; but the chief sources of his success were his faith and his sympathy, his deep conviction of the things that are not seen and an imaginative sympathy with the trials and sorrows of human nature. In all his labors day by day, whether on his knees or on his feet, one thought, one hope, one purpose inspired and preoccupied him, the sad thought of his fellow-countrymen forced to flee from Ireland, and the hope and purpose of helping them to preserve their ancestral faith, their only possession that had eluded the spoiler.

It is difficult to estimate with accuracy how many Irish emigrants or persons of Irish descent were to be found in English speaking countries at the beginning of the nineteenth century, but it is fairly certain that by 1840 there were four hundred thousand of Irish birth in England and Scotland, that Australia had received twenty thousand, that a small number had found their way to South Africa and the Argentine, that one hundred and fifty thousand had landed at Quebec and not fewer than three hundred thousand at Boston, Philadelphia, and New York.

The exodus to the United States was greatest; for the exiles, escaping from the tithe proctor, the crowbar, and the "peeler," hoped to find freedom and fair play in the new Republic which their fellow-countrymen had helped to establish. But alas, what a greeting awaited them! On arriving on the Atlantic seaboard, famished, after a seven weeks' voyage, in foodless ill-provided wooden tubs, they encountered the same hostility that they had left behind, the same "superiority," the same superciliousness, the same contempt for their speech their poverty and their rusticity.

Father Hand knew all this, and feared that as thousands of the shepherdless Irish had been absorbed by a hostile environment at the end of the eighteenth century so once again thousands might be lost. His heart was touched with pity and affection for the poor exiles, and day after day the voice, the injunction, that had come to him, before as well as after his ordination, was renewed and reiterated: "Send us priests and send them soon."

But how could he? He had no money, no friends, no influence, no position. Two things sustained him—his trust in Providence and his reliance on the generosity of the people. Accordingly he began to beg, he called on the clergy and laity, he visited fairs and markets, shops and private houses, sometimes on foot, sometimes in a rather dilapidated little gig (drawn by the most sagacious pony that ever came out of Connemara). Of course he was mocked. Not a few of his clerical brethren spoke of him as "the dreamer," and the laity smiled at him saying: No doubt the poor young priest is a little "touched," but God bless him all the same, he is so gentle, so courteous, so unassuming, so kindly. Whatever misgivings others might entertain there was one who never faltered in his conviction that the dreamer was a realist as well; and that one was the Reverend George Leonard, the wise and venerable Parish Priest of Oldcastle, in the Diocese of Meath. At a clerical gathering, in reply to a skeptical query he spoke out as follows:

> Do I know that young priest? Indeed I do well. I baptised him and watched over his boyish years, his youth and his manhood. When his rugged father tried to keep him working on the farm, I cooperated with his saintly mother in getting him to a secondary school and ultimately to Maynooth. In the national College he did so well and so won the esteem of his professors and superiors that some envious companions brought on him the humiliation of what in collegiate slang was called a "scrape." I have always observed something unique in this young man's character, and in particular an ardent personal attachment to the Son of Mary. He has vision and determination—the vision of a people perishing and the determination to rescue them. Beneath those bent shoulders and behind that calm grey eye there is the soul of an Apostle.

The old seer was right. Father Hand persevered, and left far behind him the timid and cautious, the doubters and the mockers. Within one year he secured the approval and support of the two first men in Ireland and of the supreme Head of the Catholic Church. "I rejoice," said Archbishop Murray, "that what appeared a dream has become a reality. I see the prompting of Providence in your plan. May God go with you." "Here," said Daniel O'Connell, "is my subscription, £100, and here also, as Lord Mayor of Dublin and hence landlord of your new home, I hand you a lease for nine hundred and ninety-nine years." And Gregory XVI, placing his hand on the young priest's head, said to him: "I bless you, my son, and bless your College. Even ten true missionaries would justify and reward your enterprise and zeal."

On November 1st, 1842, the young Rector opened the College with one student and four professors. He had leased a fine old Georgian mansion, situated in a spacious park in the midst of many of those splendid beeches oaks and chestnuts which are characteristic of the County Dublin. As the lands on which the mansion stood belonged before Henry VIII's confiscation to the Priory of All Hallows—supplanted by Trinity College—it was decided to adopt that name and to place the new College under the patronage of All Saints and in particular of the Virgin Mary and of St. Francis Xavier. New buildings were added, old ones repaired; the staff was enlarged, many new students enrolled. In 1843 the number had risen to forty; in 1844 to fifty-eight; in 1845 to sixty-five.

"The Professors" wrote Father Hand, and without doubt he is describing his colleagues, including Drs. Moriarty, Woodlock and Bennett, "should be men of ability, of scholarly attainments, and of high character, capable of training practical, trustworthy and unselfish missionaries. They should give their services gratuitously, and be content with food, raiment and lodging. Students should be physically fit, highly commended by their parish priest, well grounded in the classics, English and Science, and of a studious disposition. They should possess sincere and solid virtue, free from singularity and puerility. They should love everything connected with divine worship and in all things be thoughtful and serious. They should cultivate good manners, affability, propriety in dress, and restraint in matters of amusement. In fine they should acquire such a competent knowledge as will enable them to expound intelligently and interestingly the truths and moral principles of Christianity."

When, four years after the opening of the College, the young Rector lay dying of lung trouble, contracted on a begging expedition, his parting words to his colleagues, assembled around him, were: "Let mutual charity and an apostolic spirit pervade the College."

Since his death, ninety years ago, more than two thousand missionaries have gone from All Hallows to all the English-speaking countries. Each year the number averages about twenty-five. For example, last year, 1931, eight went to the Pacific coast, eight to Australia, seven to England, two to South Africa, and one to Southern Nigeria.

It may be asked what has been the concrete embodiment of Father Hand's principles and ideals; what has been the character and quality of his disciples; what has been the influence, the result, of all the missionaries who have been sent from Ireland—Maynooth, Carlow, Kilkenny, Thurles, Waterford and Wexford. To such a far reaching question a broad answer may be found in the gratitude and magnificent virility of the Irish of the Diaspora—in their gratitude to Ireland and to the priests from over the seas, and in their generous constancy, supporting their schools and churches, their priests and nuns, out of slender resources and in the face of unrelenting opposition; and also in authentic testimonies to the worth and work of Irish missionaries, testimonies which may be summed up in a few words: The typical priest from Ireland was a good man, a loyal citizen in his new home, and a faithful minister of Christ, human, tolerant, sociable, untainted by politics or graft or worldliness, a lover of his people, preserving their native purity and the decencies of life, deepening their faith, safeguarding the religious education of the young, and maintaining the reverence and dignity of Christian worship.

MARGARET MARY HALLAHAN (1803–1868)

by EVE HEALY

CATHOLICITY IN ENGLAND IN THE FIRST HALF OF THE 19th century was largely a thing of obscurity and hidden corners. Tyranny had caused Catholics to consider their religion as something to be concealed and shut away from blasphemous eyes. They had been forced to strip it of its externals. The Mass was said secretly and not always frequently; many devotions had been discontinued. Statues, sanctuary lamps, rosaries and even vestments had been locked away. In the past, there had been good cause for these precautions against sacrilege; now, however, precaution had become a habit instead of a protection. Catholics had grown used to the dinginess around them. The whole country required a clean sweep, but who could attempt it? Men whose vision had grown dim were unfitted for the work. It was obvious that a large part of the impulse would have to come from without—and so it happened.

First came Daniel O'Connell to make an opening for Catholics in their own political household. Newman was soon to follow. And there were a host of others. Among them God chose a little Irish servant girl, Margaret Mary Hallahan.

She was born in London on 23rd January, 1803: her parents were poor Irish people and good pious Catholics. Her father's name was

Edmund Hallahan; her mother's maiden name was Catherine O'Connor. Both were consumptives, so that from her earliest childhood Margaret had learnt what suffering and hardship meant. It was a continual struggle to keep the home together.

When she was nine years-old she lost her father and six months later her mother also died. On her father's death, the Abbe Carron, an émigré priest took Margaret into an orphanage in Somers Town, run by French ladies of rank, who had been forced to leave France during the Revolution. Here she remained for three years, after which she became a servant in the household of Madame Caulier, proprietress of a lace warehouse in Cheapside. This lady was a harsh mistress, owing probably to her lack of understanding of children; for, beneath all, she had a kind heart.

Margaret was not happy here, yet she faced the world boldly and cheerfully. Even at this age she possessed a supernatural courage based on an unshaken belief in God's presence within her, around her and enfolding her. Her utter confidence in God developed within her great independence of spirit; she relied on Him implicitly, casting aside all human aid or consolation. This trust sustained her not only at this time, but throughout her whole life.

When Margaret was twelve years old, she ran away from Madame Caulier. She walked gaily through the streets of London, going from door to door, and with utter childlike innocence asking whether anyone required a maid. Finally she was taken in by an innkeeper's wife who had compassion on the child. Meanwhile Madame Caulier tried to trace her, employed the Town Crier and had her publicly cried through the streets of London—an event unusual in a servant girl's life, a foreshadowing perhaps of the time when Margaret's fame should be broadcast to the whole world.

Later, Margaret went into service with a Protestant family. Here she was unable to hear Mass for two years; and she frequently had to champion the cause of the Church against the insults of the other servants. Once she successfully silenced a blasphemer by breaking a plate over his head. On another occasion a visitor to the house attempted to insult her: she promptly boxed his ears and he departed hurriedly. In neither of these circumstances was prayer her sole weapon. Margaret understood perfectly that God helps those who help themselves.

When she was about twenty years old, Madame Caulier got her into the family of Dr. Morgan, formerly physician to King George III. He was an invalid and in addition to her ordinary household work Margaret nursed him day and night. He left her a legacy of £50, the whole of which she spent in having Masses said for the repose of his soul!

She remained in service with Dr. Morgan's daughter, and with her went out to Bruges in 1826.

Before leaving England, Margaret, at the age of twenty-two, solemnly dedicated herself to God. Kneeling on an old kitchen chair, wooden like the Cross of Our Lord, she took a vow of perpetual chastity. From this time God seems to have taken her into His own Hands; He took her out of England into a Catholic country in order to mold her into that particular form of broom which was to sweep so many homes fifteen years later. Margaret herself afterwards wrote in one of her letters: "for I ever look upon myself as a sort of broom our dear Lord makes use of, to show that contemptible things can bring forth His Will and that, when done with, it may be cast like all old brooms into the fire...."

Her stay in Belgium was a time of preparation; her soul was in a restless, turbulent and unsettled state. She was continually seeking to attune herself to God's touch, ignorant of what it was that God required of her, yet eager to welcome His Holy Will and content to be His handmaid.

Bruges at that time was little different from the Bruges of today. Margaret delighted in the beautiful churches—built in fine open spaces, whereas the people of the city lived in narrow cobble-stoned streets. She loved the splendor and riches of God's house and compared them with the simplicity of the Belgian homes. In Bruges too she came to apprehend the beauty of the liturgy, devotions and services of the Church and to see God worshipped in state by all, rich and poor. At last she had found a nation in which God came first and was publicly given the place of honor amongst its people.

Her confessor, M. Versavel, one of the two English confessors then in Bruges, was attached to the Church of St. Walburga. He was a very holy man but so severe that few persevered under his direction. Margaret, however, was his penitent for fifteen years.

At first she had care of her mistress's children who all loved her dearly. Later, on account of financial losses in the family, she became maid of all work. This period of housework became for her a time of ejaculatory prayer; it was the seed which grew until one day Margaret was to remark that "for her to pray was as simple as to breathe."

She got up at 4:00 a.m. every morning to hear Mass so that her household duties were not interfered with. In her spare time, she went round Bruges, visiting the poor, nursing the sick in their homes and in hospital, and even distributing alms. For these she used to beg from house to house. Her charity became renowned throughout the city; everywhere she became known as "Sister Margarita."

Once, with the permission of her confessor, she tried her vocation as a lay sister in a convent in Bruges. But no sooner was she in than she longed to be out again. On leaving she said laughingly: "I would not remain if you were to make me Reverend Mother!" She had already made friends there for life and was to visit this convent later when she *was* a Reverend Mother!

It was about this time that Margaret first became interested in the Third Order of St. Dominic. There were many Tertiaries in Bruges and the Order was strong throughout Belgium. Margaret was thrilled with its romance, even though she had acquired the English prejudice with regard to St. Dominic! He had always been associated in her mind with the horrors of the Inquisition. On the other hand, St. Francis had always made strong appeal to her; but when faced with the question of attaching herself to one Order or the other, she was—almost unwillingly—drawn to St. Dominic. Later on she said: "I did not choose the Dominican Order, but Our Lord in His mercy and for His own wise reasons forced me into it and I have reason to bless Him for it."

For eight years she begged her confessor's permission to become a Tertiary before he finally consented. On the Feast of the Espousals of St. Catherine of Siena, 1834, she received the Scapular and on the Feast of St. Catherine, the following year, she made her profession.

Margaret's two great devotions were to Our Lady and to St. Catherine of Siena. When she first became acquainted with M. Versavel, he presented her with a carved wooden statue of Our Lady painted after the Belgian fashion. It was enshrined in her room and everyone in the house, even visitors, were invited there for the rosary or night prayers each evening. This statue was to become famous for its unpopularity in England in years to come, when Margaret's anger was to blaze at the insults offered to her Mother.

Whilst in Bruges, she diverted her love of reading into channels of ascetic literature. She taught herself both French and Flemish and became well acquainted with the best spiritual writers in both languages. She collected, amongst others, the works of St. Theresa, St. John of the Cross, Pére Surin and a little book by Boudon, entitled *Dieu Seul.* This motto, "God Alone," became Margaret's own; every thought became directed towards this end.

In the meantime she had formed various plans and schemes for inaugurating good works and had become so well known that the clergy of different Orders approached her to start charitable institutions in France, Belgium and even in America. But in all these she was continually thwarted by her confessor, who checked and curbed her ardent nature vigorously. She begged him to allow her to try her vocation again, but he was adamant in his refusal. It appears he was averse to involving her in anything that should fetter her freedom. He seems to have been certain that she was destined by God for some great work, but it had not been revealed to him what it was.

This constant checking of every active impulse to do something constructive for God caused intense pain and desolation in Margaret's sensitive soul. She was groping in the dark and each ray of light became a phantasy. She realized that when God afflicts a soul, no one can console it. This threw her back on to "God Alone" and her life and actions are an example of implicit trust in God.

At length with the encouragement of M. Versavel, she gathered together a few Tertiaries who were prepared to live together and devote themselves to charitable works. This, however, turned out to be a failure. Promised financial help did not mature; a prominent priest actively opposed her; her plan was ridiculed throughout the city; finally, M. Versavel himself turned against her. The whole thing was a fiasco and Margaret was left without a friend. Forsaken and desolate, the anguish of her soul was indescribable.

At this time a Mrs. Amherst who had visited her in Bruges wrote from Coventry begging her to come to England and promising to find employment of some kind for her. Margaret went to M. Versavel and obtained his permission to go. He gave it so readily that she felt he was glad to be rid of a restless, troublesome soul. Later he was to remind her of this thought of hers.

She crossed to England on the Feast of St. Catherine, 1842, and entered the household of Dr. Ullathorne, O.S.B., priest in charge of the Church at Coventry. He engaged her as mistress of the girls' school, which was not yet in being! She had been asked beforehand what wages she required? She answered quite simply—her board and lodging—adding that she had a supply of clothes for five years, after which she would require some new ones! She resided in Dr. Ullathorne's house, shared the kitchen with a crotchety cook and slept in a tiny attic. Later she became housekeeper. Our Lord completed thirty years in the home of Mary and Joseph; Margaret, too, had worked for the same period in the homes of His people. Now her ministry was to commence!

Almost as soon as she arrived Dr. Ullathorne had to go to Rome, so Margaret was left to find her own way about her work. She set about it in her characteristic way, working amongst the poor, nursing the sick and winning over the factory girls by her simple motherly ways. She collected the ribbon weavers and other factory hands together and formed a night school for them. When Dr. Ullathorne returned he was astounded to find her running a school of 200. She had divided the school into six classes and had appointed a monitor for each. She herself then taught one class in succession each day, setting work for the monitors of the other classes so that they could carry on. In this way she knew every individual in the school.

Coming fresh from a Catholic country, she was distressed to see the timidity of Catholics in England. She was indignant beyond words to find that the Blessed Sacrament was usually kept in a cupboard in the sacristy and, as she often remarked, a "dirty one at that!" The old tradition of a sanctuary lamp was practically forgotten and Benediction was seldom given. When there was a tabernacle it was invariably of wood. This reversal of the Belgian order of things incensed Margaret, for even the poor classes used mahogany for their furniture: and that people were content to have Our Lord rest in *pewter* chalices whilst most families used silver on their dining-tables, was a meanness she simply failed to understand.

The rosary, she found, had fallen into disuse: and she was surprised, too, to find that Catholics were unfamiliar with the use of statues: they were practically unknown to the ordinary Catholic who had not travelled. Sister Margaret, as she was called throughout Coventry, set about putting all these things in order and with the help of Dr. Ullathorne re-introducing old Catholic devotions.

She had brought with her from Bruges her carved statue of Our Lady. At first, Dr. Ullathorne warned her not to display it too publicly. Then she used to take visitors to her room to show her statue and say a prayer. To most, however, the shrine was just a foreign notion, while some even regarded it with suspicion. Later Dr. Ullathorne gave permission to set up an altar to Our Lady in the schoolroom. Sister

Margaret had a triptych carved for the statue. Anxious to make the altar as worthy as possible, she bought two lovely branch candlesticks for it. When the bill was sent in she was horrified to find they cost £8. Knowing that Dr. Ullathorne would consider this extravagance, she made a door to door collection and all was paid off within a month. When the school altar was complete, her joy was childlike. A lady who afterwards joined her community was astonished to find Sister Margaret one day executing a little dance before it.

Dr. Ullathorne entered whole-heartedly into all her work and every encouragement was given her by the Dominican Fathers at St. Peter's Priory, Hinckley. On Rosary Sunday, 1842, after many refusals, permission was given by the Bishop to place a cut glass lamp in front of the Tabernacle in the Church at Coventry. Sister Margaret bought the first pint of oil for it, filled the lamp, lit it, and saw that it never was allowed to go out. This was the first Sanctuary Lamp in Coventry since the Reformation. Dr. Ullathorne began courses of lectures on the books of the Bible, on the ceremonies and ritual of the Church. People flocked to these weekly instructions. Work and devotion made great strides at Coventry; it was like a wonderful revival of Catholicity. Sister Margaret was working silently in the homes of the people, influencing them by the strength and simplicity of her character and persuading them to attend the lectures and services in the Church. In the meantime she carried on her domestic life with complete simplicity, sharing the kitchen with a little servant girl.

Once a week she had an hour's talk with Dr. Ullathorne. It was out of these talks that the idea of forming a religious community was conceived.

About this time a lady of means applied to Dr. Ullathorne for permission to try her vocation. He spoke to her of Sister Margaret's scheme for starting a conventual community of Dominican Tertiaries. She was anxious to join at once and Dr. Ullathorne pressed Margaret to found her community. She desired with all her heart to be one of the religious, but she humbly declared herself incapable of leading others. She was prepared to organize it and set it going, but she pleaded to be allowed to join the Novitiate.

Finally, with the approbation of both Dominican and Benedictine authorities, arrangements were made for Dr. Ullathorne to take postulants under his own roof. Sister Margaret and three others took up residence; only one had means and these were quite insufficient for all the others. So Dr. Ullathorne placed both house and purse at their disposal. He himself acted as Novice Master, explaining the constitutions and rules, teaching them the Office and encouraging them in all their work. Thus were the children of St. Dominic nurtured and reared in their religious nursery by a son of St. Benedict!

Sister Margaret had now taken the first practical step in the great work she was to accomplish for the Catholic Faith in England. The first act of the community was to take in three motherless Irish children, and as the care of orphans was Sister Margaret's favorite work, she was quite put out when later the father came from Ireland and took them home.

The little band of sisters soon were known to every poor family in Coventry; they visited homes, taught the children in the schools and nursed the sick in the hospitals. All, both Catholic and Protestant, made Sister Margaret their confidante. It is impossible to overestimate the power she had of speaking directly to the soul: she had the capacity of awakening the most dormant instincts of Faith sometimes by sheer downright talk, sometimes by her mere homeliness. Souls were attracted to her and she was noted for her sympathetic understanding of scrupulous people. She possessed a keenness of insight, which gave her an added confidence and strength in facing many of the difficult problems of her everyday work. Her judgments were always sound and her methods practical.

An event which caused Sister Margaret great concern took place in 1844. Every third year in Coventry (always within the Octave of Corpus Christi) there is enacted the disgraceful procession of Lady Godiva. It dates back to the time of Charles II and was performed, originally, as a mockery of the Catholic Procession of the Blessed Sacrament. Sister Margaret suggested that as a counter attraction the Catholics should have a procession of their own. She adorned her beloved Belgian statue of Our Lady with lights and flowers and it was carried shoulder high. Children dressed in white walked in front and the priest and congregation followed, all singing hymns. The procession which took place on two successive days went outside the church and round it. It caused a sensation in Coventry.

In 1845 Dr. Ullathorne was consecrated Bishop of the Western District, which meant his removal to Clifton. The house had to be given up and the members, now increased to six, were homeless. Hospitality, offered by the Dominican nuns of the Second Order at Atherstone, was accepted for the community by Sister Margaret. She, however, remained behind in Coventry to look for a house and to find funds.

Prior to the dispersion of the sisters, the Constitutions of the Second Order of St. Dominic had been adapted to their needs. Now that the role of Superioress fell entirely on Sister Margaret's shoulders she was anxious that the formalities should be completed before Dr. Ullathorne's departure. On 8th December, 1845, Sister Margaret was professed before Rev. Father Dominic Aylward, O.P., representing the Provincial of the Order. The other sisters took their vows to "Sister Margaret, Prioress of the Community of St. Catherine of Siena." Later, her nomination as Superioress received the approval of the Master-General of the Order.

Left alone in Coventry, Mother Margaret found herself in a state of real poverty and, in obedience to her confessor, she appealed for assistance to a complete stranger—the Prioress of St. Benedict's Priory, Rugeley. Her letter was shy and diffident but it received a warm and hearty response. Later, a brother of the Prioress sent Mother Margaret a donation of £500. Unable to find a suitable house in Coventry, Mother Margaret moved to a house in Bristol. The Community were brought together once more and schools were again started. Bishop

Ullathorne meanwhile bought some property for a Cathedral at Clifton with space available for the building of a convent. Mother Margaret, without delay, arranged to have the convent built and when it was completed the chapel was used as a public one until the Cathedral was finished.

The Belgian statue of Our Lady was erected in the Lady Chapel, but so unused were the people to images that this statue caused a grievance amongst various members of the congregation. Whilst Mother Margaret was away in Belgium on one of her begging missions the nuns were forced to take it down. On her return she immediately replaced the statue, angry at the insult offered Our Lady in her absence. She introduced the recitation of the rosary and the congregation, at first small, soon grew in numbers until finally the chapel was crowded out. She next petitioned the Bishop for more frequent Benediction and this devotion soon became a favorite with the laity. In 1849 she erected a Crib; it was the first ever seen in Bristol.

As the work progressed she desired to spread her convents all over the country and when Bishop Ullathorne was transferred to Birmingham she decided to have a convent in his diocese. So Longton was fixed for the next foundation and in 1850 she took a house there. She found the place practically pagan; hardly anyone had ever heard of a crucifix. This promised to be a good field for her labors, and once more schools were started, the poor and sick cared for in their homes and 80 girls, who were employed during the day in the potteries, attended religious instruction in the evening.

At this time one of Mother Margaret's ambitions—the foundation of a Mother House—was to be realized. Unexpectedly she was offered land at Stone—and thither she moved the novitiate in 1853. The Priory was never completed in her lifetime, but it was always the Mother House until her death.

In 1857 she made another foundation at Stoke in the Potteries and the remaining years of her life were occupied in founding convents at Leicester (1860), Rhyl (1864), St. Mary Church (1864), Bromley

(1866), Walthamstow (1866), and, finally, Bow (1867).

The founding of these new convents was no easy matter and it is a curious fact that each foundation cost the life of one of the community. Usually one or two nuns went with Mother Margaret to prepare a house and to make it ready for the little band of sisters who were to form the community. Often there was no furniture to put in it—in fact only in two instances, Rhyl and St. Mary Church, was there anything ready for the house. With all the other foundations for the first few weeks packing cases were used for chairs and tables whilst cupboards often afforded their only place for sleeping. Apart from this there was little or no food and they had to beg for it—or rather, pray for it. Always there was a want of money! Mother Margaret never worried about these things—she knew God would provide. Proof of this was given time after time in her lifetime.

Once at Walthamstow, when at the request of Cardinal Wiseman she undertook to take charge of a hundred children to be sent to her by the Poor Law Guardians, a hitch occurred in the arrangements and the authorities at the last moment refused to hand over the children. For three days Mother Margaret waited and watched anxiously at the doorway for their arrival. Impatient at this inaction, she went off to the parish priest and begged him to find her some destitute children. That evening she saw him coming down the road holding one child in each hand. She ran to meet them and welcomed them joyfully. The sister in the kitchen, however, was very perturbed—there was scarcely any food in for the next day's dinner, but Mother Margaret told her not to worry. That evening a boy appeared with a large leg of mutton to which a sovereign was attached. It had been sent anonymously.

From Walthamstow Mother Margaret went on to found another convent at Bow, just when the finances of the Congregation were in a very low state. The other prioresses used to remonstrate with her over this reckless expenditure and wanted to show her the accounts. But she abhorred accounts and would say serenely: "If I stop doing something for God, the money stops coming in." As Mother Margaret foretold, funds always turned up at the last moment and from the most unexpected quarters. Again and again she was criticized by outsiders for that generosity of heart which seemed to many simply folly, especially when she spent money lavishly in providing the poor churches around with vestments, altar linen, chalices or ciboriums.

The only time her nuns knew her downcast was when she was planning a new foundation and was going through all the initial stages. On such occasions Mother Margaret was anxious and depressed; it was always a time of concentrated prayer. She would often sink into a state of great mental stress—her time of travail until the birth of her new offspring! All depression, however, passed away the moment she went into the house. She was the heart and soul of the place during the first weeks of trial, when many hardships had to be borne, and she never left until all was in order and the new community settled in comfortably.

When debts had to be settled she would go to Belgium on a begging tour. One of these she made in 1856. Whilst there she visited an exhibition held in the Town Hall at Bruges and was greatly attracted by a beautiful carved oak statue of Our Lady of Victories. Realizing the impossibility of buying such a work of art, she—to use her own expression—just "*invited* Our Lady to Stone." Some years later the statue was brought to England and was presented to the community by a generous benefactor. It was found difficult, however, to place such a large statue in the chapel at Stone and someone suggested its removal to Stoke—"No, on no account," said Mother Margaret emphatically, "it was to Stone I invited her and to Stone she has come." Finally it was erected in the garden in the chapel of St. Ann.

This was not the only work of art she invited to Stone. On another occasion she visited Alton Towers, the seat of the Earl of Shrewsbury, and in looking round the famous gallery, she fell in love with a beautiful reproduction of Sassoferrato's celebrated picture—"The Giving of the Rosary." She loved the figures of St. Dominic and St. Catherine and once again, in her childlike way, she *invited* the painting to Stone.

Some years later the picture came into the market and Mother Margaret arranged with friends to bid for it up to £30. Hearing privately, however, of a purchaser who was prepared to give £300, she withdrew her bid. Actually the picture was knocked down for £25 to one of the trustees of the estate. He was a party in a lawsuit and he appealed to the community to pray for an adjournment, promising if he obtained this to present the community with the picture. A novena was started immediately, the lawsuit was postponed and the painting arrived at Stone.

It was the custom for Dominican houses of the Second Order to be absolutely independent of one another and self-supporting. Mother Margaret, however, wanted to keep her convents under one Mother-General and one novitiate house. It was necessary, therefore, to obtain the Pope's permission for this and also his sanction to the Constitutions. So in 1858 Mother Margaret, although in poor health at the time, set out on her first and last visit to Rome.

The city itself seems to have disappointed her. She was accustomed to the Gothic style of architecture in Belgium and admired it above all other. She could not get used to the contrast in the Roman churches. Added to this, she was disgusted with the dirty narrow streets, the unkempt looking shrines and the dusty statues. When asked to start a community in Rome, she replied—"I would found a confraternity of *scavengers*, as that seems the only kind of confraternity that Rome requires!"

But for all her love of Gothic her admiration of St. Peter's was unbounded, and most of her time was spent within its walls. She had an audience with the Pope, who received her kindly and promised to give full consideration to the objects of her mission.

After a tedious wait of five months she was obliged to return home before the matter was decided. Shortly after her arrival at Stone news came through that the Constitutions had been ratified by the Pope and that the "Congregation of St. Catherine of Siena" was to be placed under the direct authority of the Master-General of the Dominican

Order. This latter announcement was an unasked-for honor which caused great joy to Mother Margaret and her community. Following this came a letter from the Master-General himself, appointing Mother Margaret first Mother-General of the English Convents.

On her return she took in five homeless Irish boys, who would otherwise have gone to the workhouse. These formed the beginning of St. Vincent's Orphanage, a work to which Mother Margaret particularly devoted herself. She was pressed to send filiations to Ireland, Italy, California and Australia; her name could have been famous throughout the world, but she knew God wanted her to work in England and she had no desire for notoriety. The work in hand was all-important to her; it was for "God alone."

To her nuns she taught that the preserving of their individual and their communal religious life should be their first concern; she desired them to be nuns first of all, and schoolmistresses, nurses and the rest afterwards. She maintained that it was possible to lead a contemplative life whilst engaged in active good works. This could be attained only by rigidly keeping the rule with as few dispensations as possible.

In 1855, after a Triduum to St. Catherine of Siena, permission was given to the Community by the Bishop to substitute the Divine Office for Lady Office. To Mother Margaret, who had petitioned again and again for this, the Divine Office represented the shining armor of a true spouse of Christ. She loved all the liturgy of the church and prided herself that all the Church services at Stone were carried out correctly in every detail.

To her novices she taught that the Religious Life was the love of the Cross, with its ideal, Christ crucified: each was to be absorbed in Him. She never disguised its hardships or its trials, but she made her children realize the Cross could be borne lightly and cheerfully when carried in company with Our Lord. Of the Rule of St. Dominic she would quote St. Catherine of Siena—"the spirit of his Rule is so large and joyous as to be odoriferous as a pleasant garden."

When Mother Margaret was satisfied that an aspirant to the

Religious Life really had a vocation, nothing was allowed to stand in the way. Sickness was only a bar when it incapacitated the individual from *all* active work. Several people were received in the Novitiate already broken in health—even consumptives—and it seemed as if God accepted these as victims for the success and spread of the Congregation.

Mother Margaret liked her nuns to be natural above all things and to possess a certain religious dignity; this latter came naturally, she used to say, from mortification of nature. She detested the habit of keeping the eyes cast down, which often meant "peeping round the corners of them," and she hated anything which savored of the unreal or of pose. "I never like you less," she said to one of her young sisters, "than when you are trying to be extra good."

She steeped her novices in the true Dominican spirit which never cramps or fetters the individual soul, which roots out only that which is bad and develops that which God has implanted therein. She never wanted them to change, but rather to perfect their own nature. She wished each to become a saint and spoke of the Novitiate as her nursery of saints. Her form of dismissal always was—"God bless you and make you a Saint!"

To the people in the world who knew her she became a second mother, alternately scolding and consoling according as she considered they needed it. She was loyal and sympathetic and her friendships embraced people of every class. Her letters are remarkable for their natural simplicity and singular beauty. To one who suffered a great deal she once wrote—"He must be very near to us when we feel the thorns with which He is crowned."

Her views on education were considered old-fashioned by the educationists of the day. Her greatest care was for the souls and characters of the children she sent into the world. The primary end of education, in her eyes, was to turn out good Christians.

The care of orphans came first in her heart. She delighted in seeing them dressed nicely—not dressed so that they bore the stamp of poverty as was the custom amongst the orphanages of that time. She dreaded, however, educating any child above its station and never wanted to turn out children who would afterwards look down on their people and thus create discontent in their homes. They were all trained for some trade or work and equipped to step into a position directly they left school.

She was shocked at the modern trend of education in the higher schools. Hearing, while in London, that girls were now playing cricket and other boys' games, she looked upon this with dismay and wrote back to Stone—"even the gentlemen say, 'We don't want wives of our own sex!'"

She thought every Catholic child should be taught Latin and predicted that the language of the Church would soon be the only distinguishing mark between our church services and those of the new Anglican party.

She abhorred anything to do with Government grants or control. Although she never set down her reasons against State aid, she distrusted the motives behind it, and was unable to reconcile the idea of a Protestant Government being prepared to help a Catholic school. At this time great agitation was going on in Parliament, and attempts had been made to bring in a Bill to allow annual inspection of convents by Government Officials. We can well understand, therefore, Mother Margaret's feelings with regard to inspection of schools also.

When we consider the work accomplished by her in establishing her community, in spreading her convents in a few years over the country, in conducting schools and orphanages, in nursing, in carrying on as a counterpart an intense religious life of prayer and fasting, we might imagine that such energy could be found only in one who enjoyed sound good health. Yet Mother Margaret's strength lay in her will, charged with desire to act for God alone, and in her heart, consumed with love of God alone. She experienced great suffering throughout her life. No one knows when it started; but, as early as the days of Coventry, one who afterwards joined her community discovered that she was covered with a distressing skin eruption. This never spread to her face or hands, but her whole body, arms and legs were covered with angry discharging sores, which caused constant irritation and discomfort. She, herself, once said it felt "as if the evil one had peppered her from head to foot." The pain was aggravated by the habitual wearing of St. Dominic's wool next her skin. Added to this she had always suffered from slight spinal trouble which grew worse as she grew older; nobody knew the agonies she suffered, for she always remained cheerful and never allowed her pain to show in her face.

On 7th November, 1867, however, she took to her bed and from it she never rose again. The pain in her back had increased almost beyond endurance, aggravated by a large abscess. For seven months she lay in what she herself described as "a pool of fire" saying that her back was being "pulled to pieces by hot burning plates." Sometimes she would ask God to ease the pain adding continually "Thy Will be done." She used to beg her sisters to pray that her Faith would not fail. She, herself, prayed unceasingly for this and was, apparently, left without any spiritual consolation. Only those who know suffering realize the agony of that loneliness of being left alone by God: it is desolation. And it must have been intensified in the soul of Mother Margaret, who all her life had depended on no one except "God alone."

One of Mother Margaret's medical advisers confessed he had never witnessed such a course of suffering. Yet, up to within a month of her death, she continued to administer the affairs of the community and to be conscious of every movement within the congregation. She never complained, but she often said: "It is God Who has been good to us—He has made use of me as you might use a broom-stick and that is all..."

Worn out, the old broom was burning, set on fire by the consuming love of "God alone."

Mother Margaret died peacefully on 11th May, 1868.

WILLIAM DOYLE, S.J. (1873–1917)

by JAMES BRODRICK, S.J.

PERHAPS THE IRISH WAY OF BEING CATHOLIC MIGHT best be described as the Way of the Cross. Ireland, indeed, has had no monopoly of martyrdom, but her share of it has been very great and almost unique in comprehensiveness. It is understandable, though wonderful and admirable, that a mighty people like the Germans should suffer economic martyrdom and yet come through triumphantly, but there are worse forms of martyrdom than the economic, and Ireland, puny and weak as a nation, suffered them all. She was robbed of her lands, her industries, her distinctive culture, once among the finest in Europe, her language, so full in its simplicities of God and His Mother as to be almost liturgical and, heaviest deprivation, the vast majority of her children. That this terrible spoliation, unparalleled in history, was in the main suffered for religion's sake is the verdict of impartial research. Thus Arthur Young, the famous English Protestant traveler, says as the result of his tour of the country, at the end of the eighteenth century:

> The history of the two religions in Ireland is too generally known to require any detail introductory to the subject.... Upon the whole nineteen-twentieths of the kingdom changed hands from Catholic

> to Protestant. The lineal descendants of great families, once possessed of vast property, are now to be found all over the kingdom in the lowest situation, working as cottiers for the great-grandsons of men many of whom were of no greater account in England than these poor laborers are at present on that property which was once their own. So entire an overthrow and change of landed possession is, within the period, to be found in scarce any country in the world.... The poor Catholics in the South of Ireland...are under such discouragements that they cannot engage in any trade which requires both industry and capital. If they succeed and make a fortune, what are they to do with it? They can neither buy land nor take a mortgage nor even sign down the rent of a lease... The system pursued in Ireland has had no other tendency but that of driving out of the kingdom all the personal wealth of the Catholics and prohibiting their industry within it. The face of the country, every object, in short, which presents itself to the eye of the traveler, tells him how effectually this has been done. Oppression has, moreover, reduced the major part of the Irish Catholics to a poor ignorant rabble.

And yet the "rabble," having been despoiled of all the precious things by which nations keep their souls alive, all except one, remained vitally a nation, a fact explicable only by some extraordinary quality in their Catholicism, in the special Irish Way of being Catholic.

That Way the Irish people learned from their own great Saints, beginning with St. Patrick. The distinctive mark of those Saints was their austerity and heroic love of the Cross. Notwithstanding disadvantages of climate, the Irish hermits of old "successfully rivalled, in their extraordinary penances and austerities and vigils, the hermits of Egypt and even those of Syria."[1] While in the Middle Ages, says an expert French authority, "it is quite certain that the Island of Saints was the most ascetic country in Europe." That this very full acceptance

1. *Cambridge Mediaeval History*, Vol. I., p. 1534.

of Our Lord's condition for discipleship did not lessen in subsequent centuries is written plain in Ireland's history. No soft or self-indulgent people, no people without the spirit of true Christian asceticism in their bones could have lived out the sixteenth century in Ireland unwaveringly loyal to their Faith. This they did, too, for the most part, without either spiritual or political leadership, since there is sad evidence to prove that the Irish bishops and priests of the mid-sixteenth century were no better than their brethren of Bavaria and Austria at that period. Bavaria and Austria, however, had powerful Catholic sovereigns to pull them through, whereas Ireland had only some squabbling chieftains for whom the survival of Catholicism was but a minor interest of warfare. It must, then, have been some quality in the common people that worked the miracle, and what that quality was is indicated by the observations of Barnaby Rich, a Protestant soldier in the army of Essex, who afterwards wrote a description of his Irish experiences. Naturally he found the common people of Ireland a murderous, plundering lot—but when it came to fasting and penitential exercises he was compelled to admit that not even Cardinal Bellarmine outshone them in austerity.[2]

But asceticism, the readiness to endure pain and privation for the sake of an ideal, would not have been enough to save Ireland's soul. There has always been a more positive element—a glad acceptance of suffering, a holy eagerness for it, not merely as a spiritual drill or tonic, but as a participation in the Divine experience of Him Who, having joy set before Him, endured the Cross. An attentive reader of St. Patrick's *Confession* must notice how full it is of St. Paul, how utterly Pauline St. Patrick himself was at heart. Through Patrick the teaching of the great Epistles on the Mystical Body of Christ and the *Pleroma* passed into Irish Catholicism, creating a tradition of personal devotion to Our Divine Lord and His Church which made everything

2. Cardinal Bellarmine, now St. Robert Bellarmine, Doctor of the Church, was alive when Rich wrote, and the best known Catholic in the world.

suffered for His Name's sake not only tolerable, but sweet. This trait of loving intimacy with Christ appears in the rhyme of an old chronicler about St. Comgall, the Founder and first Abbot of Bangor:

Amavit Deus Comgallum
Bene, et ipse Dominum.

It is the explanation, too, or the best part of the explanation, of Ireland's missionary effort from the days when St. Columbkille, St. Columbanus and St. Gall founded their famous monasteries abroad[3] to our own day when there is hardly a mission field in the world without its contingent of Irish priests and nuns.

Nor in the most modern times, in this present generation when we seem to be heading for the ghastly, painless *Brave New World* of Aldous Huxley, has Ireland forgotten the marked Christian asceticism and expiatory devotion of the past.[4] Other nations have their great shrines of Our Lady or the Saints to which the sick are brought from all over the world. Ireland has Lough Derg, but Lough Derg is not for the sick. They would be dead after a day of it. Lough Derg is unique in the world as being primarily and of set purpose a place of stern penance and expiation, and it is significant that stalwart Irishmen and Irishwomen flock thither in ever increasing numbers for a period of spiritual purgation as drastic as the ancient Fathers of the Desert could have desired.[5]

In other and more general practices, too, the same ascetic and penitential spirit is evident. Certainly no country in the world observes

3. At least two hundred and fifty different localities in France, Belgium, Switzerland, Italy and Germany, are associated with the names and ministry of old Irish Saints.
4. In this connection it is interesting to note that the one sane man in Mr. Huxley's fierce satire on Fordian civilization reverts in disgust to the ascetical practices of Christian monasticism.
5. It was a great wish and, indeed, determination of our present Holy Father, Pope Pius XI, to make the Lough Derg pilgrimage, until his election to St. Peter's Chair rendered the project impossible.

the Church's fasting legislation with the strictness of Ireland. Only a generation or two ago it was a common thing for men and women, including the aged, to touch no food during Lent until after sunset, and the writer has painful memories, dating from very tender years, of the black, sugarless tea and dry bread by which the significance of Ash Wednesday and Good Friday was burned into the small understanding of a child.

Another general feature of Irish Catholicism which the careful observer cannot fail to note is what might be called its starkness and independence of all that is not strictly essential. Thus, the Irish people as a whole have no marked devotion to the solemn liturgy of the Church. But it was of them that the Nonconformist English statesman was speaking when he said: "It is the Mass that matters"—the ordinary Low Mass which, in penal times, they risked their lives to hear as it was said by some hunted priest on a bare rock of the hillside. Those Mass-rocks of Ireland are truly symbolic of the Irish Way. Again, devotion to the Mother of God is certainly no less strong in Ireland than in any Catholic country, yet Ireland has never had a famous shrine of Our Lady such as pre-reformation Walsingham. Finally, nothing in her religion has meant more to Ireland than the Passion of Our Divine Lord. It has, of course, meant the world to other peoples, too, to the peasantry of the Black Forest, for instance, but with a remarkable difference. The Black Forest is positively sown with wayside Calvaries and there are practically none of them in Ireland. These are but a few instances of a phenomenon noticeable in Irish Catholicism, a restraint in the externalization of devotional impulse which may be due in part to the repression of penal times, but it is almost certainly mainly rooted in the ascetical spirit of the people. Like their beloved Mother Mary, they keep these things in their hearts. It would probably not be very far out to say that the true Irishman is austere by nature despite the gaiety with which he is credited. When that austerity is pressed into the service of an ideal, whether of this world or the next, it easily becomes heroic, as witness cultured, Protestant

Mitchel, rotting on a felons' hulk, but magnificently defiant of "Gaffer Bull" to the last; one-armed Davitt lecturing to his pet blackbird in Portland Gaol; saintly Pearse struggling against poverty and derision in his Gaelic school, and then with his toy sword and box of soldiers challenging Great Jove himself to the encounter.

Of their breed was Father Willie Doyle, though the cause for which he lived and died had no visible flag to assert its nobility. Speaking of Father Doyle's earliest days in the Dalkey of the seventies, his old nurse reported: "His love to be a soldier even from his babyhood was wonderful—to fight for Ireland," and long afterwards as a man, it was his "burning love for Ireland" that, next to his sanctity, most impressed his dear English friend, Father Charles Plater.[6] Indeed, Willie Doyle was Irish to the core of him, and more Irish in the profoundest, Catholic sense than any but a few intimates suspected, until after a German shell had sent him to heaven, his biography dropped like another one in the midst of our Christian complacencies.

William Doyle, educated in England by the sons of Antonio Rosmini, on whom the Jesuit Liberatore had waged fierce, philosophical war, entered the Irish Novitiate of the Society of Jesus in March, 1891, as the direct result of reading a small book on the religious life by the Founder of the Redemptorists. After following the normal Jesuit course of college work and study, he was ordained a priest in 1907. Between 1908 and 1915 he gave 152 missions and retreats, characterized, say those who made them, by amazing energy and devotedness, though his health was very bad. In 1916 he went to the Front as chaplain to an Irish Regiment, and in August of the following year was killed during a battle while out in the open ministering to a wounded soldier.

6. These and all the following details of Father Doyle's life are, of course, taken from Professor O'Rahilly's Classic biography (4th ed., 1930), one of the finest, wisest, most inspiring and learned religious books ever published. It has been translated into the principal European languages and has made Father Doyle the possession not only of Irish, but of universal Catholicism.

That is the outline of Father Doyle's story, forty-four years of humdrum existence with no great learning nor achievement of beauty to crown it, and for romance, only a flash at the end. Of course, even during his lifetime it was known to those who lived with him or came under his influence that he was an exceptionally holy and zealous priest. At the time of his death, too, newspapers of every complexion rang with praise of his matchless courage and devotion to duty, and a brother chaplain, a Scotsman, published his considered judgment that he had merited the V.C. "not once alone, but twenty times," though he never received it. But these facts by themselves would not have sent Father Doyle's name round the world, for there were other priests who lived holily and died heroically without anybody knowing except their immediate circle and God. What caused the stir in Father Doyle's case and made the reviewers gasp was the revelation in Professor O'Rahilly's book, first published in 1920, of a hidden life of prayer, penance, expiatory suffering and divine love that seemed to have come straight out of the deserts of Egypt or the cloisters of the Middle Ages. The surprise could hardly have been greater in some quarters if Simeon Stylites had been found one morning on the top of Nelson's Pillar in O'Connell Street, or Trafalgar Square. Was not this the twentieth century, and was not Father Doyle, by all accounts, a perfectly normal Roman priest, handsomer, perhaps, and better groomed than most, a good mixer, jolly and humorous, a gentleman and man of the world? … It was and he was; and so, by the testimony of St. Athanasius, was St. Anthony of Egypt a gentleman and man of the world. Such a life as Father Doyle's makes hay of our narrow categories. It was a life externally full of human charm, for like his great brother Jesuit, St. Robert Bellarmine, Father Doyle was emphatically "*D'humeur fort gaie*,"[7] and loved innocent fun, sweet cakes and Irish butter as well as any man. "Violent temptation to eat cake and resisted several times," is one of the entries in his spiritual diaries, which, but

7. The words of Bishop Camus who knew St. Robert personally.

for the accident of his death on the battlefield, might never have been published, as he had left instructions that they were to be burned. Professor O'Rahilly explains the reasons which caused relative and superiors to overrule the dead man's wishes and to any fair-minded reader they must appear perfectly convincing. Father Doyle had kept such records for a long period as a check on his progress in the love and service of God. It was a common practice with the great Saints. Among the earliest of the documents is the following scrap, written when he was a novice:

> A.M.D.G. ac B.V.M.
>
> My Martyrdom for Mary's Sake.
>
> Darling Mother Mary, in preparation for the glorious martyrdom which I feel assured thou art going to obtain for me, I, thy most unworthy child, on this the first day of thy month, solemnly commence my life of slow martyrdom by earnest hard work and constant self-denial. *With my blood I promise thee to keep this resolution. Do thou, sweet Mother, assist me and obtain for me the one favor I wish and long for: To die a Jesuit Martyr.* May 1st, 1893.

The words here given in italics were written by Father Doyle in his own blood, and far from being a mere specimen of noviceship heroics, they registered one of the dominant desires of his life. Even as a boy he had begun to hunger after hardship, and to school his ardent and restive young heart. Very impetuous by nature, hot-tempered and active-minded, he soon realized that only by a steady, ruthless process of self-discipline could he find his own soul and the fulness of God. So he set to work in the way taught by St. Ignatius, taking this fault and that, one at a time, making resolutions, breaking them, and making them again, giving his natural appetites and inclinations a thousand pin-pricks a day till they were forced into the service of the great love that encompassed his being. Like the child of the ballad, not through a summer's day, but for a score of years, he

> Piled up small stones to make a town,
> And evermore the stones fell down
> And he piled them up again.

The story of his daily denials, kept a guarded secret from those around him, and still more the story of his self-inflicted sufferings, all to satisfy the love of his Crucified Master, which more and more devoured him, read like chapters from Blessed Henry Suso or St. John of the Cross. "Last night I rose at twelve," he wrote in 1915, "and knelt in the cellar for an hour to suffer from the cold. It was a hard fight to do so, but Jesus helped me. I said my rosary with arms extended. At the third mystery the pain was so great that I felt I could not possibly continue; but at each *Ave* I prayed for strength and was able to finish it. This has given me great consolation by showing the many hard things I could do with the help of prayer." The many hard things, what a list they make! They are Father Doyle's "holy follies," the very exuberance of love which as à Kempis says, "often knows no measure but grows fervent beyond all measure." He would rise at midnight, tie his arms in the form of a cross and remain before the Blessed Sacrament in that position for three hours on end. During the winter he used to slip out of the house in his nightshirt at 3:00 a.m. in the morning, and stand, up to his neck, in a frozen pond, praying for sinners. Several times he undressed and rolled in furze bushes "for Jesus' love," and he adds in his record. In an intimate letter he recalls certain day on which "the love of Jesus Crucified was burning in my heart with the old longing to suffer much for Him, and even give Him my life by martyrdom. This thought was in my mind when, crossing a lonely field late that evening, I came across a forest of old nettles. Here was a chance. Had not the saints suffered in this way for Him with joy and gladness of heart? I undressed and walked up and down until my whole body was one big blister, smarting and stinging. Words could never describe the sweet but horrible agony from that moment till far into the next day.... More than once I knelt by my bed and offered Him my life, as I felt I could not live, and then in my weakness begged Him to have pity on me and yet the moment after He gave me strength to murmur: 'Still more, dear Lord, a thousand times more for Your dear love.'" To apply the maxims of jog-trot prudence to such deeds is about as helpful as trying to find the temperature of the sun with a clinical thermometer. And there were hundreds of such deeds in Father Doyle's life, efforts of finite love to come to terms with the Infinite. As the Curé of Ars used to say: "To be a saint it is necessary to be beside oneself, to lose one's head entirely." Father Doyle's one aim in all his terrible wooing of pain was to fill up what is wanting in the sufferings of Christ, to be clothed, as the Jesuit rule demands, in His garment and livery, to make reparation to His Sacred Heart for the neglect and outrages of a sinful, ungrateful world. "He seems pleased," he wrote, "when I am alone in the chapel, if I kneel close to Him, uncover my breast and ask Him again to pour His grace and love into my heart. I often press my throbbing heart to the door of the Tabernacle to let Him hear its beats of love; and once to ease the pain of love, I tried with a penknife to cut the sweet Name of Jesus on my breast. It was not a success, for I suppose my courage failed; I did try a heated iron, but it caused an ugly sore." On another occasion he said: "I know not why I am writing this except it be to ease my straining heart, for at times I feel half mad with the love of God."

So the grain of wheat that had died in the ground ripened to its golden maturity. The Irish Way of being Catholic, the good and gallant old way of mortification and self-denial proved once again in Willie Doyle its perennial efficacy. Matt Talbot and he both went the way of the Irish Saints, and it led them, as it will any man who follows it steadily and bravely, beyond all petty skepticisms and hesitations to the top of God's mountain. There is no word in Father Doyle about the Mystery of Suffering with which the modern world is so anxiously and unavailingly concerned. He had found his way to the Heavenward side of the mystery and discovered, like so many great and simple souls whose metaphysics were negligible, that its other face is love.

That is, perhaps, the greatest lesson which his life and the history of Catholicism in his country teach us. The solution of our trouble is under our noses: *Solvitur patiendo.*

MATT TALBOT (1856–1925)

by F. J. SHEED

THE UNIQUE THING IN IRISH CATHOLICISM IS THE LAITY. Taken all through history the Irish priesthood has been magnificent: yet, Catholic priests tend to a certain magnificence wherever you find them: it is the occasional dimming of that magnificence, in a particular place at a particular time, that is exceptional, not its presence. But the thing that strikes everyone who comes new to the vision of Catholic Ireland—the thing that lends the savor of miracle to the story of the Faith in Ireland—is the great nameless mass of the Irish faithful.

The strong and persistent feature in them is their utter and fundamental religiousness—I do not say holiness, for that varies from man to man, and no nation is of necessity holier than another; but in the Irishman, even in the Irish sinner, there is this "religiousness,"—a supernatural thing that seems to have become natural—an instinctive awareness of God's presence as something actual and obvious, a taking for granted of the spiritual world. It issues most characteristically in their devotion to the Blessed Sacrament—for the special note of that devotion is not adoration, though adoration is, of course, there, but sheer companionability. Even the priests are not so obviously Irish Catholic priests as Irish Catholic men, nor is there the same gap in devotion between the mass of the people and their clergy as you would reasonably expect to find and normally do find. Yet, if the strange persistence through the centuries of the rank and file seems a miracle, it is an anonymous miracle. No Irish layman has been canonized: till our own day no Irish layman had even been thought of for canonization. Bishops, abbots, nuns: but not a layman. That, it may be, is the significance of Matt Talbot. He may or may not come to be canonized: but saint or not he is a superb symbol—the adequate and satisfying representative of that special quality of Irish Catholicness. He is authentically the Irish Catholic layman—the thing itself concentrated, stripped of irrelevance. In a sense he is scarcely an Irishman: he is the Irish Catholic. He has no meaning save a religious meaning. Take away from him what is Catholic and there is nothing left. He is totally Catholic, and his Catholicity is totally of the Irish sort.

Thus the story of his life has no features save religious. A simpler story cannot be imagined.[1] He was born in 1856 (and he who was so essentially Irish in all things, was essentially Irish in this—that he had a good mother). He went to work at twelve: worked at a variety of jobs: he was a bricklayer's laborer from the age of seventeen until at thirty-six he became a laborer in a timber-yard and so remained until he died at sixty-nine. Nothing ever happened to him. He seems to have had no accidents: nor, till the last couple of years, even an illness. He wrote one letter in his life. He never went outside Dublin. He never married, nor had he so much as a love affair. Not one man in a thousand has so eventless a life: and when you find such a man, he is usually pallid to match, lifeless and featureless. But *this* man was all strength and luminousness: the natural life meant so little because the religious life meant so much: the wire was lost in the light—a light

1. For my knowledge of Matt Talbot, I, in common with hundreds of thousands of others, am immensely in the debt of Sir Joseph Glynn, author of the standard Life published by the Veritas Co. of Ireland. My quotations of things said or written by Matt Talbot are drawn from it and my essay has no higher ambition than to persuade every Irishman to read that wonderful book.

so tiny and hidden that the eye might miss it altogether, but in itself sheer white light.

The atmosphere of his childhood made for a solid Catholic life. His father was steadily faithful in the practice of his religion, while his mother was a woman of real holiness, endlessly praying. In that household of many children—there were twelve of them—the Rosary was said every night. Matt left the Christian Brothers' school when he was twelve: became a messenger to a firm of wine-merchants, and within a year was drinking heavily. His drinking was marked by the thoroughness which was later to carry him so far in sanctity. His practice was to hand his wages to the publican on pay day and then drink through them. Beyond that we find the whole sickening normal round of the man held by drunkenness—the week's wages spent in half a week, the pawning of clothes, the reliance on chance generosity—*anybody's* generosity. So for fifteen years: and then, at twenty-eight, conversion.

The decision was sudden. Craving for a drink, he had failed to get one: his friends had passed him by. That afternoon he told his mother that he was going to take the pledge. "Go in God's name," she said; "but don't take it unless you are going to keep it." He answered, "I'll go in the name of God." As he was leaving the house his mother said, "God give you strength to keep it."

What moved him to his decision there is no certain way of knowing. But its suddenness should not deceive us: the causes that produced it may well have been working obscurely in his soul for a long time. It is at any rate a possibility that the process may have started with the shock of something done when he was drunk and seen in its true light when he was sober. We know of such an incident: Matt and a number of others, drinking with a fiddler, pawned his fiddle: with the money, they bought more liquor, which the fiddler, knowing nothing of his loss, helped them to drink. It was a great night: and the fiddler had lost the thing that brought him his living. We know that the incident preyed on Matt Talbot's mind, and that later he searched the city—fruitlessly—to find the victim, and had many Masses said for him.

He took the pledge for three months: then for a year: then for life. This gradual feeling of his way was the last sign of indecision he was ever to show. Everything that follows is clean-cut and irrevocable. But it may well be that nothing he was ever to do was as difficult as this first step. It cost him agonies. But from the beginning he planned his warfare with superb commonsense. It is the way of the strong man to run away from temptation. The man who sets out to look temptation in the face and stare it down is certain to lose. Since every street had its bar and every bar was a temptation, he decided that he must be in the streets as little as possible. Again, since his own nature was agonizing for drink, he must get help from outside himself. In the church, before the Blessed Sacrament, he was out of the way of the bar, in the way of the help of God. He began to haunt the churches of Dublin. Before the day's work he went steadily to the five o'clock Mass at Gardiner Street: after the day's work, and at the weekend, he spent every moment in one church or another.

But his difficulties were immense. It was a question not only of an old habit that would not easily release its grip but of a new habit that would not easily take hold. Prayer is one of the hardest of the works of man. Matt Talbot, trying to grow into the life of prayer, had years of leeway to make up (since he had given up receiving the Sacraments these years past). And he had the maddening distraction of his craving. In the early weeks he had the hopeless feeling that once the three-month period was up the craving would have its way. But gradually prayer won. He had asked God, he said later, for the gift of prayer and had got it in abundance. From now on prayer figured in his life not as conquering drink, but as conquering him.

The abolition of the five o'clock Mass at Gardiner Street set him a problem: his work started too early to allow of his going to a later Mass. He solved the problem by finding work with new employers: and with them he stayed for the thirty-three years of life that remained to him. The external framework of his life thus stabilized, the life of prayer was able to grow undisturbed. In the beginning there was a mysterious occasion when unseen hands tried to hold him back from entering the church: and a morning when he almost succumbed to the most appalling despair. But such troubles seem to have passed from him early.

His day began at 2:00 a.m. when an alarm clock woke him for prayer. For anything up to two hours he prayed, kneeling on his bed or face downwards on the floor. Sometimes he slept for a while after these first prayers: sometimes not. At 4:00 a.m. he rose for good, dressed, and prayed till just before 5:00 a.m. Then he set out for Mass. Normally he reached the church at 5:00 a.m. and knelt outside until it opened at 5:30 a.m. Mass was at 6:15 a.m. He returned home for breakfast: then set out again, and was at work by 7:45 a.m. At 6:00 p.m. he left the timber-yard, and returned home for his evening meal. After the meal he either went to church for the devotions of one of his confraternities or spent the evening in prayer and the reading of theological, ascetical or mystical books. Between 10:30 and 11:00 p.m. he went to bed, to sleep until a new day should begin at 2:00 a.m. On Sundays he remained in the church for one Mass after another from the opening till the end of Benediction—roughly about half-past one—returning home to break his fast at two, and spend the remainder of the day as he spent his evenings through the week. In a sense the Sunday was more totally a day of prayer: yet it is doubtful if the working days yielded to it in completeness. On his way to and from work there was a visit to the Blessed Sacrament in the church of St. Laurence O'Toole: between loads at work there was prayer in the solitude of his shed: and work itself was not an interruption but rather an outflowing or a special directing of the steady fixedness of the soul in God. Praying or working, it was all of a piece.

Prayer, I have said, is one of the hardest of the works of man: it demands a strict training of the whole man. The mystic *must* be an ascetic: there is no mystical way for the comfortable. Matt Talbot knew it: and he had, as we have seen, a tendency to thoroughness. When he reached the church, wet or fine, he knelt on the steps for the half hour till the church opened: inside the church, save when he was making the stations or approaching the communion rail, he still knelt—knelt the whole time—on Sundays seven or eight hours. Now kneeling is hard work: not as hard as praying, but hard. Matt Talbot knelt upright, with not so much as his hand resting on any support: and he knelt on his bare knees, for he had slit the knees of his trousers—lengthwise, so that when he stood upright, the gap closed and the slit was not seen.

He had begun by denying his body drink: he proceeded to deny it food—for fasting is of all forms of mortification the one the Church knows best and practices most, so that among mortifications it holds a kind of primacy. Every day in Lent, every day in the month of June, every Saturday, every vigil of a feast, and on a variety of other occasions, he fasted on two slight meals without meat, butter or milk. Even when he was not thus observing a black fast, he denied himself rigorously. For nine months of the year he never ate meat. His midday meal on working days was a slice of dry bread and a cup of tea; from 1920—five years before his death—he introduced a variation by mixing cocoa with the tea. This unpleasing mess he drank cold.

We have already seen that in the hours of his sleep as in the matter of food and drink he had succeeded in imposing his own terms upon the body. Consider now the bed on which he had that shadow of a night's rest: under him two bare planks, unplaned, and a wooden pillow; over him half a blanket: on very cold nights an old sack. And he slept in chains.

From Blessed Grignon de Montfort's book *True Devotion to the Blessed Virgin* he had adopted the practice. When his body was taken to the mortuary there were found on it chains, the size of a large dog's chain, ropes and beads. Round his waist were two chains, intertwined with a knotted rope, and with medals tied to them. The chains were deeply embedded in the flesh and rusted. Above the left elbow a light chain was wound tight: above the right arm a knotted cord, and the same on the right leg: on the left leg a chain bound round with a cord.

The fullness of what all this mortification meant to Matt Talbot we cannot know: more than most men he could say *secretum meum mihi*—his secret was his. Yet the elementary things about it can be known. He was trying to master the body for the liberation of both soul and body. Now all bodies are not equally clamorous, nor clamorous for the same things. It is to be noted that even in his drinking days, Matt Talbot was untouched by sexual sins. But celibacy, which in the supernatural order normally goes with virility, sometimes does so in the natural order too—in the Irish more so perhaps than in most races. From the certain absence of sexual sin—even from the presumed absence of sexual temptation—no man acquainted either with Catholics in a state of grace or with Irishmen in any state whatever would argue to an absence of virility. The man who drank as Matt Talbot did, certainly had a sufficiently clamorous body: and the man who disciplined the body as he did certainly had an immense store of vital energy. But notice the quality of his mortification. The mastering of Matt Talbot's body, it would seem, demanded a certain steady, unrelaxing pressure. To apply his own phrase "it is constancy God wants." Thus he did not scourge himself: for scourging, however frequent, is an incident, an *event*: but chains are a *state*. Just as his day had, in a sense, no high points of spirituality but he lived at his maximum: so it had no high points of mortification—no moments when the suffering bit more fiercely: nor any moment when the iron pressure relaxed. Throughout, the word of his mortification is pressure—not violence. There was nothing that could even look like morbidity. His body he kept scrupulously clean. When the chains rusted beyond a point, he changed them for fresh. His was a mastered, not precisely a tortured body.

Right asceticism never means *less* than the conquest of self for the liberation of self. So much it certainly meant for Matt Talbot. It can mean much more—suffering offered in union with the sufferings of Christ for his own sins and for the sins of others: that, too, it must have meant for him: but there is no sure way of following him into the deepest parts of his spiritual life. He was not given to analyzing his spiritual states: of direct statement about himself he has left almost nothing. What we have is a few actions, a few things said, a handful of extracts copied from spiritual books, the names of some books he read.

This question of his reading is very significant. There are those who see no point in theology for the laity and set against the ideal of a laity deeply instructed in the Faith the picture—by now traditional—of "the good old Irishman saying his Rosary." It is an unfortunate line of argument, since it seems to suggest that further knowledge of the Faith means giving up the Rosary: as though the Rosary—given to the world by St. Dominic—is a prayer for the ignorant only, or at any rate a prayer in the saying of which ignorance is an advantage. In truth ignorance of God's teaching is never an advantage: and the Rosary is a prayer that no theologian ever outgrows. One man of less knowledge may pray better than another man with more: but not *because* his knowledge is less. The faith and love of "the old Irishman saying his Rosary" is marvelous: but he would be the last person to agree with his eulogist that a deeper and deeper study of Catholic dogma is a thing unnecessary. Matt Talbot sums up the position with rare perfection. He did not repine because his school education had stopped when it did: "God knew what was best"; but neither did he stay at that point. He read immensely, and not the easiest books: "whenever he read a book he always prayed to God to give him light to understand it, or at least to understand the main points…he thought he got enough of light to understand most of what he read."

There is no keeping track of the books he borrowed. But among the books he owned were Newman's *Arians of the Fourth Century*, *Essays on Miracles*, and *Present Position of Catholics in England*, Mary of Agreda's *Mystical City of God*, Père Grou's *Manual for Interior Souls*, and *The School of Christ*, Bishop Hedley's *Our Divine Saviour*,

Montalembert's *St. Elizabeth of Hungary*, St. Francis de Sales' *Introduction to the Devout Life*, and, of course, the Bible.

That he was not wrong in thinking he was given light to understand appears from the extracts he copied down, some in a notebook, others on the back of scraps of paper. Among the transcripts are statements of universal application on dogmatic and mystical theology—on the hypostatic union, the nature of miracles, grace, sin, the Papacy, purgatory and venial sin, the meaning of mystical theology, the distinction between meditation and contemplation. There are also some which bear specially on the way of his own life:

> The sons of man neither know what is the greatness of what is eternal nor the baseness of what is temporal. The time of life is but a career of death in which no man is permitted to make a stay.

> At present the human body is an animal body inasmuch as to preserve its life on this earth, so it is (necessary) to nourish it with earthly food.

On the elementary purpose of asceticism, there is the prayer:

> O Most Sweet Jesus, mortify within me all that is bad—make it die. Put to death in me all that is vicious and unruly. Kill whatever displeases Thee, mortify within me all that is my own...

And, as a hint of the deeper purpose in asceticism:

> O Blessed Mother obtain from Jesus a share of His Folly.

In such a collection there is always an element of chance; as between one passage and another, the chance of a handy piece of paper may decide. But these forty or fifty scraps—written in a shapeless hand and oddly spelt—are indications of an educated mind, a mind with a massive view of life as a *whole*, with the great things in their right relation to the whole and to each other, and the lesser things known to be lesser.

But whatever part reading played in Matt Talbot's formation for prayer, it played only a minor part in his actual praying. In church he did not use a prayer book, but prayed for hour after hour with eyes closed. Of his early morning prayer we know from the description given by his mother, who for years slept at the other end of the same room. He seemed to be in ecstasy and he spoke to Our Lady at great length, not simply as one praying, but as one conversing, as one *seeing*. That is all we know on this question of seeing, for he himself never spoke.

One curious thing must be noted of his life of prayer. He, who was so continuously in the company of Our Lady and in the presence of the Blessed Sacrament, was shy of priests. The priests at Gardiner Street did not know him: nor did the priests at the Franciscan Church, though he belonged to a Sodality at the one church and the Third Order at the other. In hospital he did not talk of spiritual things with the nuns. He received Holy Communion with the rest on Monday, but never asked for it on other days: only, if it were being brought to another patient and he were asked if he wished to receive it, he always accepted. He knew one or two priests, but for the greater part of his life certainly—and possibly for all of it—he had no spiritual director. Humility is an obvious explanation; yet it remains mysterious. All that he received from the Church, measureless as it was, he received as a Catholic, a member of the body, never as Matt Talbot. Confession he went to at the hours fixed for hearing confessions; he received Our Lord sacramentally when Communion was being given; he listened to the Church's teaching as one of a congregation; all these things at times fixed for the general convenience, none of them at any time arranged for himself alone. There is a curious impersonality about it, curious and very significant.

In the sacramental system Christ Our Lord uses the humanity

of the priest—consecrated to His use—as a means by which His life is given to the soul. Beyond that, as a secondary means, Christ uses the *personality of* the priest—this or that gift of character or temperament, of wisdom or learning or experience—to help souls individually. The first way is universal, open equally and without distinction to every member of the Church, it being a matter of no importance whether a man goes to one priest or another: for Christ is all and the priest simply an instrument in His hands. The second way varies from priest to priest, and a member of the Church might conceivably, if God so shapes his life, get little or no help of this sort. Matt Talbot's life is proof that the first way can be all-sufficing.

He said little of himself. Yet he said enough to show the note of his life of prayer. Once, speaking of St. Mary Magdalen, St. Mary of Egypt and other saints of penance, he said "They were great girls"—a pleasant phrase, probably never used before or since in that connection. It is familiarity carried to its last point. Now the one place where familiarity does not breed contempt is in the family. Matt Talbot was of the family. In him there is, at its highest pitch, the note of companionability which marks the Irishman at prayer. It blazed out in his reply to one who complained of being lonely: "Lonely! How could you be lonely? That's nonsense, and Our Lord in His Tabernacle." In themselves the words might mean little enough; one has heard such things said, but Matt Talbot lived them.

Just how completely he lived them brings us to another point: his attitude to men. The words just quoted deny the actual need of human companionship. One of his penciled notes has this: "What do I want to speak to you, when I have Jesus to speak to me?" The distinction between the two phrases is a delicate one, and might easily be missed: but there is a long stride between "Why do I *need* men?" and "What do I *want* with men?"

We have seen the face he turned to God: what face did he turn to the world?

First note this: that the work he had to do for a living he did carefully and well. He was never late; perfectly poised in his dealings with those set over him: not disrespectful, nor subservient. When he was in charge of stores, not even waste could be taken away without authorization. To his fellows he was kindly, considerate, generous in lending money—very direct in speech where direct speech was called for, capable, surprisingly enough, of sudden heat of anger. A great hater of lying. But he avoided all close intimacy with men. When life brought him into contact with others, he was ready to act: but he never sought contact with others as a means to action. Within the family circle he advised on business matters with much commonsense: to the lodge-keeper's children at the timber yard he was most tenderly affectionate: to men who spoke profanely or indecently in his presence, he spoke bluntly and directly of Christ dying on the Cross, so that profanity and indecency died out where he was: to charities he gave largely, for he lived on anything up to ten shillings a week: to those he met who seemed to him likely to make progress in the spiritual life he spoke, lent books, and even revealed something of the prayer and the rigor of his own life. And this last is significant: for normally he concealed his way of life very closely: if he had a meal at the house of a friend, he ate as much as the others ate, and those who thought they knew him well knew nothing of the reality of his life. In short, he loved men but felt no direct sense of mission to them, and as far as life would allow him he avoided them. He acted *for* them but not *upon* them: his action was upon God. There is one kind of man who deliberately goes apart from men to serve God, and thereby to serve men too—and that is the contemplative.

If his action upon individuals was thus secondary, his attitude to the general frame of the natural life was still more remote. In politics he had no interest whatever: he never voted, never even talked of them. He had schooled himself not to look at the placards of the newspapers: the anti-conscription campaign of 1916–1917 had run six months of its course before he had heard of it. Of the troubles in the years just before and just after the Treaty he said nothing. When his union called a strike he went on strike with the others, having satisfied himself that strikes could be justified, and that knowing nothing of the matter he might in conscience trust his fellows: but he refused to picket. And the men decided that, even so, he should receive his full strike pay: they recognized that he was different: for this was Ireland.

This deliberate withdrawal from things, like that other withdrawal from men, is the mark of the contemplative. Why did Matt Talbot not join a contemplative order—the Trappists or the Carthusians? That is God's secret; obscurely one feels that it is bound up with the vocation of the Irish people: less obscurely that it is bound up with the special need of our day. For action fills the whole horizon and to the man of our time contemplation smells musty, of a dead age. Concentration upon God is possible in the world—possible in some measure to everyone. From this point of view Matt Talbot was a living parable: for living in the world, he was totally contemplative. In one sense he did not need an enclosure: he was his own enclosure and the world could not come in to him. There is no photograph of him: and the fullest verbal description of a man leaves him vague and almost invisible.

Yet of the description we have, something stands out: he was a small slight man and he walked through the streets with long strides, his eyes fixed on the ground. Thus he avoided looking at the world: but not in order that he might look at the ground. There is great significance in the names he chose when he joined the Third Order—Joseph Francis. For both St. Joseph and St. Francis lived in the world, in contact with men but with eyes fixed on God.

The life of Matt Talbot startles the onlooker at first sight. But, by dint of long looking, the eye gets accustomed to it and to an eye so accustomed Matt Talbot seems the very embodiment of sound commonsense: it is we who seem distorted and even eccentric. For he, knowing the goal of life, bent every energy towards it, while we, knowing as well as he, go waveringly at best. In the very beginning of his conversion he had that healthy terror of hell which is so much dimmed in men to-day. He read the book *Hell open to Christians* and "it frightened the life out of him." It is the fashion to be superior to the horrors of hell and talk as though we had outgrown them. But the only way to outgrow them is to grow into a deeper love of God: to lose the one without gaining the other is not growth at all. Matt Talbot never lost the fear of hell and grew steadily in the love of God.

Along with the steady growth in love was a steady growth in freedom: and by that the commonsense of his conduct appears unmistakably. He had burst the bonds of a score of servitudes. All the tyranny of the body he had broken: whether he ever lost the craving for drink we do not know: what agony the conquest of sleep cost him we do not know. He was not communicative. The clamors of his body may or may not have died away: what is certain is that they had no dominion over him.

That greater tyranny of human respect he had likewise broken. He did not want man's good opinion: he did not even want man's contempt. He was a free man.

It has already been observed that everything he received from the Church he received not as an individual but along with others, at the Church's times. But there is one Sacrament which a man receives as himself, at a moment settled by *his* needs, not by the Church's timetable. The best-run parish does not set aside one particular hour in the week for the giving of Extreme Unction. This Sacrament Matt Talbot received, though not at the time of his death. In the last two years of his life illness came. His body, as we have seen, for all that it was mastered, was not tortured—nor was it broken. Towards the end the muscles of his face were affected by the wooden pillow, and he tended to deafness. But at 67 he was still doing his heavy laboring work. In 1923, he went to the Mater Misericordiae Hospital with an affection of the heart. Here it was that he received the Last Sacraments. He was twice in hospital that year. Through 1924 he suffered greatly, but he resumed the chains he had taken off to go to hospital and continued his fasting, watching and praying: yet he was no longer able to spend the Sunday mornings as of old, finding it necessary to come home for breakfast after the early Mass before proceeding to complete the morning in church. In April, 1925, he went back to work. On June 7th—Trinity Sunday—he went to an early Mass; came home to breakfast: and set out for St. Savior's. Near the church he fell: a woman ran across to him: he died without speaking. A man on his way from the church made the Sign of the Cross over the dead body with a crucifix. One of the Dominican fathers knelt and recited prayers. At the mortuary they found upon his body the chains which in life he had always removed for his visits to hospital. On the feast of Corpus Christi, dressed in the Franciscan habit, he was buried with his chains in Glasnevin Cemetery.

There is no looking at Matt Talbot without feeling that he is a perfect symbol of the Irish people at prayer: not one sort of Irishman but the Irishman as such—the Irishman stripped down to his Catholicism.

Suffering and prayer have been the lot of Ireland for seven centuries: mixed with them have been a score of other things, good and less good: but those two steadily. And they have produced a strongly marked type of Catholicism. Every one of us knows the type—the Irishman in youth and middle age regular in the practice of the Faith, developing in old age into a life that is only prayer: at every point of life marked by a certain decisiveness as of men who do not so much as *see* the alternative. It is of this abiding type that Matt Talbot is the perfect representative. He is essence of Irishman: every Irishman smells a little of Matt Talbot unless he is lost altogether. And if he is canonized a host of unknown Irishmen will be raised to the altars with him.

CLUNY MEDIA

Designed by Fiona Cecile Clarke, the Cluny Media *logo depicts a monk at work in the scriptorium, with a cat sitting at his feet.*

The monk represents our mission to emulate the invaluable contributions of the monks of Cluny in preserving the libraries of the West, our strivings to know and love the truth.

The cat at the monk's feet is Pangur Bán, from the eponymous Irish poem of the 9th century. The anonymous poet compares his scholarly pursuit of truth with the cat's happy hunting of mice. The depiction of Pangur Bán is an homage to the work of the monks of Irish monasteries and a sign of the joy we at Cluny take in our trade.

"Messe ocus Pangur Bán,
cechtar nathar fria saindan:
bíth a menmasam fri seilgg,
mu memna céin im saincheirdd."

Made in the USA
Middletown, DE
07 March 2025

72279980R00184